MW00616802

PENNSYLVANIA GUN LAW

Armed And Educated

A Complete Guide To Gun Law In Pennsylvania

2016 Edition

By Attorneys Justin McShane and
Michael Giaramita, Jr.

Copyright © 2016 by Stanley Marie, LLC
First Printing

All rights reserved. No part of this book may be reproduced in any form or by any means without permission in writing from the publisher.

Written by Justin McShane and Michael Giaramita, Jr., and published in the United States of America
By U.S. Law Shield
ISBN 978-0-692-68011-7

To order additional books by phone or for wholesale orders call (877) 448-6839.

TABLE OF CONTENTS

PREFACE

As lawyers with years of representing law-abiding gun owners in cases all over the State of Pennsylvania, we have seen how well intended folks exercising their Second Amendment rights get mixed up in the legal system through just plain not understanding the law. For that reason, we set about creating a one volume resource that provides any gun owner with a base level of knowledge about laws that gun owners need to know.

The law can be complicated, overlapping, hard to understand, and in some cases, completely arbitrary to the point of confusion. Laws are often written by lawyers for lawyers or are the result of political compromises generating confusing laws that the courts are left to interpret. After years of legal work in the arena of firearms law, we found there did not exist a resource that explained gun law in a manner that was easy for everyone to understand, because understanding the law goes far beyond just reading statutes or regulations. If you do not know either the process by which the law is being administered or how the courts are interpreting the meaning of the law, then you don't understand the full legal story.

That is why we wrote *Pennsylvania Gun Law: Armed And Educated.* It is a one volume guide to the minimum law every gun owner needs to know to stay legal. Whenever appropriate, we tried to present useful analysis and real world applications. Our goal was to explain the "law" so gun owners who wanted to could inform and educate themselves. Thousands of attorney hours have gone into producing this resource, always with the goal in mind of education. Our collective legal experience has taught us well that anyone can become ensnared in the legal system. Many people firmly believe that "it" can't happen to them. Even people who have never been in trouble before find themselves in the world of law, lawyers, and law enforcement through ignorance of the law.

We are committed to helping protect Second Amendment rights for all legal gun owners. It is our passion and our mission. We want people to know the law, because only through eternal vigilance will we protect our cherished right to bear arms. If you own a gun, the laws concerning firearms and their use apply to you. Ignorance of the law is not a valid legal excuse. Therefore, if you want to stay legal, know the law!

CHAPTER ONE
BRIEF LEGAL HISTORY OF THE RIGHT TO BEAR ARMS AND THE LAWS REGULATING FIREARMS

I. Introduction and overview

Before there was the Second Amendment to the United States Constitution, there was the Pennsylvania Declaration of Rights (the Pennsylvania Constitution of 1776). Clause 13 of the Pennsylvania Declaration of Rights recognized that "the people have a right to bear arms for the defense of themselves and the state." Pennsylvania was the very first state to use this language which later influenced our Federal Second Amendment right, as well as most other state constitutions when it comes to gun rights.

The Second Amendment was adopted on December 15, 1791, as part of the first Ten Amendments comprising the Bill of Rights. The Pennsylvania Declaration of Rights was published in 1776. As such, Pennsylvanians hold an ancient right to gun ownership.

In 1790, Pennsylvania adopted one of the most strongly worded phrases that has ever been written anywhere when it comes to law-abiding citizens and gun rights. This language is found in Article I, Section 21 of the Pennsylvania Constitution. Article I, Section 21 as it exists now reads: "The right of the citizens to bear arms in defense of themselves and the State shall not be questioned." Those 19 words form the basis of the power that we as citizens have.

To fully understand our federal rights, one should start first at the beginning: the formation document for our federal government, the United States Constitution. The Constitution was written without any enumerated individual rights. The Founding Fathers thought it obvious and apparent that individuals had rights; therefore, there was no reason to spell them out in a document that was supposed to control the government. James Madison also thought that by naming certain rights, it would imply that those were the only rights an individual possessed. After much discussion, and a complete change of opinion by Madison, the lack of enumerated rights was remedied in the first Congressional session and by the state ratification process. When the dust settled, ten amendments were added to the Constitution; these ten amendments are the Bill of Rights. It is the Second Amendment that concerns firearms specifically, though throughout this book we will reference many others, including the Fourth and Fifth Amendments, that both affect your rights to bear arms and the fundamental rights for us all.

II. Do I have a constitutional right as an individual to keep and bear arms?

Yes. The Supreme Court of the United States has decided that an individual has a constitutionally given right to keep and bear arms that flows from the Second Amendment, which states simply:

> *A well-regulated Militia, being necessary to the security of a free State, the right of the people to keep and bear Arms, shall not be infringed.*

From a plain reading, there are two important parts to this amendment: first, that a well-regulated militia is necessary to the security of a free state, and second, that there is a right of the people to keep and bear arms. For years before the issue was decided, anti-gun activists have tried to argue that the Second Amendment only applied to "militias" and not to individuals. Luckily, this argument is not the law. Nevertheless, despite the Supreme Court of the United States rulings stating otherwise, this myth seems to persist. What do these parts of the Second Amendment mean? Are they the same, or are they different?

A. *What is a "Well-Regulated Militia?"*

As we discussed earlier, the first part of the Second Amendment references a "well-regulated militia." What is a well-regulated militia? The U.S. Supreme Court has held what this phrase does and does not mean. In 1939, in the case of *United States v. Miller*,

307 U.S. 174 (1939) (ironically, a ruling that upheld firearms regulation), the court defined a Militia as comprising "all males physically capable of acting in concert for the common defense." Based on how the amendment was drafted, the Court stated, it was clear that the Militia pre-dated Article I of the Constitution, because unlike armies and navies, it did not have to be created by Congress. What then is "well-regulated" per the Court? It is exactly what it sounds like: the imposition of discipline and training. So, is this just the National Guard? No.

In the case of *D.C. v. Heller*, 554 U.S. 570 (2008), the Supreme Court stated that the well-regulated militia is not the state's military forces, but a separate entity altogether. The Supreme Court of the United States stated that the word "militia" referred to the body of the people, and they—the people—were required to keep a centralized government in check. The Supreme Court considered and rejected the position that the National Guard is the current militia under the Second Amendment.

B. *How has the phrase "right to keep and bear arms" been interpreted by the courts?*

One of the first cases to directly deal with the Second Amendment was *United States v. Miller*. In *Miller*, the Supreme Court found that the National Firearms Act ("NFA"), which imposed registration requirements on machine guns, short-barreled weapons, destructive devices, and other similarly unique firearms, did not violate the Second Amendment. The Court used the reasoning that possession of weapons regulated by the NFA did not reasonably relate to the preservation or efficiency of a well-regulated militia, therefore, the NFA was held constitutional.

Court fight where it all began: *United States v. Miller*

United States v. Miller **(1939)**

The Facts

Defendants, Miller and Layton, transported a double barrel 12-gauge shotgun with a barrel length of less than 18 inches from Oklahoma to Arkansas, and were being prosecuted under the

National Firearms Act (which required certain types of firearms to be registered and a tax to be paid). Defendants challenged the NFA as an unconstitutional violation of the Second Amendment.

The Legal Holdings

Upheld the National Firearms Act as Constitutional.

An interesting quirk of history in the *Miller* case (and not a shining moment for the legal system) is that Miller's attorney never appeared at the arguments before the Supreme Court of the United States because he was court-appointed and had not been paid. There was no written brief and no legal representation at oral arguments by the party arguing that the law was unconstitutional. The Court only heard the government's side. To make matters worse, Miller was shot to death before the decision was rendered.

C. *69 years later, the Supreme Court interprets the Second Amendment again: D.C. v. Heller*

It would be 69 years after *Miller* that the Supreme Court of the United States addressed the Second Amendment directly again, except this time the Court would hear both the government's and Heller's arguments. Fortunately, freedom and Second Amendment rights prevailed in court that day. The Court held that individuals have a right to keep and bear arms.

District of Columbia v. Heller (2008)

The Facts

Heller applied for a handgun ownership permit and was denied; without such a permit, D.C. required that all firearms (including rifles and shotguns) be kept unloaded and disassembled, or bound by a trigger lock, even in a person's own home.

The Legal Holdings

1. The Supreme Court found that the Second Amendment protects an individual right of firearms ownership for purposes of self-defense, not connected with any militia or military purposes; it further elaborated that individual self-defense is "the central component" of the Second

Amendment. Further, handguns are the primary defensive weapon of choice and are protected by the Second Amendment.

2. A well-regulated militia is not the state's military forces.
3. The Court also discussed what the phrase "bear arms" meant: "wear, bear, or carry... upon the person or in clothing or in a pocket, for the purpose... of being armed and ready for offensive or defensive action in a case of conflict with another person."
4. The D.C. regulation was held to be unconstitutional.
5. The Court concluded that like other rights, the right to bear arms is not completely absolute. Reasonable provisions and restrictions have been upheld.

Keep in mind *D.C. v. Heller* was a split 5-4 decision; only one justice away from a completely different outcome, where the Second Amendment (according to the dissent) had "outlived its usefulness and should be ignored."

D. *Can states ignore the Second Amendment? McDonald v. City of Chicago*

D.C. v. Heller was fantastic, but there was a slight quirk: The District of Columbia is under the exclusive jurisdiction of Congress and is not part of any state. Therefore, the case shed no light on the question of what states can do when it comes to regulating or banning firearms. How do state constitutions interact with the Second Amendment and can states ban guns outright? *McDonald v. City of Chicago* sought to answer these questions.

McDonald v. City of Chicago, (2010)
The Facts
McDonald v. City of Chicago was decided in 2010; Chicago ordinance banned handgun possession (among other gun regulations). McDonald was a 76-year-old retired maintenance engineer who wanted a handgun for self-defense. Chicago required that all handguns had to be registered, but refused all handgun registration after a 1982 citywide handgun ban.

> **The Legal Holdings**
> The Supreme Court of the United States held that the Second Amendment is fully applicable to the States and that individual self-defense is "the central component" of the Second Amendment. Therefore, the Second Amendment prohibits states from enacting bans on handguns for self-protection in the home.

E. _Legal limitations of the right to keep and bear arms_

The Supreme Court of the United States has stated: "Of course the right [to keep and bear arms] was not unlimited, just as the First Amendment's right of free speech was not." Courts may have struggled over the years with what the Second Amendment means, but they have been resolute that there is an element of self-defense. The _Heller_ Court stated that, "The Second Amendment does not protect the right to carry arms for any sort of confrontation," focusing their decision on self-defense. Further, the _Miller_ Court stated that the weapons protected were those "in common use at the time" of the decision. This is supported by historical traditions of prohibiting the carry of "dangerous and unusual weapons" that are commonly used by criminals offensively, as opposed to by law-abiding citizens for defensive purposes.

The Second Amendment does not protect against prohibitions on firearm possession by felons and the mentally ill; _Heller_ made this point in its decision, and many circuit court cases such as _U.S. v. Everist_ follow the same reasoning. The Court of Appeals in _U.S. v. Everist_ stated that the Second Amendment is subject to, "limited narrowly tailored specific exceptions or restrictions for particular cases that are reasonable; it is clear that felons, infants and those of unsound mind may be prohibited from possessing firearms." _U.S. v. Everist_, 368 F.3d 517, 519 (5th Cir. 2004). Along this same train of thought, the _Heller_ Court did not want to eliminate laws that imposed conditions and qualifications on the commercial sales of firearms.

It also does not mean that the Second Amendment includes the right to carry anywhere a person wants. The *Heller* Court stated that their opinion was not meant to allow the carrying of firearms in sensitive places such as schools and certain government buildings.

Practical Legal Tip:

Currently, the two most important court decisions fortifying our gun rights are *Heller* and *McDonald*. But those cases were very, very close to going the other way! Both were decided by a 5-4 majority, meaning that if only one other Supreme Court Justice had decided differently, our individual right to possess and carry firearms could have been severely limited. -*Justin*

III. Major firearms statutes every gun owner needs to know
At the federal level, there are plenty of laws and regulations that concern firearms, but this section will focus on some of the more major legislative actions that all gun owners need to know.

A. *Gun Control Act of 1968*
The Gun Control Act of 1968 ("GCA") was enacted by Congress to "provide for better control of the interstate traffic of firearms." This law is primarily focused on regulating interstate commerce in firearms by generally prohibiting interstate firearms transfers except among licensed manufacturers, dealers, and importers. However, interstate commerce has been held by the courts to include nearly everything. It also contains classes of individuals to whom firearms should not be sold. For the specifics of who can and can't purchase a firearm, please refer to Chapter Three. Among other things, the GCA created the Federal Firearms License ("FFL") system, imposed importation restrictions on military surplus rifles

(adding a "sporting purpose test" and a "points system" for handguns), and marking requirements.

B. *The Brady Handgun Violence Prevention Act*

The Brady Handgun Violence Prevention Act, commonly referred to as the Brady Law, instituted federal background checks (the National Instant Criminal Background Check System or NICS) for firearm purchasers in the United States. It also prohibited certain persons from purchasing firearms. For more information on who can or cannot purchase a firearm, *see* Chapter Three.

C. *The Firearm Owners' Protection Act*

The Firearm Owners' Protection Act ("FOPA") revised many provisions of the original GCA, including "reforms" on the inspection of FFLs. This same Act updated the list of individuals prohibited from purchasing firearms that was introduced by the GCA. The FOPA also banned the ownership by civilians of any machine gun that was not registered under the NFA as of May 19, 1986. FOPA created what is called a "safe passage" provision of the law —18 U.S.C. §926A— which provides a specific, lawful method for traveling *through* states with strict gun laws with a firearm. Finally, FOPA prohibited a registry for non-NFA items that directly linked firearms to their owners.

D. *The Public Safety and Recreational Firearms Use Protection Act*

The Public Safety and Recreational Firearms Use Protection Act, commonly referred to as the *Federal Assault Weapons Ban*, was a subsection of the Violent Crime Control and Law Enforcement Act of 1994. It banned outright the manufacture and transfer of certain semi-automatic firearms and magazines. This ban grandfathered-in previously legally owned weapons, but no prohibited firearm could be acquired or manufactured after September 13, 1994. With great foresight, the drafters of this law included a so-called "sunset provision" that stated the ban would expire ten years later unless renewed. The ban expired in 2004, and all attempts to renew it have been unsuccessful.

E. *The National Firearms Act*

The National Firearms Act ("NFA") regulates and imposes a statutory excise tax on the manufacture and transfer of certain types of firearms and weapons: machine guns, short-barreled weapons, suppressors, explosive devices, and "any other weapons" (AOWs can range from everyday objects that are actually firearms, such as an umbrella that can fire a round, to other weapons the ATF decides to place in this category, such as wallet holsters). The tax is $200 if you make or transfer an item (other than for the transfer of AOWs). The tax for transferring AOWs is $5. The NFA is also referred to as Title II of the federal firearms laws. For more information on how to navigate the NFA while remaining legal, please *see* Chapter Fourteen.

IV. Do Pennsylvanians have a right to keep and bear arms in the Pennsylvania Constitution?

Yes. The Pennsylvania Constitution acknowledges the right to keep and bear arms in Article I, Section 21. The Pennsylvania Constitution predates the United States Constitution, and the provisions of Article I, Section 21 existed prior to the Second Amendment. Article I, Section 21 reads:

> *The right of the citizens to bear arms in defense of themselves and the State shall not be questioned.*

The Pennsylvania Constitution guarantees the right to bear arms more clearly than the United States Constitution. As discussed above, the Supreme Court of the United States has wrestled with whether the Second Amendment protections apply to private citizens (remember, *Heller* was decided by a one vote margin!). The Pennsylvania Constitution leaves no room for this argument, as it plainly applies to "the citizens," and makes no reference to militia. Moreover, Article I, Section 21 specifically provides a purpose for this right in "defense of themselves and the State."

Despite its strong wording, the Supreme Court of Pennsylvania has held that the right guaranteed in Article I, Section 21 is "not beyond regulation," much like that of the Second Amendment. Further, the Commonwealth Court of Pennsylvania has held that the right to bear arms "may be restricted in the exercise of the police power for the good order of society and protection of the citizens." *Gardner v. Jenkins*, 541 A.2d 406, 409 (Pa. Cmwlth. 1988).

A. *Can Pennsylvania prohibit local municipalities from making certain gun laws?*

Yes. The Pennsylvania Legislature can and does expressly prohibit local governments from making certain gun laws by the legal doctrine known as "preemption." A preemption statute is a mechanism by which the Pennsylvania Legislature sets certain areas off-limits to local government regulation. This helps ensure the uniformity of law across the state, in this case, firearms law.

Uniformity of law can be extremely important when it comes to firearms law. For example, some of Pennsylvania's neighboring states have firearms laws that are very different —and exponentially more restrictive— than those of Pennsylvania. As a result, some gun owners from Pennsylvania have inadvertently become criminals by crossing the wrong state lines. Considering there are over 2,000 municipalities in Pennsylvania, preemption prevents inadvertent criminal activity *within* the Commonwealth.

B. *What local governments may not regulate*

In 1974, the Pennsylvania State Legislature enacted 18 Pa.C.S. §6120, which is Pennsylvania's preemption law. Today, the main provision reads:

> §6120. Limitation on the regulation of firearms and ammunition
>
> a) General rule.—No county, municipality or township may in any manner regulate the lawful ownership, possession, transfer or transportation of firearms, ammunition or ammunition components when carried or transported for purposes not prohibited by the laws of this Commonwealth.

Pennsylvania courts have interpreted section 6120 to have a broad preemptive effect. Most clearly, Pennsylvania law specifically denies "all municipalities the power to regulate the ownership, possession, transfer or [transportation] of firearms." *Nat'l Rifle Ass'n v. Phila.*, 977 A.2d 78, 82-83 (Pa. Cmwlth. 2009) (quoting *Ortiz v. Commonwealth*, 545 Pa. 279, 681 A.2d 152 (1996)).

While local governments have contended that municipalities may regulate *unlawful* activity, the Commonwealth Court of Pennsylvania has determined otherwise. *See Nat'l Rifle Ass'n v. Phila.*, 977 A.2d 78 (Pa. Cmwlth. 2009). Accordingly, Pennsylvania courts have found that local governments cannot regulate the ownership, possession, transfer or transportation of firearms, even if the conduct they're attempting to regulate is already unlawful under state law.

Local governments have additionally tried to argue that preemption is limited to activities that include "carry or transport." Again, the Commonwealth Court has disagreed with this. *See Clarke v. House of Representatives*, 957 A.2d 361, 364 (Pa. Cmwlth. 2008) *aff'd sub nom. Clarke v. House of Representatives of the Commonwealth*, 602 Pa. 222, 980 A.2d 34 (Pa. 2009). As a result, local governments are forbidden from regulating the ownership, possession, transfer or transportation of firearms, regardless of whether the activity includes carry or transport.

C. *What local governments may regulate*
It is important to note that the Commonwealth Court has used strong language confirming the broad authority afforded by section 6120. Particularly, it has reasoned "Section 6120(a) preempts all firearm regulation." *Dillon v. City of Erie*, 83 A.3d 467 (Pa. Cmwlth. 2014).

By statute, however, state law permits local governments to "regulate or to prohibit and prevent . . . the unnecessary firing and discharge of firearms in or into the highways and other public places thereof." 53 P.S. §3703.

D. _Beware of defiant local governments_
Although local firearms regulation has been illegal since 1974, some local governments continue to enact, uphold and enforce ordinances that blatantly restrict ownership, possession, transport and transfer of firearms in some manner. Unfortunately, lawsuits—which are very costly and time-consuming—are really the only way citizens can demand compliance from local governments. Because local governments are aware of these practical impediments, there has been little incentive for them to follow the law.

In January of 2015, U.S. Law Shield of Pennsylvania took action and filed a lawsuit against the City of Harrisburg challenging five illegal firearms ordinances. Ultimately, there is much more work to be done, and many lawsuits against many local governments will likely follow. The bottom line is that until the courts force these local governments to repeal illegal ordinances, local governments may continue to enforce them. So even though these ordinances are illegal under state law, violators may very well find themselves becoming a "test case."

CHAPTER TWO
LEGAL DEFINITIONS AND CLASSIFICATIONS OF FIREARMS: WHAT IS LEGAL?

I. Introduction and overview

Before discussing the law of firearms and all its different facets, it is important first to understand what the law defines as a "firearm." Firearms laws are governed on both the federal and state levels; therefore, throughout this chapter we will explore the interactions federal and state law have on the purchase and possession of firearms.

A. *What is a firearm?*

Federal definition
Under the federal law, a firearm is defined as "any weapon (including a starter gun) which will or is designed to or may readily be converted to expel a projectile by the action of an explosive." 18 U.S.C. §921(a)(3). The federal definition of a firearm also includes the frame or receiver of any such weapon, any firearm muffler or silencer, or any "destructive device."

Pennsylvania definition
Section 6102 of the Uniform Firearms Act of Pennsylvania defines a firearm as "any pistol or revolver with a barrel length less than 15 inches, any shotgun with a barrel length less than 18 inches or any rifle with a barrel length less than 16 inches, or any pistol, revolver, rifle or shotgun with an overall length of less than 26 inches. The barrel length of a firearm shall be determined by measuring from the muzzle of the barrel to the face of the closed action, bolt or cylinder, whichever is applicable."

The takeaway is that the Pennsylvania definition of what is a "firearm" is a subset of the federal definition of "firearm." Therefore, all items that meet the Pennsylvania definition of "firearms" are covered by the federal definition of what is a "firearm." But, not every item classified under the federal definition of "firearm" is a "firearm" under Pennsylvania law.

NOTE: While the definition above generally applies to the Uniform Firearms Act, other Pennsylvania laws—even certain specific laws in the Uniform Firearms Act—define "firearm" more broadly. Although the specific wording of the definition may vary slightly, the broader definitions include long guns, and closely resemble the federal definition. The laws which use a more broad definition of "firearm" include: 18 Pa.C.S. §908 (Prohibited offensive weapons); 18 Pa.C.S. §913 (Possession of firearm or other dangerous weapon in court facility); 18 Pa.C.S. §2707.1 (Discharge of a firearm into an occupied structure); 18 Pa.C.S. §3901 (Definitions [related to Theft and Related Offenses]); 18 Pa.C.S. §6105 (Persons not to possess, use, manufacture, control, sell or transfer firearms); 18 Pa.C.S. §6107 (Prohibited conduct during emergency); 18 Pa.C.S. §6111 (Sale or transfer of firearms); 18 Pa.C.S. §6111.2 (Firearm sales surcharge); 18 Pa.C.S. §6111.4 (Registration of firearms); and 18 Pa.C.S. §6113 (Licensing of dealers).

Why might it be important to know the different ways the term "firearm" is defined under federal and state law? There are different actions that you may be permitted to take under federal law, but not under Pennsylvania law. It all focuses around the definitions. Just because something is legal under federal law does not make it legal under Pennsylvania law.

It also matters because if a person finds themselves charged with a crime by federal authorities, the federal definition of a firearm will apply. Likewise, if the charge is a violation of state law, then the Pennsylvania definition will apply. Thus, the primary difference in the definitions and their impact on an accused charged with a crime involving a firearm lies with how a person may be in trouble with the law. As we will see in the next section, the definitions of what does and does not constitute a firearm, although similar in many aspects, contain a lot of differences that make violating the law surprisingly easy.

B. *Definitions for handguns, rifles, and shotguns*
In addition to defining what constitutes a firearm, federal and Pennsylvania laws further classify and define weapons into categories of firearms and long guns (rifles and shotguns). This section will provide an overview of how federal and state laws classify firearms and other weapons as well as the physical requirements for a weapon to be legal under federal law and under Pennsylvania law.

1. <u>What is a handgun?</u>
This is where the basic definitions and distinctions between the Pennsylvania definition of "firearm" and the federal definition are most realized. In Pennsylvania, there is no definition for "handgun." However, in Pennsylvania, a revolver and a pistol fall under the definition of a "firearm" as long as the barrel length is less than 15 inches.

However, under federal law, a handgun simply refers to any firearm that is designed to be fired by using only one hand (*i.e.*, pistol and revolvers). While it is true that most individuals will use two hands when firing a handgun for safety and accuracy purposes, the emphasis in the legal definition of a handgun under federal law rests purely in its design to be held or fired with a single hand, whereas the Pennsylvania definitions primarily focus upon the length of the weapon.

Federal definition
The United States Code of Federal Regulations defines a handgun as "(a) any firearm which has a short stock and is designed to be held and fired by the use of a single hand; and (b) any combination of parts from which a firearm described in paragraph (a) can be assembled." 27 CFR §478.11.

Pennsylvania definition
As mentioned, there is no specific definition under Pennsylvania law for a handgun. Instead, all revolvers and pistols meet the definition of "firearm" in Pennsylvania. Other items also meet the

Pennsylvania definition of "firearm" as we will see later when we talk about National Firearms Act (NFA) weapons.

2. What is a rifle?

Federal law defines a rifle as "a weapon designed or redesigned, made or remade, and intended to be fired from the shoulder, and designed or redesigned and made or remade to use the energy of the explosive in a fixed metallic cartridge to fire only a single projectile through a rifled bore for each single pull of the trigger." 27 CFR §478.11. In addition, a non-NFA regulated rifle must have a barrel length of 16 inches or greater, and includes any weapon made from a rifle which is at least 26 inches overall in length. Pennsylvania law does not provide a specific definition for a rifle under the Uniform Firearms Act, but it does include Short Barrel Rifles (SBR) (*i.e.*, rifles that have a barrel that is under 16 inches or an overall length less than 26 inches) within the Pennsylvania definition of "firearm."

Minimum lengths
In order for a rifle to not be subject to the NFA, it must have a *barrel* of at least 16 inches in length. The ATF procedure for measuring barrel length is accomplished by measuring from the closed bolt (or breech-face) to the furthermost end of the barrel or permanently attached muzzle device. Below is an example of a rifle that does not meet the minimum barrel length requirement after measurement:

Per the ATF, the barrel is to be measured by inserting a dowel rod into the barrel until the rod stops against the bolt or breech-face.

The rod is then marked at the furthermost end of the barrel or permanently attached muzzle device, withdrawn from the barrel, and then measured. Any measurement of less than 16 inches will classify the rifle as being an SBR under federal law and subject the firearm to the NFA. For SBRs and other NFA weapons and the laws concerning them, *see* Chapter Fourteen. *Note:* for overall length, rifles with collapsible/folding-stocks are measured from the "extreme ends," unless the stock is "easily detachable," in which case it is measured without the stock.

The Pennsylvania measurement method for what constitutes a "firearm" is determined by a specific means of measurement. We can find this method in section 6102 of the Pennsylvania Uniform Firearms Act, which reads "The barrel length of a firearm shall be determined by measuring from the muzzle of the barrel to the face of the closed action, bolt or cylinder, whichever is applicable." The Pennsylvania method is silent in terms of specific guidance for the determination of overall length.

3. <u>What is a shotgun?</u>

The federal definition of a shotgun is "a weapon designed or redesigned, made or remade, and intended to be fired from the shoulder, and designed or redesigned and made or remade to use the energy of the explosive in a fixed shotgun shell to fire through a smooth bore either a number of ball shot or a single projectile for each single pull of the trigger." 27 CFR §478.11. Like rifles, under federal law, non-NFA regulated shotguns have requirements for minimum barrel and overall lengths. Shotgun barrels must be at least 18 inches long and must also comply with the same 26 inch overall length requirement.

In Pennsylvania, there is no specific definition of shotgun. A non-NFA governed shotgun (*i.e.*, the barrel length is over 18 inches and the overall length is greater than 26 inches) is not considered a "firearm" under the definition provided in the Pennsylvania Uniform Firearms Act.

Minimum lengths

In order for a shotgun to not be subject to the NFA, it must have a barrel of at least 18 inches in length. The ATF procedure for measuring the barrel length of a shotgun is the same as it is for a rifle. Below is an example of a shotgun that does not meet the minimum barrel length requirement after measurement:

Per federal law, any shotgun with a measurement of less than 18 inches (or overall length of less than 26 inches) will classify the shotgun as a short-barreled shotgun (SBS) under federal law and as a "firearm" under Pennsylvania law. For SBSs and other NFA governed weapons, *see* Chapter Fourteen. *Note:* under federal law, the collapsible/folding-stock rule that applies to rifles applies to shotguns as well. Pennsylvania offers no such guidance in how the overall length is measured.

C. *Antique firearms and replica firearms*

When is a firearm not legally a "firearm?" It is when the law defines it as not being one, such as with "antique" firearms.

    1.   Federal definition of "antique firearm"

1898 or prior

The federal definition of firearm under Title 18, Section 921 of the United States Code specifically excludes "antique firearms." Even though an antique firearm still functions ballistically similar to a "modern" firearm, under federal law, antique firearms are regulated differently, if at all. An antique firearm under federal law includes any firearm with a matchlock, flintlock, or percussion cap, or similar type of ignition system manufactured in or before 1898 or any replica of a firearm just described so long as the replica "is not designed or redesigned for using rimfire or conventional centerfire fixed ammunition, or uses rimfire or centerfire ammunition that is no longer manufactured in the United States and is not readily available in ordinary channels of commerce." 18 U.S.C. §§921(16)(A) and (B). So, an "antique firearm" is not a "firearm" for purposes of federal regulation; it is an "antique firearm."

Muzzle loading
In addition, federal law does not consider "any muzzle loading rifle, muzzle loading shotgun, or muzzle loading pistol, which is designed to use black powder, or a black powder substitute, and which cannot use fixed ammunition" as a firearm. Be aware, however, that the term "antique firearm" does not include any weapon which incorporates a firearm frame or receiver, any firearm which is converted into a muzzle loading weapon, or any muzzle loading weapon which can be readily converted to fire fixed ammunition by replacing the barrel, bolt, breechblock, or any combination of these parts. 18 U.S.C. §921(a)(16)(C).

2. Pennsylvania definition of "antique firearm"
The Pennsylvania definition of "antique firearm" is almost identical to the federal definition. While the Uniform Firearms Act generally does not apply to antique firearms, there are explicit exceptions to this general rule. Pennsylvania law makes it clear that certain provisions of the Uniform Firearms Act do apply to antique firearms (§6106 related to firearms not to be carried without a license and §6105 related to persons not to possess firearms). As a result, per Pennsylvania law, when one is in Pennsylvania, one may not conceal an "antique firearm" without a License to Carry Firearms, and those prohibited from possessing firearms under Pennsylvania law may not possess an antique firearm. Even though an "antique firearm" is generally not considered a "firearm" under Pennsylvania law, these specific restrictions apply to antique firearms.

It is important to note that persons prohibited from possessing firearms *under Pennsylvania law* cannot possess a muzzle loader. In 18 Pa.C.S. §6105 (persons not to possess firearms), "firearm" is defined as "any weapons which are designed to or may readily be converted to expel any projectile by the action of an explosive or the frame or receiver of any such weapon." Because Pennsylvania law does not specifically exclude muzzle loading firearms, and a muzzle loading firearm meets that definition, those prohibited from possessing firearms under Pennsylvania law cannot lawfully possess muzzle loading firearms.

D. *What firearms are legal under federal law but are illegal under Pennsylvania law?*

None. There are no non-NFA governed items that are illegal in Pennsylvania. There is only one sub-set of NFA governed items that are possibly legal to possess and use under federal law that are not legal under Pennsylvania law. *See* Chapter Fourteen where we discuss this further.

There is no specific provision of the Pennsylvania Uniform Firearms Act that makes it illegal to possess an unregistered NFA firearm (*e.g.*, possess a SBR without a Form 4 and a tax stamp). Instead, prosecutors must resort to a charge outside of the Pennsylvania Uniform Firearms Act and the more general charge under the Pennsylvania Crimes Code called "Prohibited Offensive Weapons" or POW. 18 Pa.C.S. §908. Under section 908, an offensive weapon is specifically defined as "Any bomb, grenade, machine gun, sawed-off shotgun with a barrel less than 18 inches, firearm specially made or specially adapted for concealment or silent discharge, any blackjack, sandbag, metal knuckles, dagger, knife, razor or cutting instrument, the blade of which is exposed in an automatic way by switch, push-button, spring mechanism, or otherwise, any stun gun, stun baton, taser or other electronic or electric weapon or other implement for the infliction of serious bodily injury which serves no common lawful purpose." Aside from a "bomb, grenade or incendiary device," compliance with the National Firearms Act serves as a defense to this general charge.

Under federal law, the NFA governed weapons include:

- short-barreled shotguns;
- short-barreled rifles;
- machine guns;
- firearm silencers or suppressors;
- weapons or devices capable of being concealed on the person from which a shot can be fired;
- pistols or revolvers having a smooth bore (as opposed to rifled bore) barrel designed to fire a fixed shotgun shell;
- pistols or revolvers with a vertical handgrip;
- destructive devices; and
- weapons classified as "Any Other Weapon," or AOWs.

See 26 U.S.C. §5845. For more information on these weapons, *see* Chapter Fourteen discussing the National Firearms Act.

On the surface, our reader may think that owning a NFA-governed item is difficult in Pennsylvania. Nothing can be further from the truth. Applying for and receiving permission to own a NFA-governed weapon is easy to do in Pennsylvania. It just takes time and patience. For more information on these prohibited weapons and the NFA, *see* Chapter Fourteen.

E.   *How big of a gun can a person possess?*
Federal law dictates that any firearm which has any barrel with a bore of more than one-half inch in diameter is a "destructive device" and is subject to the NFA. Possession of any such firearm without the proper paperwork associated with NFA firearms is illegal under federal law. Note, however, that some shotguns are regulated differently. For more information on destructive devices and the NFA, *see* Chapter Fourteen. Pennsylvania has no similar restriction based on barrel size. However, all people in Pennsylvania must follow federal restrictions or they will be subject to prosecution in federal court.

II. Ammunition and the law

No discussion concerning firearms laws would be complete without examining laws concerning the ammunition that goes into a firearm. Just like firearms, the law regulates the possession, sale, and even composition of "legal" ammunition. This section addresses the essential aspects of the law concerning ammunition and what gun owners need to know, both under federal and Pennsylvania law.

A. *How does the law define ammunition?*

Under federal law, the term ammunition is defined under 18 U.S.C. §921(a)(17)(A) and means "ammunition or cartridge cases, primers, bullets, or propellant powder designed for use in any firearm." Thus, the federal definition of ammunition includes the finished product and all of the components in making a round of ammunition. However, the federal definition of ammunition does not include (1) any shotgun shot or pellet not designed for use as the single, complete projectile load for one shotgun hull or casing, nor (2) any unloaded, non-metallic shotgun hull or casing not having a primer. *See* 27 CFR §478.11. In other words, individual ammunition components are legally defined as ammunition themselves, even if they are simply parts, except that shotgun ammunition components, if not completely assembled, are not ammunition.

Under Pennsylvania law, there is no statutory definition for mere "ammunition."

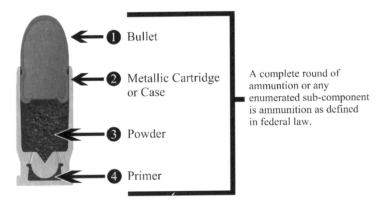

1. Bullet

2. Metallic Cartridge or Case

3. Powder

4. Primer

A complete round of ammuntion or any enumerated sub-component is ammunition as defined in federal law.

B. *Is there a difference in ammunition that is used in different types of firearms?*

Yes. Ammunition can be divided into two classifications: ammunition for handguns and ammunition for long guns. Long gun ammunition can be further divided into ammunition for rifles and ammunition for shotguns.

Handgun ammunition means ammunition that is meant to be fired from a handgun, and it comes in many different calibers. Rifle ammunition is meant to be fired from a rifle and is similar to handgun ammunition in that it comes in many different calibers. Shotgun ammunition, on the other hand, comes in self-contained cartridges loaded with some form of shot or a shotgun slug which is designed to be fired from a shotgun.

Practical Legal Tip:

Even with firearms, having the right tool for the job is important. Practically speaking, you should choose the firearm and ammo that you feel most comfortable using. At the end of the day, *why* you started shooting is always more important than *what* you chose to shoot with. -*Mike*

C. *What ammunition is illegal?*

Armor-piercing handgun ammunition is the only ammunition which has explicit prohibitions under federal law when used in certain circumstances.

The federal definition of armor-piercing ammunition is found in 18 U.S.C. §921(a)(17)(B) and means "[1] a projectile or projectile core which may be used in a handgun and which is constructed entirely (excluding the presence of traces of other substances) from one or a combination of tungsten alloys, steel, iron, brass, bronze, beryllium copper, or depleted uranium; or [2] a full jacketed projectile larger than .22 caliber designed and intended for use in a handgun and whose jacket has a weight of more than 25 percent of the total weight of the projectile."

Federal law

Under federal law, while there is no blanket prohibition on the mere possession of armor-piercing ammunition, it is prohibited under four conditions:

1. *Prohibition one: it is illegal to make or import armor-piercing ammunition.* Under 18 U.S.C. §922(a)(7) it is unlawful for any person to manufacture or import armor-piercing ammunition unless (1) the

manufacture of such ammunition is for the use of the United States, any department or agency of the United States, any state, or any department, agency, or political subdivision of a state; (2) the manufacture of such ammunition is for the purpose of exportation; or (3) the manufacture or importation of such ammunition is for the purpose of testing or experimentation and has been authorized by the United States Attorney General.

2. *Prohibition two: it is illegal for manufacturers and importers to sell or deliver armor-piercing ammunition.* Federal law states that it is unlawful for any manufacturer or importer to sell or deliver armor-piercing ammunition unless such sale or delivery is (1) for the use of the United States, any department or agency of the United States, any state, or any department, agency, or political subdivision of a state; (2) for the purpose of exportation; or (3) for the purpose of testing or experimentation and has been authorized by the United States Attorney General. *See* 18 U.S.C. §922(a)(8).

3. *Prohibition three: an FFL or other license-holder cannot sell or deliver armor-piercing ammunition without the proper documentation.* Under 18 U.S.C. §922(b)(5), it is unlawful for any licensed importer, licensed manufacturer, licensed dealer, or licensed collector to sell or deliver armor-piercing ammunition to any person unless the licensee notes in his records, as required under 18 U.S.C. §923, the name, age, and place of residence of such person if the person is an individual, or the identity and principal and local places of business of such person if the person is a corporation or other business entity.

4. *Prohibition four: it is illegal to possess armor-piercing ammunition if a person is involved in a crime of violence or a drug-trafficking crime.* Pursuant to 18 U.S.C. §924(c)(5), it is unlawful for "any person who, during and in relation to any crime of violence or drug trafficking crime (including a crime of violence or drug trafficking crime that provides for an enhanced punishment if committed by the use of a deadly or dangerous weapon or device) for which the person may be prosecuted in a court of the United States, uses or carries armor piercing ammunition." Individuals who use or carry armor-piercing ammunition in the commission of a crime of violence or during a drug-trafficking crime are subject to heightened sentencing standards should they be found guilty.

Pennsylvania law

Pennsylvania does not have any general restrictions on any type or kind of ammunition. It does restrict the possession of certain types and kinds of ammunition in certain situations: (1) while subject to a Protection From Abuse (PFA) order, and (2) while committing or attempting to commit a crime of violence.

The only restriction on the total possession of ammunition occurs when a person is under an active Protection From Abuse (PFA) order. In that circumstance, the target of the PFA is restricted from owning or possessing ammunition (or weapon or scope, or sight, or bipod, or sling, or light, or magazine, or clip) during the period that the PFA is in effect.

In Pennsylvania, it is unlawful for any person to possess, use or attempt to use a KTW teflon-coated bullet or other armor-piercing ammunition while committing or attempting to commit a crime of violence.

D. *Does modifying traditional ammunition make it illegal?*
No, outside of armor-piercing ammunition in certain circumstances, or persons under an active PFA order, there is no handgun or long gun ammunition that is prohibited under the federal or Pennsylvania law. Modified or other than traditional ammunition is perfectly legal in Pennsylvania.

Factory and Expanded Hollow Point Rounds

E. *What about "armor-piercing" rifle rounds when you are not committing a crime?*
This is perfectly legal in both Pennsylvania and under federal law. This is because the federal definition of armor-piercing ammunition contemplates handguns only, and there are no restrictions on types or kinds of ammunition in Pennsylvania so long as you are not committing a crime of violence. Armor-piercing ammunition for a rifle is perfectly legal, though it may complicate matters at trial in trying to demonstrate to the jury any differentiation. Beyond armor-piercing ammunition, it is legal to use ammunition that is available in common calibers and that functions in revolvers, pistols, shotguns, and rifles.

With a solid understanding of what is and is not a firearm and ammunition, as well as what firearms and ammunition a person may legally possess without the necessity of obtaining additional documentation, we are now ready to move to the next chapter discussing the purchase and possession of firearms.

CHAPTER THREE
PURCHASING, TRANSFERRING, AND POSSESSING FIREARMS

I. Laws of purchasing and possessing: the basics

The laws of purchasing, selling, gifting, or otherwise transferring a firearm are distinct and different from the laws of possessing a firearm. It may be legal for someone to possess a firearm, and it still be illegal for them to "purchase" the firearm. Further, each of these sets of laws for "purchasing" or "possessing" has a federal and a state component both of which must be satisfied in order to start on the right side of the law. As we all recently learned through the Supreme Court of the United States case of *Henderson v. United States*, ownership does not necessarily equal possession. Even a convicted felon maintains a level of lawful ownership over firearms that he or she once lawfully possessed so as to allow the lawful sale or transfer of the firearms. Since the felon can no longer legally possess the firearms, the trial court must be satisfied that the buyer/recipient will not give the felon control over the firearms, so that the felon could either use them or direct their use.

On the federal level, the Bureau of Alcohol, Tobacco, Firearms and Explosives ("ATF") is charged with regulating firearms including sales, purchases, and transfers through Federal Firearms Licensees ("FFLs" or "dealers"). However, a multitude of federal agencies can be involved in any given firearms law investigation or police function most currently falling under a branch of the U.S. Department of Homeland Security. Pennsylvania has no direct state-level counterpart to the ATF.

A. *What is an FFL?*

An FFL or Federal Firearms License is a license required by federal law for those persons or entities that are engaged in the business of buying and selling firearms. A federal firearms licensee is often called an "FFL" or "dealer." When an individual purchases, sells, or transfers a firearm through a dealer, the FFL and the individual must both comply with specific federal law requirements, paperwork, and procedures concerning the buying, selling, or transferring of those firearms. These requirements will be addressed throughout this chapter.

B. _Who must obtain an FFL?_

Federal law requires a federal firearms license if a person is engaged in a _business_ as a firearms dealer, manufacturer, or importer. For the purposes of our discussion in this chapter, a person is engaged in the business when the person "devotes time, attention, and labor to dealing in firearms as a regular course of trade or business with the principal objective of livelihood and profit through the repetitive purchase and resale of firearms, but such term shall not include a person who makes occasional sales, exchanges, or purchases of firearms for the enhancement of a personal collection or for a hobby, or who sells all or part of his personal collection of firearms." 18 U.S.C. §921(a)(21)(C). There is no exact number of sales or transfers that constitutes "occasional sales, exchanges, or purchases of firearms."

C. _What are the different types of FFL?_

There are nine different categories of FFLs. The most common of which are the Type 01-Dealer in Firearms/Gunsmithing and Type 07-Manufacturer of Firearms/Ammunition. The Type 01 (01 FFL) is a dealer license that allows one to conduct the business of selling or transferring firearms other than destructive devices. It allows the 01 FFL licensed person to conduct business involving revolvers, pistols, rifles, shotguns, and some gunsmithing activities, such as basic repair. If the 01 FFL has a _Special Occupational Tax_ (SOT), then it allows for the selling and transferring of National Firearms Act (NFA) items. Note, the 01 FFL may not manufacture or create firearms, or deal or create destructive devices. (_See_ Chapter Fourteen for more information on the NFA and Destructive Devices). The 07 FFL allows for all of the level of activity allowed under a 01 FFL, but, in addition, allows for the licensee to make and manufacturer firearms and ammunition. If you apply for an SOT when you have a 07 FFL, you can legally make machine guns, suppressors, short barrel rifles, and short barrel shotguns subject to certain restrictions outlined in Chapter Fourteen.

D. *I want to become an FFL. How do I do it?*
It can be an amazingly simple process, for those who have not applied for a FFL, it can be rather daunting. There is an application process, an interview, and a lot of aspects about being an FFL that you should know about. One thing that you should know is that an FFL must be in business (which generally means for a profit) and cannot use the FFL simply for his or her own personal collection efforts.

E. *What is a private sale?*
A private sale is just what it sounds like: a sale, purchase, or transfer of a firearm by parties that are not licensed dealers. For long guns in Pennsylvania, a private sale need not involve an FFL or the sheriff's office, as long as all other legal requirements are met. An FFL or the sheriff's office must be involved in all transfers or sales of "firearms" as defined by the Uniform Firearms Act (*i.e.,* modern handguns, short-barreled rifles, short-barreled shotguns) except for "transfers between spouses or to transfers between a parent and child or to transfers between grandparent and grandchild." 18 Pa.C.S. §6111(c). We will discuss the ins-and-outs of private sales in greater detail in this chapter under section IV.

The Pennsylvania law requiring that all private "firearm" transfers go through an FFL or the sheriff's office does not apply to:
1. Any firearm manufactured on or before 1898.
2. Any firearm with a matchlock, flintlock or percussion cap type of ignition system.
3. Any replica of any firearm described in paragraph (1) if the replica:
    (i) is not designed or redesigned to use rimfire or conventional center fire fixed ammunition; or
    (ii) uses rimfire or conventional center fire fixed ammunition which is no longer manufactured in the

United States and which is not readily available in the ordinary channels of commercial trade. 18 Pa.C.S. §6111(e).

Private transfers of these types of firearms are not subject to this requirement. For the purposes of this discussion, we will refer to the firearms subject to this requirement as "modern handguns."

F. *What is the legal age to purchase a firearm?*

Federal law controls all FFL firearms transactions and requires that a person be 21 years of age or older before they may purchase a handgun or 18 for the purchase of a long gun. Pennsylvania follows the federal FFL provisions. However, Pennsylvania differs slightly from the federal provisions when it comes to private sales. As noted above, all handgun purchases in Pennsylvania must go through an FFL or the sheriff's office for a background check, unless the sale or transfer involves "transfers between spouses or to transfers between a parent and child or to transfers between grandparent and grandchild." 18 Pa.C.S. §6111(c). Therefore, it is perfectly legal for a person under the age of 18 to have a handgun transferred to him or her provided that the transfer is conducted through the sheriff's office. In Pennsylvania, if there is a purchase of a modern handgun, then an SP 4-113 must be filled out.

Under federal law, a person must be at least 18 years of age in order to possess a handgun or ammunition for a handgun. *See* 18 U.S.C. §922(x)(2). Unlike the law on purchasing a long gun, there are no federal age requirements for the possession of a rifle or shotgun. There is a Pennsylvania law directly specifying that a person under 18 may not possess or transport a firearm anywhere in the state unless:

- The minor is under the supervision of a parent, grandparent, legal guardian or an adult acting with the expressed consent of the minor's custodial parent or legal guardian and the minor is engaged in lawful activity, including safety training, lawful target shooting, engaging in an organized competition involving the use of a firearm or the firearm is unloaded and the minor is transporting it for a lawful purpose; or

- The minor is lawfully hunting or trapping in accordance with 34 Pa.C.S. (relating to game) [18 Pa.C.S. §6110.1].

You will note above that the use of a firearm in self-defense is not specifically mentioned in section 6110.1 of the Pennsylvania Uniform Firearms Act. There are no reported Pennsylvania appellate cases or Third Circuit cases that address this question directly. However, there is clear tension between the general applicability of the affirmative defense of self-defense (*see* Chapter Four for more details) and the specific prohibition against juveniles possessing a firearm. There seems at the very core of the holding in *United States v. Heller* a transferable concept that, at least while in the home, a juvenile exercising reasonable self-defense may avoid prosecution for violation of section 6110.1. The Third Circuit has recognized "justification" defenses in federal felon in possession cases. It is very rare, short of "immediate emergencies," and they have provided a test. *See United States v. Dodd*, 225 F.3d 340, 344 (3d Cir. 2000) and *United States v. Paolello*, 951 F.2d 537, 539 (3d Cir. 1991). Although these cases deal with federal law, they found the justification to exist even though it isn't enumerated in the federal statute.

G. *Special duty of firearms dealers involving minors*
Federal law requires that FFLs who deliver handguns to non-licensees display at their licensed premises (including temporary business locations at gun shows) a sign that customers can readily see. These signs are provided by the ATF and contain the following language:

1. The misuse of handguns is a leading contributor to juvenile violence and fatalities.
2. Safely storing and securing firearms away from children will help prevent the unlawful possession of handguns by juveniles, stop accidents, and save lives.

3. Federal law prohibits, except in certain limited circumstances, anyone under 18 years of age from knowingly possessing a handgun, or any person from transferring a handgun to a person under 18.

4. A knowing violation of the prohibition against selling, delivering, or otherwise transferring a handgun to a person under the age of 18 is, under certain circumstances, punishable by up to 10 years in prison.

In addition to the displayed sign, federal law requires FFLs to provide non-licensee customers with a written notification containing the same four points as listed above as well as sections 922(x) and 924(a)(6) of Title 18, Chapter 44 of the United States Code. This written notification is available as a pamphlet published by the ATF entitled "Youth Handgun Safety Act Notice" and is sometimes referred to as ATF information 5300.2. Alternatively, this written notification may be delivered to customers on another type of written notification, such as a manufacturer's brochure accompanying the handgun or a sales receipt or invoice applied to the handgun package. Any written notification delivered to a customer other than the one provided by the ATF must include the language described here, and must be "legible, clear, and conspicuous, and the required language shall appear in type size no smaller than 10-point type." 27 CFR §478.103(c).

II. Federal law disqualifications for purchasing and possessing firearms

Federal law lists categories of persons disqualified from legally *purchasing* and *possessing* a firearm. This list comprises disqualifications that come from several different pieces of federal legislation including the Gun Control Act of 1968, the Brady Handgun Violence Protection Act, and the Violence Against Women Act. If a person buys or attempts to buy a firearm from an FFL, they must not be disqualified under any of the laws. Before an FFL may sell or otherwise transfer a firearm, the purchaser must fill out an ATF Form 4473. This form has questions concerning each of the criteria that disqualify a person to purchase a firearm under federal law. These disqualifications include:

1. if the person is not the actual purchaser of the firearm—also known as a "straw man purchaser;"
2. if the person is under indictment or information in any court for a felony or any other crime for which the judge could imprison the person for more than one year;
3. if the person has ever been convicted in any court for a felony or other crime for which the judge could imprison the person for more than one year;
4. if the person is a fugitive from justice;
5. if the person is an unlawful user of, or addicted to, marijuana, or any depressant, stimulant, narcotic drug, or controlled substance;
6. if the person has ever been adjudicated as mentally defective or has been committed to a mental institution;
7. if the person has been dishonorably discharged from the Armed Forces;
8. if the person is subject to an active protective order restraining the person from harassing, stalking, or threatening the person's child, or an intimate partner or child of such partner;
9. if the person has been convicted in any court for a misdemeanor crime of domestic violence;
10. if the person has ever renounced their United States citizenship;
11. if the person is an alien illegally in the United States; and
12. if the person is admitted under a non-immigrant visa and does not qualify for an exception.

The purchaser must legally affirm that they are not subject to any of the criteria listed above before they may purchase a firearm. If a prospective purchaser answers any question on the form in a manner that indicates they are legally disqualified, it is illegal for the FFL to sell that person the firearm, and it is illegal for the purchaser to complete the transaction or possess the firearm.

A. *Understanding who is disqualified*
   1. Can I buy a firearm for another person?

No. This would be a "straw purchase." In order to legally purchase a firearm from a dealer, you must be the "actual purchaser or transferee." If you are not the actual purchaser or transferee, it is illegal for you to complete the transfer or sale under federal law. Purchases for third persons are often called "straw purchases" and are illegal. Legitimate gifts are not considered straw purchases under federal law, as discussed below. As previously discussed, Pennsylvania law strictly governs the transfer of handguns, which may impact how you must legally transfer a "gift." In fact, SP 4-113 contains the following question:

Are you the actual buyer of the firearm(s), as defined under 18 Pa.C.S. §6102 (relating to definitions), listed on this application/record of sale? Warning: You are not the actual buyer if you are acquiring the firearm(s) on behalf of another person, unless you are legitimately acquiring the firearm as a gift for any of the following individuals who are legally eligible to own a firearm:
   1. spouse;
   2. parent;
   3. child;
   4. grandparent; or
   5. grandchild.
If you are not the actual purchaser, beware!

In fact, the ATF has a campaign called "Don't Lie for the Other Guy" that is targeted at (as they term it on their website) detection and deterrence of straw purchases. The ATF website lists numerous examples of prosecutions for straw purchases and a United States Supreme Court case examined and upheld federal law on this matter. *Abramski v. United States*, 134 S.Ct. 2259 (2014).

Pennsylvania also has its own government-funded Straw Purchase Prevention Education Program.

So who is the "actual" buyer or transferee so as not to be a "straw man?" The ATF states that you are the actual "transferee/buyer if you are purchasing the firearm for yourself or otherwise acquiring the firearm for yourself (*e.g.,* redeeming the firearm from pawn/retrieving it from consignment, firearm raffle winner)." The ATF goes on to state "you are also the actual transferee/buyer if you are legitimately purchasing the firearm as a gift for a third party."

Example:

> Mr. Smith asks Mr. Jones to purchase a firearm for Mr. Smith. Mr. Smith gives Mr. Jones the money for the firearm. Mr. Jones then buys the firearm with Mr. Smith's money and gives Mr. Smith the firearm.

Mr. Jones is not the "actual buyer" (he is legally a "straw man") of the firearm and if Mr. Jones indicates that he is the "actual buyer" of the firearm on ATF Form 4473, he has committed a federal crime. The Supreme Court ruling in *Abramski*, however, did not make "gifts" of firearms illegal.

When completing ATF Form 4473: if a person checks "yes" to the box asking if the person is the "actual purchaser," then that person cannot have engaged in a separate transaction to sell or transfer the firearm privately. Please note: The Supreme Court's ruling held that a person cannot legally purchase a firearm on behalf of another even if the person receiving the firearm would not otherwise be prohibited from making the purchase themselves. So don't buy a firearm for another person no matter how good a friend, relative, or person they are—it is a crime!

FREQUENTLY ASKED QUESTIONS FROM ATF WEBSITE

Q: May I buy a firearm from an FFL as a "gift" for another person?
A: Yes.

Editor's note: Instead of the previous example where Mr. Smith paid Mr. Jones to purchase a firearm for him, if Mr. Jones decides to buy a firearm with his own money and then give the firearm to

Mr. Smith as a present, then Mr. Jones is the actual buyer/transferee of the firearm. Since Mr. Jones is the actual buyer, there exists no sham or "straw man," and the purchase is legal. Beware that all transfers of modern handguns are subject to Pennsylvania's restrictions. Barring certain specific exceptions, these must go through an FFL or the sheriff's office.

Q: May a parent or guardian purchase a firearm as a gift for a juvenile?

A: Yes, however, possession of handguns by juveniles is generally unlawful under federal law. Juveniles may only receive and possess handguns with the written permission of a parent or guardian for limited purposes.

See www.atf.gov.

2. <u>A person cannot purchase a firearm if they have been convicted or are under "indictment or information" for a felony or certain misdemeanors</u>

If a person has been convicted of a felony or other crime for which a judge may sentence, or could have sentenced the person to more than one year imprisonment, that person may not legally purchase a firearm (unless the crime was a state misdemeanor punishable by imprisonment of two years or less). *See* 18 U.S.C. §921(a)(20)(B).

In Pennsylvania, this means that if one is charged or arrested or convicted for a crime that is a misdemeanor of the first degree or higher (*e.g.*, felony of the third degree, felony of the second degree, felony of the first degree, inchoate murder or murder) then one cannot purchase or possess a firearm.

More people get charged with firearm related felonies or misdemeanors because they misunderstand this part of the law than any other federal or state law involving firearms. It is vitally important to point out that the *actual sentence* received is *not* the determining factor for disqualification. Rather, it is the possible maximum sentence. A person may have only been sentenced to 30 days imprisonment, but if the crime for which they were charged allowed a maximum penalty of five years, then that person is disqualified. *See Schrader v. Holder*, 831 F.Supp.2d 304 (D.D.C. 2011, *aff'd*, 704 F.3d 980 (D.C. Cir. 2013)). Even if your charges are still pending and you have been offered the Accelerated Rehabilitation Disposition (ARD) program, but have not formally entered it, you still cannot purchase or possess a firearm if the charges are a misdemeanor of the first degree or higher. Even if the FFL says "just fill it out and we'll see," that is not a defense to incorrectly answering the question and certifying it as a true answer on the Form 4473.

3. <u>What does it mean to be a "fugitive from justice" so as to be disqualified from purchasing a firearm?</u>

A "fugitive from justice" is a person who, after having committed a crime, flees from the jurisdiction of the court where the crime was committed. A fugitive from justice may also be a person who goes into hiding to avoid facing charges for the crime of which he or she is accused. Such individuals are not eligible to purchase or possess firearms.

Under Pennsylvania law, a state-based disqualification as a "fugitive from justice" does not apply to an individual whose fugitive status is based upon a nonmoving or moving summary offense under Title 75 (relating to vehicles). *See* 18 PA.C.S. §6105(c)(1).

4. <u>Unlawful users of or persons addicted to drugs are disqualified from purchasing firearms</u>

Federal law is very broad in that it disqualifies persons from the purchase of firearms if they are either illegal users of or addicted to marijuana or any depressant, stimulant, narcotic drug, or any controlled substance. Under federal law, an "addict" is defined as a person that "habitually uses any narcotic so as to endanger the public morals, health, safety, or welfare, or who is so far addicted to the use of narcotic drugs as to have lost the power of self-control with reference to his addiction." 21 U.S.C. §802(1). However, in using the terms "users of," no such frequency or dependence seems contemplated in the words, nor did Congress give further guidance. Illegal users and addicts are prohibited from purchasing firearms from any person under federal law, and are likewise prohibited from possessing firearms. *See* 18 U.S.C. §§922(d) and (g). For the purposes of this prohibition, the Pennsylvania State Police consider a person an "unlawful user" for one year following any drug-related conviction, even if the conviction itself does not otherwise qualify as prohibitive.

5. A person can't legally buy or possess firearms if they are "mentally defective"

What does "mentally defective" mean? A person is considered to have been adjudicated as "mentally defective" if there has been a "determination by a court, board, commission, or other lawful authority that a person, as a result of marked subnormal intelligence, or mental illness, incompetency, condition, or disease: is a danger to himself or others, or lacks the mental capacity to contract or manage his own affairs." The term "mentally defective" includes "a finding of insanity by a court in a criminal case, and those persons found incompetent to stand trial or found not guilty by reason of insanity or lack of mental responsibility." 27 CFR §478.11.

"Mentally defective" also includes a person who has been committed to a mental institution by a court, board, commission, or other lawful authority, or a commitment to a mental institution involuntarily. The term includes commitment for mental defectiveness or mental illness, and also includes commitment for other reasons, such as drug use. However, it does not include a person in a mental institution for observation or a voluntary admission to a mental institution. Individuals who have been adjudicated as mentally defective are also prohibited from possessing firearms under federal law. *See* 18 U.S.C. §922(g)(4).

In the federal statutes there is supposed to be an avenue for a person who meets the federal definition of "mentally defective" to petition to have that status removed. *See generally*, 18 U.S.C.

§925(c) and the NICS Improvement Amendments Act of 2007, Public Law 110-180. However, at this time, there has been zero funding or effort by the ATF to implement the program.

If the mental health adjudication or commitment was imposed by a federal department or agency, the person affected can also be relieved from this "mental defective" disability only if the:

- Adjudication or commitment was set aside or expunged;
- Person was fully released from mandatory treatment, supervision, or monitoring;
- Person was found to no longer suffer from the disabling mental health condition;
- Person has otherwise been found to be rehabilitated; or
- Adjudication or commitment was based solely on a medical finding without opportunity for hearing.

Pennsylvania has a series of laws that govern voluntary and involuntary commitments called the Mental Health Procedures Act, found in Title 50 of the Pennsylvania Statutes. This is an exceedingly murky area of the law in practice. For example, if someone is initially involuntarily committed to a mental health treatment facility under an emergency petition (called a 302 commitment), does he or she meet the definition of mentally defective? Under federal law, there is no existing case law and the answer remains unclear. As a result, Pennsylvanians are encouraged to treat these as prohibitive under federal law. But under Pennsylvania law, the person is expressly prohibited from possessing a firearm. There is a procedure in place where a person who was involuntarily committed under section 302 may apply for rehabilitation of his or her rights to own, possess, and use a firearm under state law. However, this procedure does not impact any federal prohibitions that may exist. In order to clear one's record of an involuntary commitment under section 302, one must instead prove that the commitment itself was invalid. In 18 Pa.C.S. §6111.1, the Court of Common Pleas is granted the authority to "review the sufficiency of the evidence upon which the commitment was based." If the Court of Common Pleas finds that "the evidence upon which the involuntary commitment was based was insufficient," the court must order the records expunged.

It is clear that a section 303 or a section 304 commitment are clearly disqualifiers under both federal and state law. Although a section 306 commitment is not specifically named in the state statute, it is still a disqualifying event under both federal and state law, because in order to have a lawful 306 commitment, one must have had a lawful 304 commitment (recall that a 304 commitment is specifically mentioned in the state statute as a disqualifying event). If a person is initially certified under section 302 but then is "allowed to change that to a voluntary commitment" after the fact, which is something that some institutions try to do, it does not remove this disability. The initial section 302 commitment papers still exist, unless the expungement process is successfully completed in state court by a judge within the committing jurisdiction.

6. A person subject to a restraining order may not purchase or possess a firearm

Under 18 U.S.C. §922(g)(8), firearms may not be sold to or received by person subject to a court order that: (a) was issued after a hearing which the person received actual notice of and had an opportunity to participate in; (b) restrains the person from harassing, stalking, or threatening an intimate partner or child of such intimate partner or person, or engaging in other conduct that would place an intimate partner in reasonable fear of bodily injury to the partner or child; and (c) includes a finding that such person represents a credible threat to the physical safety of such intimate partner or child; or by its terms explicitly prohibits the use, attempted use, or threatened use of physical force against such intimate partner or child that a person would reasonably be expected to cause bodily injury. An "intimate partner" of a person is the spouse or former spouse of the person, the parent of a child of the person, or an individual who cohabitates with the person.

Pennsylvania has very specific provisions when it comes to restraining orders. Unlike other states, Pennsylvania does not allow for general restraining orders and only allows Protection From Abuse (PFA) orders in limited circumstances. To be eligible to obtain a PFA order, the applicant must be a person 18 or over or an emancipated minor. The applicant can only seek legal protection from acts of domestic abuse done to them personally or to that person's minor child by a family or household member. It does not include protection from stranger violence. It does include a spouse or former spouse; a person who lives or lived with you as a spouse; a brother or sister; a parent or child; a family member related to the applicant by blood or marriage; a current or former sexual or intimate partner; and/or someone the applicant has a child in common with. *See* 23 Pa.C.S. §6102(a). An applicant can apply for a PFA to cover a current or former same-sex partner. 23 Pa.C.S. §6102(a). An unemancipated minor child can obtain a PFA, but only if a parent or a guardian ad litem files for the PFA on that person's behalf.

In addition to who the applicant may seek protection from, there is a narrow scope of behavior that can give rise to a proper PFA. To be proper, a PFA must allege and prove that the target of the PFA:

1. Is attempting to cause or causing (with or without a deadly weapon):
    1.1 Bodily injury or serious bodily injury;
    1.2 Rape;
    1.3 Involuntary deviate sexual intercourse (oral sex, anal sex, vaginal or anal penetration with a foreign object performed under force or the threat of force, or while unconscious or with someone not capable of granting consent due to age or mental infirmity);
    1.4 Sexual assault or statutory sexual assault;
    1.5 Aggravated indecent assault (vaginal or anal penetration with a finger or other body part under force or threat of force, or while unconscious with

someone not capable of granting consent due to age or mental infirmity);

   1.6 Indecent assault (touching a person's intimate parts for the purposes of arousal without consent, under force or threat of force, or while the person is unconscious or with someone not capable of granting consent due to age or mental infirmity);

   1.7 Incest; or

2. Placing another in reasonable fear of immediate serious bodily injury;
3. False imprisonment;
4. Physical or sexual abuse of a child; or
5. Engaging in a course of conduct or repeatedly committing acts toward another person, including following the person, under circumstances which place the person in reasonable fear of bodily injury.

In general, there are three types of PFA orders: Emergency PFA Orders, Temporary *ex parte* PFA Orders, and Final PFA Orders. An Emergency PFA is a very short-term PFA that is provided for when or if the Court of Common Pleas is closed. A lower court judge (called a Magisterial District Judge or MDJ) will determine if you are in immediate danger and whether or not, if believed, you meet the criteria for issuance of a PFA. If so, the MDJ will issue an emergency PFA that is only in effect until the moment that the Court of Common Pleas opens again. The target of the PFA (the person sought to be restrained) has no right to notice of the hearing before the MDJ, cannot be present during the hearing, and has no opportunity to be heard or submit a counter narrative in an Emergency PFA action.

A Temporary *ex parte* PFA Order is an emergency order that is based upon a sworn written application by the accuser. Again, the target of the PFA (the person sought to be restrained) has no right to notice of the application, has no opportunity to be heard, and is not allowed to submit a counter narrative before the judge renders a decision based upon the sworn declarations in the application.

The Temporary *ex parte* PFA Order is only in effect for a maximum of 10 days unless agreed to by the parties. In terms of a Final PFA Order, there are generally two types: Final PFA Orders where there is a finding of facts, and a Stipulated Final PFA Order with no finding of facts. In the ordinary course of affairs when a Final PFA Order is sought, a full contested hearing with full due process rights, where the accuser has to provide proof and sworn testimony to satisfy the burden to get a PFA, will occur unless the PFA is withdrawn or the parties agree to a Stipulated Final PFA Order with no finding of facts. A Stipulated Final PFA Order with no finding of facts is where both the accuser and the accused agree to the length and terms of the PFA order, but the court and the accused do not agree to any of the allegations of fact. A Final PFA Order can last up to 3 years and can be extended under limited circumstances.

Besides the implications mentioned above forced on those who are subject to a current PFA order, Pennsylvania law allows for a MDJ or a Judge of the Court of Common Pleas to forcibly and physically dispossess a gun owner who is subject to a current PFA from his or her firearms and/or ammunition (sometimes called a "no guns, no ammo provision"). This is so even for an Emergency PFA Order or a Temporary *ex parte* PFA Order where the gun owner does not have a say in the process whatsoever. If an MDJ or a Judge of the Court of Common Pleas enters an Emergency PFA Order or a Temporary *ex parte* PFA Order, the "no guns, no ammo provision" can be challenged. Although, a "no guns, no ammo provision" should not be automatic and should be rationally related to the alleged harm, in reality many, if not most, MDJs or judges of the Court of Common Pleas will simply sign such a provision out of routine or a feeling of "better safe than sorry."

Under Pennsylvania law, when a "no guns, no ammo provision" is entered, the target of the PFA has to dispossess himself or herself of the guns and ammo within 24 hours of the time the judge makes the order or service of the order is achieved. While the PFA is in effect, in order to be in compliance of the 24-hour mandate, the person who is subject to the PFA may transfer the gun to the local sheriff, to a third party for safekeeping, or to a licensed dealer for safekeeping or sale. The law requires those who have the guns for safekeeping, namely the sheriff or the third party, to keep them until the PFA is no longer in effect. If the guns are transferred to a third party, Pennsylvania law requires that the sheriff confirm that the third party is permitted to own or possess firearms, and a certificate of safekeeping be issued that includes a process by affidavit signed by both the third party and the target of the PFA, acknowledging that, among other things, the third party is not subject to a PFA and has never been subject to a PFA, the third party accepts the temporary transfer until the safekeeping certificate is recalled, and the third party knows that the target of the PFA is not to have firearms or ammunition for the duration. If the person who is subject to the PFA transfers the guns to an FFL, the FFL must keep them until the PFA expires or until the guns are sold (subject to the wishes of the owner). *See* 23 Pa.C.S. §§6108(a)(7)(i)(B), 6108.2 (relating to relinquishment for consignment sale, lawful transfer or safekeeping) or §6108.3 (relating to relinquishment to third party for safekeeping) for greater details.

Pennsylvania state law requires that all PFA orders (regardless of type) be inputted into the NICS and PICS firearms background check within 24 hours. Generally, it is a lot sooner than 24 hours if the application and/or orders are generated through the Pennsylvania Protection From Abuse Database (PFAD) system.

7. Domestic violence issues and disqualifications

Any person who has been convicted of a crime of domestic violence may not purchase or possess firearms under federal law. These restrictions were passed in what is known as the *Violence Against Women Act* in 1994 and amended in 1996. This is an often misunderstood law, and, in fact, the ATF has numerous "Frequently Asked Questions" concerning this disqualification on its website: www.atf.gov. The ATF does a good job of explaining the scope of this subject in their FAQs. Due to the complexity of this issue, the ATF examples are included here:

FREQUENTLY ASKED QUESTIONS FROM ATF WEBSITE

Q: What is a "misdemeanor crime of domestic violence?"

A: A "misdemeanor crime of domestic violence" means an offense that:

1. is a misdemeanor under federal or State law;
2. has, as an element, the use or attempted use of physical force, or the threatened use of a deadly weapon; and
3. was committed by a current or former spouse, parent, or guardian of the victim, by a person with whom the victim shares a child in common, by a person who is cohabiting with or has cohabited with the victim as a spouse, parent, or guardian, or by a person similarly situated to a spouse, parent, or guardian of the victim.

However, a person is not considered to have been convicted of a misdemeanor crime of domestic violence unless:

1. the person was represented by counsel in the case, or knowingly and intelligently waived the right of counsel in the case; and
2. in the case of a prosecution for which a person was entitled to a jury trial in the jurisdiction in which the case was tried, either-
    1. the case was tried by a jury, or
    2. the person knowingly and intelligently waived the right to have the case tried by a jury, by guilty plea or otherwise.

In addition, a conviction would not be disabling if it has been expunged or set aside, or is an offense for which the person has been pardoned or has had civil rights restored (if the law of the jurisdiction in which the proceedings were held provides for the loss of civil rights upon conviction for such an offense) unless the pardon, expunction, or restoration of civil rights expressly provides that the person may not ship, transport, possess, or receive firearms, and the person is not otherwise prohibited by the law of the jurisdiction in which the proceedings were held from receiving or possessing firearms. 18 U.S.C. 921(a)(33), 27 CFR 478.11.

Editor's note: A significant number of people make the mistake of overlooking or forgetting about a court issue or family law judicial proceeding. However, if you meet the above criteria, you are federally disqualified from possessing a firearm. The fact that it may have happened a long time ago, or that you did not understand the ramifications, is legally irrelevant.

Q: What is the effective date of this disability?
A: The law was effective September 30, 1996. However, the prohibition applies to persons convicted of such misdemeanors at any time, even if the conviction occurred prior to the law's effective date.

Editor's note: For those wondering why this is not an unconstitutional *ex-post facto* law, multiple federal appeals courts have ruled against that argument and the Supreme Court has consistently declined to review any of those cases, effectively accepting the ruling of the courts of appeals and upholding the law.

Q: X was convicted of misdemeanor assault on October 10, 1996, for beating his wife. Assault has as an element the use of physical force, but is not specifically a domestic violence offense. May X lawfully possess firearms or ammunition?
A: No. X may not legally possess firearms or ammunition. 18 U.S.C. 922(g)(9), 27 CFR 478.32(a)(9).

Editor's note: In this situation because X's conviction for assault was against a person in the statute's protected class, the conviction would be, for purposes of firearms purchasing disqualification, a domestic violence conviction.

Q: X was convicted of a misdemeanor crime of domestic violence on September 20, 1996, 10 days before the effective date of the statute. He possesses a firearm on October 10, 2004. Does X lawfully possess the firearm?
A: No. If a person was convicted of a misdemeanor crime of domestic violence at any time, he or she may not lawfully possess

firearms or ammunition on or after September 30, 1996. 18 U.S.C. 922(g)(9), 27 CFR 478.32(a)(9).

Q: In determining whether a conviction in a State court is a "conviction" of a misdemeanor crime of domestic violence, does Federal or State law apply?
A: State law applies. Therefore, if the State does not consider the person to be convicted, the person would not have the Federal disability. 18 U.S.C. 921(a)(33), 27 CFR 478.11.

Q: Is a person who received "probation before judgment" or some other type of deferred adjudication subject to the disability?
A: What is a conviction is determined by the law of the jurisdiction in which the proceedings were held. If the State law where the proceedings were held does not consider probation before judgment or deferred adjudication to be a conviction, the person would not be subject to the disability. 18 U.S.C. 921(a)(33), 27 CFR 478.11.

Q: What State and local offenses are "misdemeanors" for purposes of 18 U.S.C. 922(d)(9) and (g)(9)?
A: The definition of misdemeanor crime of domestic violence in the GCA (the Gun Control Act of 1968) includes any offense classified as a "misdemeanor" under Federal or State law. In States that do not classify offenses as misdemeanors, the definition includes any State or local offense punishable by imprisonment for a term of 1 year or less or punishable by a fine. For example, if State A has an offense classified as a "domestic violence misdemeanor" that is punishable by up to 5 years imprisonment, it would be a misdemeanor crime of domestic violence. If State B does not characterize offenses as misdemeanors, but has a domestic violence offense that is punishable by no more than 1 year imprisonment, this offense would be a misdemeanor crime of domestic violence. 18 U.S.C. 921(a)(33), 27 CFR 478.11.

Q: Are local criminal ordinances "misdemeanors under State law" for purposes of sections 922(d)(9) and (g)(9)?

A: Yes, assuming a violation of the ordinance meets the definition of "misdemeanor crime of domestic violence" in all other respects.

Q: *In order for an offense to qualify as a "misdemeanor crime of domestic violence," does it have to have as an element the relationship part of the definition (e.g., committed by a spouse, parent, or guardian)?*
A: No. The "as an element" language in the definition of "misdemeanor crime of domestic violence" only applies to the use of force provision of the statute and not the relationship provision. However, to be disabling, the offense must have been committed by one of the defined parties. 18 U.S.C. 921(a)(33), 27 CFR 478.11.

Editor's note: This basically means that if illegal force was used against another person, regardless of the language in the underlying statute, if the illegal force was used against a member of the protected class under the statute, federal law will deem this as satisfying the requirements and disqualify the individual from purchasing and possessing firearms.

Q: *What should an individual do if he or she has been convicted of a misdemeanor crime of domestic violence?*
A: Individuals subject to this disability should immediately dispose of their firearms and ammunition. ATF recommends that such persons transfer their firearms and ammunition to a third party who may lawfully receive and possess them, such as their attorney, a local police agency, or a Federal firearms dealer. The continued possession of firearms and ammunition by persons under this disability is a violation of law and may subject the possessor to criminal penalties. In addition, such firearms and ammunition are subject to seizure and forfeiture. 18 U.S.C. 922(g)(9) and 924(d)(1), 27 CFR 478.152.

Q: *Does the disability apply to law enforcement officers?*
A: Yes. The Gun Control Act was amended so that employees of government agencies convicted of misdemeanor crimes of domestic violence would not be exempt from disabilities with

respect to their receipt or possession of firearms or ammunition. Thus, law enforcement officers and other government officials who have been convicted of a disqualifying misdemeanor may not lawfully possess or receive firearms or ammunition for any purpose, including performance of their official duties. The disability applies to firearms and ammunition issued by government agencies, purchased by government employees for use in performing their official duties, and personal firearms and ammunition possessed by such employees. 18 U.S.C. 922(g)(9) and 925(a)(1), 27 CFR 478.32(a)(9) and 478.141.

Q: Is an individual who has been pardoned, or whose conviction was expunged or set aside, or whose civil rights have been restored, considered convicted of a misdemeanor crime of domestic violence?
A: No, as long as the pardon, expungement, or restoration does not expressly provide that the person may not ship, transport, possess, or receive firearms.

See www.atf.gov.

8. <u>Illegal aliens or aliens admitted under a non-immigrant visa</u>

Persons who are illegally in the United States may not legally purchase, possess, or transport firearms. Generally, non-immigrant aliens are also prohibited from legally purchasing, possessing, or transporting firearms.

Exceptions for nonimmigrant aliens
However, a nonimmigrant alien who has been admitted under a non-immigrant visa is not prohibited from purchasing, receiving, or possessing a firearm if the person falls within one of the following exceptions:

1. if the person was admitted to the United States for lawful hunting or sporting purposes or is in possession of a hunting license or permit lawfully issued in the United States;

2. if the person is an official representative of a foreign government who is accredited to the United States Government or the Government's mission to an international organization having its headquarters in the United States;

3. if the person is an official representative of a foreign government who is *en route* to or from another county to which that alien is accredited;

4. if the person is an official of a foreign government or a distinguished foreign visitor who has been so designated by the Department of State;

5. if the person is a foreign law enforcement officer of a friendly foreign government entering the United States on official law enforcement business; or

6. if the person has received a waiver from the prohibition from the Attorney General of the United States.

See 18 U.S.C. §922(y).

III. Pennsylvania law disqualifications: who cannot buy a firearm under Pennsylvania law?

As mentioned earlier, Pennsylvania has restrictions on the sale, transfer, and possession of firearms that are separate and distinct from the federal restrictions. If a person runs afoul of the law, they could potentially face prosecution in both state and federal court.

Note: even though a person may not be disqualified from possession of a firearm under state law, that person may nevertheless still be disqualified to possess a firearm under federal law.

Pennsylvania has certain classes of people who cannot possess, use, manufacture, control, sell, or transfer firearms. These can be found in 18 Pa.C.S. §6105. These include:

- Those who are actively under a PFA Order, if the order provided for the relinquishment of firearms during the period of time the order is in effect. *See* section A6 above for greater detail and discussion on PFA matters.

- Those who are fugitives from justice (excepting those whose status is due to a nonmoving or moving summary offense under Title 75-Vehicles).
- Those who have been convicted of an offense under the act of April 14, 1972 (P.L.233, No.64), known as The Controlled Substance, Drug, Device and Cosmetic Act, or any equivalent federal statute or equivalent statute of any other state, that may be punishable by a term of imprisonment exceeding two years.
- Those who have been convicted of driving under the influence of alcohol or controlled substance as provided in 75 Pa.C.S. §3802 (relating to driving under influence of alcohol or controlled substance) or the former 75 Pa.C.S. §3731, on three or more separate occasions within a five-year period. This prohibition applies only to transfers or purchases of firearms after the third conviction.
- Those who have been adjudicated as an incompetent or who have been involuntarily committed to a mental institution for inpatient care and treatment under section 302, 303 or 304 of the provisions of the Act of July 9, 1976 (P.L.817, No.143), known as the Mental Health Procedures Act. This paragraph shall not apply to any proceeding under section 302 of the Mental Health Procedures Act unless the examining physician has issued a certification that inpatient care was necessary or that the person was committable. For more discussion, *see* section A5 above.
- Those who, being an alien, are illegally or unlawfully in the United States.

In Pennsylvania, certain types of convictions (regardless of whether they happened inside or outside of Pennsylvania) will prohibit someone from possessing, using, manufacturing, controlling, selling, or transferring firearms. These also can be found in 18 Pa.C.S. §6105. These include convictions for:
- Felony drug offenses
- Section 908 (relating to prohibited offensive weapons)
- Section 911 (relating to corrupt organizations)

- Section 912 (relating to possession of weapon on school property)
- Section 2502 (relating to murder)
- Section 2503 (relating to voluntary manslaughter)
- Section 2504 (relating to involuntary manslaughter) if the offense is based on the reckless use of a firearm
- Section 2702 (relating to aggravated assault)
- Section 2703 (relating to assault by prisoner)
- Section 2704 (relating to assault by life prisoner)
- Section 2709.1 (relating to stalking)
- Section 2716 (relating to weapons of mass destruction)
- Section 2901 (relating to kidnapping)
- Section 2902 (relating to unlawful restraint)
- Section 2910 (relating to luring a child into a motor vehicle or structure)
- Section 3121 (relating to rape)
- Section 3123 (relating to involuntary deviate sexual intercourse)
- Section 3125 (relating to aggravated indecent assault)
- Section 3301 (relating to arson and related offenses)
- Section 3302 (relating to causing or risking catastrophe)
- Section 3502 (relating to burglary)
- Section 3503 (relating to criminal trespass) if the offense is graded a felony of the second degree or higher
- Section 3701 (relating to robbery)
- Section 3702 (relating to robbery of motor vehicle)
- Section 3921 (relating to theft by unlawful taking or disposition) upon conviction of the second felony offense
- Section 3923 (relating to theft by extortion) when the offense is accompanied by threats of violence
- Section 3925 (relating to receiving stolen property) upon conviction of the second felony offense
- Section 4906 (relating to false reports to law enforcement authorities) if the fictitious report involved the theft of a firearm as provided in section 4906(c)(2)

- Section 4912 (relating to impersonating a public servant) if the person is impersonating a law enforcement officer
- Section 4952 (relating to intimidation of witnesses or victims)
- Section 4953 (relating to retaliation against witness, victim or party)
- Section 5121 (relating to escape)
- Section 5122 (relating to weapons or implements for escape)
- Section 5501(3) (relating to riot)
- Section 5515 (relating to prohibiting of paramilitary training)
- Section 5516 (relating to facsimile weapons of mass destruction)
- Section 6110.1 (relating to possession of firearm by minor)
- Section 6301 (relating to corruption of minors)
- Section 6302 (relating to sale or lease of weapons and explosives)
- Any offense equivalent to any of the above-enumerated offenses under the prior laws of this Commonwealth or any offense equivalent to any of the above-enumerated offenses under the statutes of any other state or of the United States.
- Those who are convicted of a crime of domestic violence and are prohibited from possessing or acquiring a firearm under 18 U.S.C. §922(g)(9) (relating to unlawful acts). If the offense which resulted in the prohibition under 18 U.S.C. §922(g)(9) was committed, as provided in 18 U.S.C. §921(a)(33)(A)(ii) (relating to definitions), by a person in any of the following relationships:
  - the current or former spouse, parent or guardian of the victim;
  - a person with whom the victim shares a child in common;
  - a person who cohabits with or has cohabited with the victim as a spouse, parent or guardian; or

- a person similarly situated to a spouse, parent or guardian of the victim.

It is important to note that successful completion of the Accelerated Rehabilitative Disposition ("ARD") program does not constitute a conviction for section 6105 purposes. Also a final adjudication of the charge as Probation Without Verdict, which is a rare disposition in Pennsylvania courts, will not count as a conviction for section 6105 purposes. However, a no contest plea will count as a conviction for section 6105 purposes.

Generally, under federal provisions, if any person, including a juvenile, has been convicted of a crime which carries a punishment of imprisonment for more than one year, then that person will not be permitted to purchase a firearm under either federal or Pennsylvania law unless their firearm rights are restored. *See* 18 U.S.C. §922(g); and *United States v. Walters*, 359 F.3d 340 (4th Cir. 2004).

Pennsylvania has its own way of examining the disqualification based upon juvenile proceedings. A person who was adjudicated delinquent by a court pursuant to 42 Pa.C.S. §6341 (relating to adjudication) or under any equivalent federal statute or statute of any other state as a result of conduct, which if committed by an adult would constitute an offense under sections 2502, 2503, 2702, 2703 (relating to assault by prisoner), 2704, 2901, 3121, 3123, 3301, 3502, 3701 and 3923, is prohibited for life. Likewise, any person who was adjudicated delinquent by a court pursuant to 42 Pa.C.S. §6341 or under any equivalent federal statute or statute of any other state as a result of conduct, which if committed by an adult would constitute an offense enumerated in 6105(b) (with the exception of those crimes that would constitute an offense under sections 2502, 2503, 2702, 2703 (relating to assault by prisoner), 2704, 2901, 3121, 3123, 3301, 3502, 3701 and 3923, shall be prohibited until 15 years after the last applicable delinquent adjudication or upon the person reaching the age of 30, whichever is earlier. The tricky part of juvenile matters occurs when the offenses occur outside of Pennsylvania, with the person now living in Pennsylvania. There must be an interpretation as to what constitutes a "substantially similar offense" under that foreign state's laws and/or what constitutes an adjudication procedure that is like a Pennsylvania section 6341 proceeding. This is where it is best to consult with an experienced firearms and juvenile law attorney.

IV. Understanding "private sales" laws

A. *What are the legal restrictions on "private sales" of firearms?*
Private individuals may legally buy, sell, gift, or otherwise transfer firearms to another private individual in Pennsylvania under certain circumstances. When it comes to long guns, there are no restrictions other than one cannot knowingly sell a long gun to a person who cannot possess or own a firearm. Also, in Pennsylvania, when it comes to a transfer or sale of a handgun, it must go through either the sheriff's office or an FFL unless it involves "transfers between spouses or to transfers between a parent and child or to transfers between grandparent and grandchild." However, even given all of this, when conducting a private sale, careful attention needs to be paid to not violate the laws regulating these transactions. So what are the legal restrictions? First, the ATF website has an informative pamphlet entitled "Best Practices: Transfers of Firearms by Private Sellers" located on its website www.atf.gov/files/publications. This pamphlet is a must-read before entering into a "private sales" transaction involving a firearm. So what are the rules in Pennsylvania regarding private sales?

1. Residency requirements

Under federal law, an unlicensed person (non-dealer) may only "transfer" a firearm to another unlicensed person in the *same* state. This means that if a person is a resident of Pennsylvania, federal law prohibits the person from directly (not through a dealer) selling or transferring the firearm to a resident of another state. Federal law makes these transactions illegal from both the buyer/transferee and seller/transferor perspective. It is illegal for a private individual to transport into or receive within his own state a firearm which was purchased in another state from a private seller. *See* 18 U.S.C. §922(a)(3). Likewise, it is illegal for a private seller to sell or deliver a firearm to an individual whom the private seller knows or has reason to believe is not a resident of the seller's state. *See* 18 U.S.C. §922(a)(5).

Example:

> *Bob is visiting his best friend from high school, Jim. Ten years ago after high school was over, Bob moved to Nebraska from Pennsylvania. One night, Bob and Jim decide to go to the shooting range during Bob's trip, and Bob borrows one of Jim's rifles. After shooting at the range, impressed with both the feel and action of Jim's rifle, Bob asks Jim if he could buy it from him. As they've been friends for so many years, Jim says yes, and even offers him a good price for the transaction. Before leaving to go home to Nebraska, Bob pays Jim and packs his new rifle.*

Has Jim committed a crime in selling the rifle to Bob? Has Bob committed a crime in purchasing the rifle from Jim? The answer to both questions is "Yes!" Under federal law, Bob is not allowed to privately purchase a rifle in another state and transport it back to his home state. Likewise, Jim is not allowed to sell a firearm legally to a person he knows lives in another state. In this example, both Bob and Jim *know* that Bob is not a Pennsylvania resident—the place where Jim has sold his firearm. Bob has committed the crime of willful receipt of a firearm from out-of-state by an unlicensed person while Jim has committed the federal crime of willful sale of a firearm to an out-of-state resident. *See* 18 U.S.C. §924(a)(1)(D). The penalties for these crimes include jail time up to 5 years and/or a fine of $250,000!

What if the situation is less obvious? Let's take a look at an example where "reasonable cause to believe" comes into play.

Example:

> *Frank, a Pennsylvania resident, recently posted his AR-15 for sale on an internet message board in Pennsylvania. Frank receives an email from a person named Ted who would like to buy the rifle. Frank and Ted agree, via email, on a purchase price and arrange to meet at a place in Pennsylvania one week later to facilitate the transfer. When Ted pulls up in his 1978 Ford LTD Wagon, Frank notices the car's Tennessee license plates. Nevertheless, Frank shrugs and sells Ted the gun anyway without going through any of the formalities of a bill-of-sale, or asking for identification. Two weeks later, Frank finds himself at an FBI field office in Philadelphia answering questions about a shooting that took place with his (former) AR-15.*

Is Frank in trouble? It is highly likely. Although Frank is not the center of the shooting investigation, Frank is probably the center of an investigation for illegally selling the firearm to an out-of-state resident under federal law.

2. <u>Private sales: don't knowingly sell to the "wrong" people</u>

Under federal law, a private individual may sell a firearm to a private buyer in the same state so long as the seller does not know or have reasonable cause to believe that the person purchasing the firearm is prohibited from possessing or receiving a firearm under federal or state law. *See* 18 U.S.C. §922(d). Also, see the discussion in the previous sections on "disqualifications."

Example:

> *Gordon and Josh are friends and Josh tells Gordon that he has just attempted to buy a handgun from a local FFL and that he was denied because he was disqualified for some reason under federal law (something about a conviction or restraining order or drug use or psychiatric*

problems—Josh was too mad to remember!).
Gordon says, "no problem, I'll just sell you one of
mine," and he does.

Gordon has just committed a federal and state crime, because he knew (or at least had reasonable cause to believe) that Josh was prohibited from purchasing a handgun under the law. *See* our earlier discussion concerning disqualifications. Also recall that in Pennsylvania, when it comes to a transfer or sale of a modern handgun, it must go through either the sheriff's office or an FFL unless it involves "transfers between spouses or to transfers between a parent and child or to transfers between grandparent and grandchild."

B. *How does the law determine a person's residence when buying or selling a firearm?*

1. Individuals with one residence

For the purpose of firearms purchases, the person's state of residence is the state in which the person is present and where the individual has an intention of making a home. 27 CFR §478.11.

2. What if a person maintains a home in two states?

If a person maintains a home in two (or more) states and resides in those states for periods of the year, he or she may, during the period of time the person actually resides in a particular state, purchase a firearm in that state. However, simply owning property in another state does not qualify a person as a resident of that state so as to purchase a firearm in that state. To meet the residency requirements, a person must actually maintain a home in a state which includes an intention to make a particular state a residence. *See* 27 CFR §478.11. This issue may ultimately be a fact question with evidence of residency being things like a driver's license, insurance records, recurring expenses in the state like utilities, as well as other things related to making a particular state a person's residence.

3. Members of the Armed Forces

A member of the Armed Forces on active duty is a resident of the state in which his or her permanent duty station is located. If a member of the Armed Forces maintains a home in one state and the member's permanent duty station is in a nearby state to which he or she commutes each day, then the member has two states of residence and may purchase a firearm in either the state where the duty station is located or the state where the home is maintained. *See* 18 U.S.C. §921(b). *See also* ATF FAQs on residency at www.atf.gov.

4. Nonimmigrant aliens

Persons who are legally present in the United States are residents of the state in which they reside and where they intend to make a home. Such persons, provided they meet all other requirements and are not otherwise prohibited from purchasing a firearm, are lawfully permitted to purchase a firearm.

C. *Suggestion on how to document a private firearms sale*

Protect yourself! This is practical advice that should not be ignored. If you engage in the private sale of a firearm, here are some practical tips:

- Ask for identification whether you are the buyer/transferee or seller/transferor to establish residency.
- Get and/or give a "bill of sale" for the transfer and keep a copy—identify the firearm including make, model, and serial number, as well as the date and place of transfer.
- Put the residency information on the "bill of sale" including names, addresses, and phone numbers.
- Do not sell or transfer a firearm or ammunition if you think the person may not be permitted or is prohibited from receiving the firearm.

Why do this? Not only will it help establish residency, but if you unfortunately happen to buy or sell a firearm that was previously used in a crime, or if you sell or transfer a gun that is later used in a crime, you want to be able to establish when you did and did not own or possess the firearm.

Further, as a matter of good course, if you are a seller or transferor in a private sale, you might ask whether there is any reason the buyer/transferee cannot own a firearm. Why? So that if there is an issue later, you can at a minimum say that you had no reason to know the buyer could not legally possess firearms. However, do not overlook behavior that may indicate the buyer is not telling you the truth, because law enforcement will not overlook facts that show you did know, or should have had reasonable cause to believe that the buyer/transferee could not own a firearm at the time of the transfer if a legal issue arises later.

V. Buying, selling, and transferring through an FFL
A. *Basic procedures*
Persons purchasing firearms through dealers must comply with all legal requirements imposed by federal law. These include both paperwork and appropriate background checks or screenings to ensure that the purchaser is not prohibited from the purchase or possession of a firearm under federal law.

When purchasing through a dealer, the first thing a prospective buyer will do is select a firearm. Once a selection has been made, the prospective purchaser is required to show proper identification and complete ATF Form 4473. This form requires the applicant, under penalty of law, to provide accurate identifying information, as well as answer certain questions in order to establish whether a person may legally purchase a firearm. The information provided on Form 4473 is then provided to the National Instant Criminal Background Check System (NICS) for processing and approval in order to proceed with the transfer. An FFL dealer can submit the check to NICS either by telephone or through the online website and only after the FFL completes all of these steps successfully is a purchaser/transferee allowed to take possession of the firearm. If the purchaser is in the state of

Pennsylvania, the purchaser will also have to fill out and certify as true a SP 4-113 form from the Pennsylvania State Police.

On July 1, 1998, Pennsylvania joined only a handful of states to push all intrastate FFL sales and sheriff's office transfer actions through a local check system as opposed to strictly relying upon the NICS check method. This is called the Point of Contact or POC option to comply with the Brady Bill. Here in Pennsylvania, it is called the Pennsylvania Instant Check System (PICS). PICS integrates with NICS, and is a call-center-based system that is available for service from 8:00 a.m. until 10:00 p.m. seven days a week, including holidays. If a record is identified on an individual's background check, the call is transferred to an operator. The operator then reviews the record, and if it is not prohibitive, approves the sale. If there is a question as to whether or not the record is prohibitive, the operator may place the file in research for up to 15 days. There is a method to challenge any erroneous PICS denials and/or to challenge any records that PICS relies upon to deny the transfer/sale.

B. *What is Form 4473 and SP 4-113 form from the Pennsylvania State Police?*

ATF Form 4473 is the ATF's form known as a Firearms Transaction Record which must be completed when a person purchases a firearm from an FFL. *See* 27 CFR §478.124. Form 4473 requires the applicant to provide their name, address, birth date, state of residence, and other information including government issued photo identification. The form also contains information blanks to be filled-in including the NICS background check transaction number, the make, model, and serial number of the firearm to be purchased, and a series of questions that a person must answer. *See* 27 CFR §478.124(c). This series of questions and the corresponding answers help determine a purchaser's eligibility under federal law to purchase a firearm. Once the form is completed, the prospective purchaser will sign the form and attest that the information provided thereon is truthful and accurate under penalty of federal law. This means that if you lie or make false statements on this form, the Feds can and will prosecute you for a crime!

Likewise, the dealer must also sign Form 4473 and retain it for at least 20 years. The ATF is permitted to inspect, as well as receive a copy of Form 4473 from the dealer both during audits and during the course of a criminal investigation. The 4473 records must be surrendered to the Bureau of Alcohol, Tobacco, Firearms and Explosives in the event the FFL dealer retires or ceases business.

Similar to the ATF Form 4473 is the SP 4-113 form from the Pennsylvania State Police. Only used for handgun transfers, it must be filled out and signed by the transferee certifying many of the same demographic and qualifying questions that the ATF Form 4473 does, and it consists of fewer questions than the ATF 4473. This form must also be filled out in the case of a private transfer of a handgun, unless it involves "transfers between spouses or to transfers between a parent and child or to transfers between grandparent and grandchild." Remember that all modern handgun transfers in Pennsylvania must go through either an FFL or the sheriff's office unless it is a transfer between spouses, between a parent and child, or between grandparent and grandchild.

C. _How are background checks administered when purchasing a firearm?_

As mentioned above, Pennsylvania opted to use the POC method of background check afforded under the Brady Bill. As such, the PICS method was born. It is a call center system that draws upon the Pennsylvania State Police statewide repository of records of arrests and prosecution (including juvenile actions), PFA orders, and mental health commitments. It is similar in nature to the Pennsylvania Access To Criminal History (PATCH) system. As a POC, the PICS system integrates to the NICS. As a result, we will focus much of our discussion on the NICS.

1. <u>NICS: National Instant Criminal Background Check System</u>
Background checks by dealers when transferring firearms are completed through the National Instant Criminal Background Check System or NICS, if required, prior to the transfer of a firearm from an FFL dealer to a non-dealer. When the prospective purchaser/transferee's information is given to NICS, the system will check the applicant against at least three different databases containing various types of records. Applicants are checked against the records maintained by the Interstate Identification Index (III) which contains criminal history records, the National Crime Information Center (NCIC) which contains records including warrants and protective orders, as well as the NICS Index which contains records of individuals who are prohibited from purchasing or possessing firearms under either federal or state law. In addition, if the applicant is not a United States Citizen, the application is processed for an Immigration Alien Query (IAQ) through the Department of Homeland Security's Immigration and Customs Enforcement Division.

2. <u>Responses from NICS</u>
NICS responses to background checks come in three basic forms: proceed, delay, or deny. The "proceed" response allows for the transfer to be completed. The "delay" response means that the transfer may not legally proceed. If the dealer receives a response of "delay," NICS has three business days to research the applicant further. If the dealer has not received a notice that the transfer is denied after the three business days, then the transfer may proceed. "Deny" means the transfer does not take place; a transferee's options after a "deny" are discussed later.

Practical Legal Tip:

Thinking about buying a gun on behalf of your buddy? Not a good idea! One of the purposes of ATF Form 4473 is to conduct a background check on individuals who want to purchase firearms in order to make sure they are legally allowed to do so. Acting as a "straw man" by purchasing it for your buddy circumvents this process and is a crime. -*Mike*

3. <u>What transactions require background checks?</u>

A background check is required before each and every sale or other transfer of a firearm from an FFL to a non-licensee unless an exception is provided under the law. For every transaction that requires a background check, the purchaser/transferee must also complete ATF Form 4473. This includes:

- The sale or trade of a firearm.
- The return of a consigned firearm.
- The redemption of a pawned firearm.
- The loan or rental of a firearm for use off of an FFL's licensed premises.
- Any other non-exempt transfer of a firearm.

4. <u>What transactions do not require a background check?</u>

A background check is not required under the following circumstances:

- The transfer of a firearm from one FFL to another FFL.
- The return of a repaired firearm to the person from whom it was received.
- The sale of a firearm to a law enforcement agency or a law enforcement officer for official duties if the transaction meets the specific requirements of 27 CFR §478.134 including providing a signed certification from a person in

authority on agency letterhead stating that the officer will use the firearm in official duties and where a records check reveals the officer does not have any misdemeanor convictions for domestic violence.

- The transfer of a replacement firearm of the same kind and type to the person from whom a firearm was received.
- The transfer of a firearm that is subject to the National Firearms Act if the transfer was pre-approved by the ATF.

5. <u>If a person buys multiple handguns, a dealer must report that person to the ATF</u>

Under federal law, FFLs are required to report to the ATF any sale or transfer of two or more pistols, revolvers, or any combination of pistols and revolvers totaling two or more to an unlicensed (non-FFL) individual that takes place at one time or during any five consecutive business days. This report is made to the ATF on Form 3310.4 and is completed in triplicate with the original copy sent to the ATF, one sent to the designated State police or local law enforcement agency in the jurisdiction where the sale took place, and one retained by the dealer and held for no less than five years.

6. <u>FFLs must report persons who purchase more than one rifle in southwest border states</u>

Although not something to worry about here in Pennsylvania, it is interesting to know that in Texas, Arizona, New Mexico, and California, dealers are required to report the sale or other transfer of more than one semi-automatic rifle capable of accepting a detachable magazine and with a caliber greater than .22 (including .223 caliber/5.56 mm) to an unlicensed person at one time or during any five consecutive business days. *See* 18 U.S.C. §923(g)(3)(A). This report is made via ATF Form 3310.12 and must be reported no later than the close of business on the day the multiple sale or other disposition took place. This requirement includes (but is not limited to) purchases of popular semi-automatic rifles such as AR-15s, AK-47s, Ruger Mini-14s, and Tavor bullpup rifles.

VI. What if I'm denied the right to purchase a firearm?

A. *If I am denied the right to purchase, how do I appeal?*

The Pennsylvania State Police has a method to challenge both a delay and a denial through the PICS. All appeals must be filed within 30 days of the delay or denial. However, you must be very careful. The Pennsylvania State Police and local District Attorneys' Offices are aggressive in charging people with false swearing (misdemeanor), and criminal attempt—persons not to possess firearms (felony) charges for those who are denied by PICS. While you may "get lucky" if you are denied through PICS and are not prosecuted for any charges, if you make a formal PICS appeal and you are wrong in that you have a disqualifying event or condition, you are virtually assured that you will be prosecuted. Remember ignorance of the law or your past is no excuse. This is where it is important to contact an attorney who has experience in these matters who can research your past before you make an appeal. There is also a method to challenge or verify what you believe to be an erroneous criminal history or other entry in the various federal and state computer systems that leads to a PICS denial. What we have found is that through the modernization efforts of taking decades-old paper files and translating them to the digital age, sometimes errors are made. In general, these errors can be fixed. It just takes time, patience, know-how and effort.

Persons who believe they have been erroneously denied or delayed a firearm transfer based on a match to a record returned by the NICS may request an appeal of their "deny" or "delay" decision. All appeal inquiries must be submitted to the NICS Section's Appeal Service Team (AST) in writing, either online or via mail on the FBI's website at www.fbi.gov. An appellant must provide their complete name, complete mailing address, and NICS Transaction Number. For persons appealing a delayed transaction, a fingerprint card is required and must be submitted with the appeal, although the fingerprint card is merely recommended on appeals for denied applications. This may seem counter-intuitive, but it is required per the FBI's website.

B. *What if I keep getting erroneously delayed or denied when I am attempting to buy a firearm?*

Apply for a PIN (personal identification number) that is designed to solve this issue. Some individuals may have a name which is common enough (or happens to be flagged for other reasons) that it causes undue delays or denials in the background check verification process through NICS. For that reason, NICS maintains the Voluntary Appeal File database (VAF) which allows any applicant to apply by submitting an appeal request and then obtaining a UPIN or Unique Personal Identification Number. A person who has been cleared through the VAF and receives a UPIN will then be able to use their UPIN when completing Form 4473 in order to help avoid further erroneous denials or extended delays. A person can obtain a UPIN by following the procedures outlined on the FBI's website at www.fbi.gov.

VII. Additional considerations in firearms purchasing and possession laws

A. *How can I legally purchase a firearm from someone in another state?*

Any individual who wishes to purchase a firearm from a person that lives in another state than the purchaser must complete the transaction through an FFL. Sellers or transferors are legally authorized to facilitate a private transaction or transfer by shipping the firearm to the purchaser's FFL in the recipient/buyer's state, where the FFL will complete the transfer process. It is a federal crime to sell or transfer a firearm between persons who are residents of different states, or where a transfer takes place in a state other than the transferee/transferor's singular state of residence.

B. *Can I purchase firearms on the Internet?*

Yes. However, all legal requirements for a transfer must be followed. If the buyer and seller are both residents of Pennsylvania and the sale solely involves a conventional long gun, then the two may lawfully conduct a private sale so long as all other legal issues are satisfied (*see* our earlier discussion on disqualifications to purchasing and possessing firearms in this chapter). However, if buyer and seller are not residents of the same state, the transaction can only be legally facilitated through the intervention of an FFL. If the transaction involves a handgun, then the transfer must go through either the FFL process or the sheriff's office, unless it involves a transfer between spouses, between a parent and child, or between grandparent and grandchild.

C. *Shipping firearms*
   1. Can I ship my firearm through the postal service?
Long guns: yes. Handguns: no. However, under federal law, a non-licensed individual may not transfer (and this would include shipping to someone else) a firearm to a non-licensed resident (non-FFL) of another state. However, a non-licensed individual may mail a long gun to a resident of his or her own state, and they may also mail a long gun to an FFL of another state. To that end, the USPS recommends that long guns be mailed via registered mail and that the packaging used to mail the long gun be ambiguous so as to not identify the contents. Handguns are not allowed to be mailed through USPS. *See* 18 U.S.C. §§1715, 922(a)(3), 922(a)(5), and 922(a)(2)(A). Rather, handguns must be shipped using a common or contract carrier (*e.g.*, UPS or FedEx).

   2. Shipping handguns and other firearms through a common or contract carrier
Under federal law, a non-licensed individual may ship a firearm (including a handgun) by a common or contract carrier (*e.g.*, UPS or FedEx) to a resident of his or her own state, or to a licensed individual (FFL) in another state. However, it is illegal to ship any firearm to a non-FFL in another state. It is a requirement that the carrier be notified that the shipment contains a firearm, however, carriers are prohibited from requiring any identifying marks on the package that may be used to identify the contents as containing a firearm. *See* 18 U.S.C. §§922(a)(2)(A), 922(a)(3), 922(a)(5), 922(e), 27 CFR §§478.31 and 478.30.

D. *Can I ship my firearm to myself for use in another state?*

Yes. In accordance with the law as described in the preceding section, a person may ship a firearm to himself or herself in care of another person in another state where he or she intends to hunt or engage in other lawful activity. The package should be addressed to the owner and persons other than the owner should not open the package and take possession of the firearm.

E. *If I am moving out of Pennsylvania, may I have movers move my firearms?*

Yes, a person who lawfully possesses firearms may transport or ship the firearms interstate when changing the person's state of residence so long as the person complies with the requirements for shipping and transporting firearms as outlined earlier. *See* 18 U.S.C. §922(e) and 27 CFR §478.31. However, certain NFA items such as destructive devices, machine guns, short-barreled shotguns or rifles, and suppressors require approval from the ATF before they can be moved interstate. *See* 18 U.S.C. §922(a)(4) and 27 CFR §478.28. It is important that the person seeking to move the firearms also check state and local laws where the firearms will be relocated to ensure that the movement of the firearms into the new state does not violate any state law or local ordinance. This is particularly important to remember when it comes to magazines. Some states have very strict magazine capacity laws.

F. *May I loan my firearm to another person?*

There is no federal prohibition on loaning a firearm to another adult person, so long as the person receiving the firearm may lawfully possess one.

Federal law specifically addresses loans in 18 U.S.C. §922.

(5) for any person (other than a licensed importer, licensed manufacturer, licensed dealer, or licensed collector) to transfer, sell, trade, give, transport, or deliver any firearm to any person (other than a licensed importer, licensed manufacturer, licensed dealer, or licensed collector) who the

transferor knows or has reasonable cause to believe does not reside in (or if the person is a corporation or other business entity, does not maintain a place of business in) the State in which the transferor resides; except that this paragraph shall not apply to

> (A) the transfer, transportation, or delivery of a firearm made to carry out a bequest of a firearm to, or an acquisition by intestate succession of a firearm by, a person who is permitted to acquire or possess a firearm under the laws of the State of his residence, and
>
> (B) the loan or rental of a firearm to any person for temporary use for lawful sporting purposes ...

In Pennsylvania, loans are specifically addressed in the Uniform Firearms Act. Loans to another adult person are not prohibited unless the loan violates another provision of the Uniform Firearms Act.

Although we claim that there is no prohibition at the state level for lending someone your modern handgun, there is one reported case that seems to challenge that statement. In *Commonwealth v. Corradino*, 588 A.2d 936, 940 (Pa. Super. 1991), a conviction for violation of 18 Pa.C.S.A. §6115 was upheld largely based upon the title of the statute as the heading reads "Loans on, or lending or giving firearms prohibited." *Id.* We contrast that with the analysis at the trial court level (which means that it does not carry with it statewide gravity) with another judge's interpretation of the law. That court held that "Since the Pennsylvania Uniform Firearms Act does not impose a duty upon one who delivers a firearm to first determine that the recipient has a license, the contention [that all lending, loaning or delivery of a firearm is prohibited] cannot prevail. Indeed, section 6106 of the Act clearly discloses that there are circumstances when a license is not required to be possessed by one who carries a firearm." *Commonwealth v. Rodriguez*, 15 Pa. D. & C.4th 155, 156-58 (Com. Pl. 1992). As a matter of practice, it seems quite a stretch to require that all lending of all firearms require proof of a License to Carry Firearms or be illegal.

Otherwise, in the very common scenario where the person who visits the range and lends a firearm to someone the next stall over to try for a few rounds, the person would be guilty of this crime. Such a result would violate the absurdity doctrine, also known as the "scrivener's error" exception, which is a legal theory under which American courts have interpreted statutes contrary to their plain meaning in order to avoid absurd legal conclusions. But, it is best to be on guard given the existence of the *Corradino* case. Under either interpretation, temporarily lending a firearm to another who possesses a Pennsylvania License to Carry Firearms is legal.

G. *What happens to my firearms when I die?*
Depending on the manner in which a person leaves his or her estate behind, firearms may be bequeathed in a customary manner like other personal property. However, firearms held in an estate are still subject to the laws of transfer and possession. Thus careful consideration needs to be given in estate planning with consideration for firearms law of both the jurisdiction in which the estate is located as well as consideration of who is to receive the firearms.

VIII. Ammunition: the law of purchasing and possession
A. *Who is legally prohibited from purchasing ammunition under federal law?*
Under federal law, there are six primary situations where a person is prohibited from buying, selling, or possessing ammunition (beyond armor-piercing ammunition which was discussed in Chapter Two).

1. Under 18 U.S.C. §922(b)(1), it is unlawful for a person to sell long gun ammunition to a person under the age of 18;
2. Under 18 U.S.C. §922(b)(1), it is unlawful for a person to sell handgun ammunition to a person under the age of 21;
3. Under 18 U.S.C. §922(x)(2)(B), it is unlawful for a juvenile to possess handgun ammunition;

4. Under 18 U.S.C. §922(d), it is unlawful to sell ammunition to a person who is prohibited from purchasing firearms;

5. Under 18 U.S.C. §922(g), it is unlawful for a person who is disqualified from purchasing or possessing firearms to possess firearm ammunition if such ammunition has moved in interstate commerce (which is nearly all ammunition); and

6. Under 18 U.S.C. §922(h), it is unlawful for a person who is employed by a person who is disqualified from purchasing or possessing ammunition to possess or transport ammunition for the disqualified individual.

For the statutes that involve juveniles, there are a couple of notable exceptions to the law: first, the law against selling handgun ammunition to a juvenile and possession of handgun ammunition by a juvenile does not apply to a temporary transfer of ammunition to a juvenile or to the possession or use of ammunition by a juvenile if the handgun and ammunition are possessed and used by the juvenile in the course of employment, in the course of ranching or farming-related activities at the residence of the juvenile (or on property used for ranching or farming at which the juvenile, with the permission of the property owner or lessee, is performing activities related to the operation of the farm or ranch), target practice, hunting, or a course of instruction in the safe and lawful use of a handgun. The law also does not apply to the temporary transfer to or use of ammunition by a juvenile if the juvenile has been provided with prior written consent by his or her parent or guardian who is not prohibited by federal, state, or local law from possessing firearms. *See* 18 U.S.C. §922(x)(3).

Additionally, juveniles who (1) are members of the Armed Forces of the United States or the National Guard who possesses or are armed with a handgun in the line of duty, (2) receive ammunition by inheritance, or (3) possess ammunition in the course of self-defense or defense of others are permitted to possess ammunition.

B. *When is a person prohibited from purchasing or possessing ammunition under Pennsylvania law?*

As covered in greater detail in Chapter Two, there are no specific types of ammunition that are illegal for an adult to possess or own in Pennsylvania. However, certain types of ammunition are illegal to possess or use during the course of certain felonies. Again, Chapter Two has a broader discussion on this topic.

C. *Can a person be disqualified from purchasing ammunition if they are disqualified from purchasing firearms?*

Yes, under federal law. Under 18 U.S.C. §922(g) it is unlawful for a disqualified person from purchasing or possessing firearms if the ammunition has moved in interstate commerce. Since nearly all ammunition or ammunition components move through interstate commerce in one form or another, this disqualification includes essentially all ammunition. However, there is no disqualification under Pennsylvania law.

D. *Can a person purchase ammunition that is labeled "law enforcement use only?"*

Yes. Although some handgun ammunition is sold with a label "law enforcement use," such a label has no legal meaning and is only reflective of a company policy or, viewed less positively, as a marketing strategy.

CHAPTER FOUR
WHEN CAN I LEGALLY USE MY GUN: PART I
UNDERSTANDING THE LAW OF JUSTIFICATION
SOME BASIC LEGAL CONCEPTS

I. Ignorance of the law is NO excuse!

Now we start to get into the meat of our discussion: when is it legal to use a gun as a weapon? The purpose of this chapter is to look at the essential, basic legal concepts of the law of when and under what circumstances a person is legally justified in using force or deadly force. Know when you may legally shoot, because ignorance of the law holds no weight in a courtroom! That is why it is critical you know the law so that you are in the best possible situation to preserve your legal rights if you ever need them.

II. Gun owners need to know Chapter 5 of the Crimes Code

In Pennsylvania, legal justifications appear in numerous places and areas of the law. Of particular importance to gun owners are the defenses found in Chapter 5 of the Crimes Code entitled "General Principles of Justification" which we cover in detail throughout this book. The text of relevant provisions of that chapter of the Crimes Code are found in the Appendix.

III. To legally use force or deadly force, you must be "justified." What is legal justification?

A. *Basic definition of justification: an acceptable excuse*

So, when is it legal to use force or deadly force against another person? The answer is when there is a legal "justification," or defense. A legal justification is an acceptable reason or excuse under the law for taking an action that would otherwise be a crime. Conduct which is generally illegal —such as use of force or deadly force— can be excused if there is a legal justification. The law is filled with these legally recognized reasons for engaging in conduct, which is otherwise illegal.

In the context of firearms, justification generally comes into the picture in self-defense situations. Pennsylvania courts have long recognized the use of force in self-defense, including deadly force: "a killing committed to protect one's life or limb, or to save one's self from great bodily harm, or under circumstances reasonably giving rise to fear of such injuries unless one kills his assailant is justifiable." *Commonwealth v. Capalla*, 322 Pa. 200 (1936). Justification principles involving deadly force have since been codified in Chapter 5 of the Crimes Code, specifically 18 Pa.C.S. §505: "Use of force in self-protection."

Practical Legal Tip:

A *defense to prosecution* is not the same as a *bar to prosecution*. A "bar to prosecution" is where a person can't be prosecuted for engaging in certain conduct. This means the charges cannot even be filed. Whereas a "defense to prosecution" allows the charges to be filed, a jury to hear the case, and evidence produced in court, but offers the accused an opportunity to present a legal excuse called a justification that allows that person to get completely out of trouble. *-Justin*

B. _Basic requirement: you must admit your action_

Justification is an affirmative defense. With an affirmative defense, "the defendant admits his commission of the act charged, but seeks to justify or excuse it." *Commonwealth v. White*, 342 Pa. Super. 1, 7 (1985) (quoting *Commonwealth v. Rose*, 457 Pa. 380, 387 (1974)). In other words, the person raising the affirmative defense says "Yes, I did it. But there's a lawful reason why I did it."

In raising an affirmative defense, a person doesn't claim that they didn't do it, that it was an accident, or that they didn't mean to do it. Frankly, "I didn't do it" cannot co-exist with "I did it, but there's a lawful reason why I did it."

Example:

> Jane is walking home one night, when a huge man jumps out of the bushes, grabs her by the wrist, and begins dragging her away. Jane pulls out her handgun and points it at the man, who then stops and runs away. Unfortunately, Jane does not call the police, but the criminal immediately does, reporting a crazy woman threatening him with a gun. Jane ends up charged with simple assault, even though Jane was the victim.

Because justification is an affirmative defense in Pennsylvania, Jane must *raise* it in order to gain its potential protection. If Jane's case goes all the way to trial, in order to offer a legal justification for committing "simple assault," she must admit in court that she did pull her handgun and point it at the assailant. Then, in order for the jury to consider a legal justification defense (*i.e.*, receive a jury instruction from the judge), she must offer some evidence of why she is legally justified under the law for having pulled her weapon (in this example, Jane believed that deadly force was necessary to prevent kidnapping). The result is that Jane is entitled to have the judge instruct the jury that they may find Jane not guilty because she was justified in her action. The jury will then decide whether they believe Jane and whether she is guilty or not guilty of the crime of simple assault.

One of the great advantages to a justification defense in Pennsylvania deadly force cases is that the government must disprove the justification beyond a reasonable doubt. In other words, the government must prove beyond a reasonable doubt that it was not reasonable for you to believe that deadly force was immediately necessary to avoid serious bodily injury, death, kidnapping or intercourse by force or threat of force.

On the other hand, if Jane says that she never pointed the gun at the man, or didn't mean to point the gun at the man (*i.e.*, it was an accident), she cannot raise justification as an affirmative defense. Legal justification is, therefore, literally the law of "Yes, I did it, BUT…" And further it is like saying in addition to that "Go ahead and prove my belief at the time as I understood it to be unreasonable beyond a reasonable doubt, I dare ya."

Practical Legal Tip:

A *jury instruction* is a statement of law the judge makes to the jury that the jury must listen to and follow. -*Mike*

IV. Categories of force for justification under the Crimes Code
Anytime a person takes a physical action against another person, they have used force. Chapter 5 of the Crimes Code divides or categorizes uses of force into two different levels. Whether or not a use of force was justified under the law often depends on how that force is categorized. These categories, which we will address throughout this book, are: 1) *force* and 2) *deadly force.*

A. *What if a person uses greater force than the law allows?*
In Pennsylvania, the use of force is justified when a person believes that the force to be used is immediately necessary to protect himself or herself against unlawful force. Simply put, use of force in self-defense must be proportional. The force used in self-defense must be of a similar kind used or threatened in the first place.

If a person uses deadly force, and the law allows only for the use of force, that person will not be legally justified. Likewise, if a person uses force when no force is legally allowed, that use of force will not be legally justified.

Example:

> Paul the Power Walker — an elite athlete at the pinnacle of his career — is enjoying a power stroll in Center City Philadelphia. Sammy the Slapper is a mischievous 91-year-old very frail man who lives in the area. When Sammy is bored, he regularly participates in a popular "game" in which he and his cohorts slap random pedestrians in the face. Sammy approaches Paul and raises his hand, preparing to deem Paul the latest loser in the slap game.

Sammy is clearly about to use unlawful force against Paul! What degree of force may Paul use to protect himself from being slapped? The law, as discussed later, will show that Paul is not allowed to use deadly force unless he has a reasonable belief that it is necessary to prevent death, serious bodily injury, kidnapping or intercourse by force or threat. Here, Sammy is incapable of delivering death or serious bodily injury with a mere slap. If Paul uses deadly force against Sammy, he will not be legally justified and would be guilty of using unlawful force against him. Ultimately, using the correct degree of force is critical in determining whether a person has committed a crime or a legally justified action.

B. *What is the legal definition of "force?"*
Surprisingly, "force" is not defined in the Pennsylvania Crimes Code. However, "deadly force" is defined. Under Chapter 5 of the Crimes Code, a precondition for being able to legally use deadly force is the requirement that a person must be able to use "force" in the same situation. Therefore, one may conclude that mere force must be something less than deadly force. How much less "force" is than "deadly force" is not defined in the case law or in the Crimes Code in Pennsylvania.

As discussed earlier, in Pennsylvania, the use of force is justified when a person believes that the force to be used is immediately necessary to protect himself or herself against unlawful force.

Example:

> *Timmy is being harassed and insulted by a bully, when the bully suddenly clenches his fist and takes a swing at Timmy. Before the bully connects, Timmy reacts by punching the bully in the face.*

Timmy used force to protect himself against unlawful force from the bully (the bully's punch). Even though the bully never connected, Timmy had a reasonable belief that he had to punch the bully to protect himself from the bully's unlawful force (*i.e.*, the inbound attacking punch). Timmy's action of striking the bully was a use of force, but because it was immediately necessary to prevent unlawful force, it is legally justified (excused).

C. *What is deadly force?*

Definition of Deadly Force; 18 Pa.C.S. §501
"Deadly force" means force which, under the circumstances in which it is used, is readily capable of causing death or serious bodily injury.

1. Deadly force does not have to cause death!

On the surface, the legal definition of deadly force seems simple. However, the meaning of what is and is not deadly force can be legally tricky. A particular action does not necessarily have to result in death to be legally defined as deadly force—it just needs to be *capable* of causing death or serious bodily injury. *Note*: although serious bodily injury is not defined in Chapter 5 of the Crimes Code, Chapter 23 defines serious bodily injury as "bodily injury which creates a substantial risk of death or which causes serious, permanent disfigurement, or protracted loss or impairment of the function of any bodily member or organ." This provides some guidance. While serious bodily injury is less than death, it must be beyond temporary discomfort or pain. So a typical bruise will not be considered serious bodily injury under the law. The same is true when it comes to cuts. The general rule of thumb is that a typical cut that does not require stiches will not be serious bodily injury.

Example:

> Jim is being robbed and beaten by a group of individuals when he manages to draw his .45 caliber handgun and fires it at one of the most aggressive assailants. His shot misses his intended target but breaks the group up, causing the would-be robbers to flee.

In our example, even though the bullet did not kill or even strike any of his assailants, Jim legally used deadly force because his conduct —shooting a gun at the assailant— fits the legal definition of "capable of causing death or serious bodily injury." Thus, actual death is not a requirement for the action of the shooter to be considered deadly force! Even objects, which are not designed to be weapons, can be "capable of causing death or serious bodily injury." For example, a typical heavy lamp on an end table is not designed to be a weapon. However, if one is to pick it up and hit someone hard on the head, it is certainly "capable of causing death or serious bodily injury." Therefore, in that context, the swinging of the heavy lamp hard at someone's head is considered deadly force. Given the definition of deadly force, which includes using any object in a way that it is "capable of causing death or serious bodily injury," in almost every context foreseeable, shooting a handgun, rifle or shotgun will be considered deploying "deadly force." There is some support in Pennsylvania court decisions that even a BB gun can be "capable of causing death or serious bodily injury" (the old "You'll shoot your eye out!") and hence classified as using deadly force. This is to be contrasted with something like a rubber band gun which has no foreseeable method of being "capable of causing death or serious bodily injury" when it simply shoots a rubber band.

D. *Warning shots*

First, under Pennsylvania law, there is no requirement that before you intentionally deploy deadly force on a person that you provide any sort of warning, including a warning shot. If deadly force is justified legally in a given situation, then it may be deployed without an oral warning or a physical warning such as a warning or grazing shot.

Warning shots get a lot of good folks in legal trouble! Warning shots are commonly portrayed in movies and television as a good idea—and people like to mimic what they see in movies and on TV! Leaving completely aside all tactical issues of whether under a particular set of circumstances a warning shot is a good idea (and almost all tactical instructors and our personal experience has taught us that very rarely, if ever, are they a good idea as you will "flag" yourself and you will lose any tactical advantage of surprise), what does Pennsylvania law say about warning shots?

1. Are warning shots a use of deadly force?

First, the term "warning shot" does not appear in the Crimes Code. Without clear guidance from statutory law or in the case law, courts are left to determine if the action of firing a warning shot is to be considered under either the "use of force" standard explained above or the "use of deadly force" standard explained above. Recall the litmus test is whether, as deployed, the force is "capable of causing death or serious bodily injury."

There is little definitive appellate court case law demonstrating how Pennsylvania courts have addressed the issue of warning shots. When cases involving warning shots have come before Pennsylvania courts, the person firing the warning shot has usually either claimed to have "accidentally" shot the person they intended to warn (*see Commonwealth v. Sattazahn*, 631 A.2d 597 (Pa. Super. 1993)) or proceeded to intentionally shoot the person they initially "warned" (*see Commonwealth v. Scott*, 389 A.2d 79 (Pa. 1978)). As a result, Pennsylvania courts have not provided clear guidance as to whether warning shots in and of themselves constitute deadly force. This means it will typically be left to the discretion of the prosecutor's office; and without clear guidance from the appellate courts, it is not good legal advice to suggest that you deploy a "warning shot."

Every gun owner should be aware that one likely argument a prosecutor may put forth against an accused at trial is that the simple discharge of a firearm is an action that is capable of causing death or serious bodily injury. Such an argument, if successful, will shift the analysis of warning shots into the much harder to defend area of justified use of deadly force where the accused will have to articulate the reasonableness under the circumstances of his or her belief that deadly force was necessary to prevent serious bodily injury, death, kidnapping or intercourse by force or threat of force.

Why is it important whether the law classifies a warning shot as a use of force or a use of deadly force, even if no one is injured? Let's take a look at an example:

Example:

> Harry Homeowner looks outside during broad daylight and sees a trespasser on the edge of his property. Not knowing what the trespasser is doing, Harry grabs his .223 AR-15 rifle to investigate. Harry confronts the trespasser and demands that he leaves the property, but the trespasser ignores Harry. Being both scared and agitated, Harry fires a "warning shot" in the air, but not directly at the trespasser to get the trespasser's attention and compliance.

Does Harry's discharging his gun into the air fit the definition of the use of deadly force? Likely, yes. Is deadly force justified under these circumstances? No. There is no indication that Harry had a reasonable belief that deadly force was necessary to prevent death, serious bodily injury, kidnapping or intercourse by force or threat. Harry very likely may be guilty of a crime and not have a justification available as a defense, because he used a higher degree of force than the law allows.

2. Warning shots: "But, I never meant to hurt anyone!"

Going back to our example, assume Harry will say he intentionally and knowingly fired the warning shot (*i.e.*, it was no accident), but that he never aimed at or even meant to hit anyone. In fact, assume Harry will say he only shot into the dirt mere feet away to get the trespasser to leave. He will further say that if he meant to hurt or kill the trespasser, he would have hurt or killed the trespasser because he is a "crack shot" and is a competitive tactical shooter. How will the law view Harry's "warning shot?"

First, Harry Homeowner was confronted in this example with a mere trespasser. As we will see later, under Pennsylvania law a person may legally use force, *but not* deadly force to remove a trespasser on his or her land. The "warning shot" that was fired by Harry described above will most likely be legally classified as deadly force by the prosecutor. You are likely thinking to yourself: "But come on! Harry is a 'crack shot' and a competitive action shooter, he deployed the warning shot in such a way that he intentionally knew that the bullet was not capable of hurting, or killing!" But under the legal definition, the force only needs to be "capable of causing death or serious bodily injury." It doesn't necessarily matter whether or not the way that it was deployed; the bullet was intended to be capable of causing death or serious bodily injury. If it is determined to be deadly force in this circumstance, Harry will not be legally justified because he cannot articulate that it was reasonable to believe that under the circumstances, deadly force was immediately necessary to prevent bodily injury, death, kidnapping or intercourse by force or threat of force, and instead, a jury may decide he is guilty of a crime. So, the classification of force vs. deadly force is the difference between guilty and not guilty in this example.

Now, let us change the example a bit to see how things may get even more complicated:

Example:

> *Harry Homeowner confronts the same trespasser (Tom) as before and fires a warning shot. This time, however, the shot startled Tom out of his zoned state of self-meditation and wandering in which he likes to contemplate the universe. Tom was so deep in his personal world, he didn't realize he had accidentally wandered onto Harry's property. In fact, Tom the trespasser was so deep in meditative strolling and enjoying the Pennsylvania air that he didn't even hear Harry's verbal demands, but, the sound of Harry's .223 AR-15 rifle got Tom's full attention! As a result, Tom does exactly what his 25 years of police training have taught him—he draws and fires at Harry, believing that Harry's shot had meant to end his days of strolling and meditation!*

Where do we start the legal analysis? First, Harry Homeowner is in what Pennsylvania legal circles often call a "big mess!" Harry has very likely used unlawful deadly force against a mere trespasser on his land. After Harry's shot, does this turn our absent-minded wandering Tom into a victim who reasonably believes his life is threatened? Does this fact then allow Tom the trespasser some legal justification to return fire, *etc.*?

Continuing the issue, if our wandering Tom Trespasser then returns fire at Harry, is Harry then legally justified in using deadly force to defend himself? Or, because Tom is an accidental trespasser, is Tom required to retreat first before he takes any action? Keep in mind that Harry knows nothing about Tom's meditation or walks—he is just confronted with a trespasser who did not respond to verbal requests, but has now responded to Harry's "warning shot" with muzzle flashes from a pistol. Ultimately, you can see how messy this type of scenario can become, which all started with a well-intentioned "warning shot."

After the dust clears (assuming perfect knowledge), Harry likely used a higher degree of force than the law allows, as it will be classified as deadly force. But who decides if a "warning shot" is a "warning shot" and not a shot at someone that simply missed? Who decides if a response to a situation is reasonable? In the vast majority of cases in Pennsylvania, a jury ultimately decides. There are no bright lines on warning shots, so be advised that a warning shot can potentially be viewed as a use of deadly force, whether you subjectively intended it to or not, and, therefore, should never be used without careful consideration.

3. Beware of Bystanders

Another problem with "warning shots" under Pennsylvania law is tied to the crime of Recklessly Endangering Another Person ("REAP"). This particular crime covers a number of different circumstances and scenarios, and basically imposes a duty on citizens not to put others in harm's way of serious bodily injury or death. It most importantly covers reckless behavior. Many prosecutors will resort to this charge in the case where a warning shot is used such as the case with Harry in the last two examples. With warning shots, REAP charges will look to how the conduct affects everybody around, not just the person being "warned." So it provides a very wide net. A person can be convicted of REAP if he "recklessly engages in conduct which places or may place another person in danger of death or serious bodily injury." 18 Pa.C.S. §2705. Recklessly Endangering Another Person is a misdemeanor of the second degree and is punishable by a term of incarceration not to exceed two years. Again, it will not be a defense to REAP if there is a simple trespasser on land.

Can firing a warning shot constitute conduct which places or may place another person in danger of death or serious bodily injury? Of course it can, depending on the circumstances. Many people have no idea of the fact that .223 ammo or 9mm ammunition will go through dry wall or other intermediate barriers quite easily without losing too much transfer of its power, and can kill people on the other side of that intermediate barrier or cause them serious bodily injury. So this leads to concerns about over-penetration where the bullet continues well past the target. This is especially so in the case of an intentional miss which is really what a warning shot is.

Even if you do not know the terminal ballistics of your bullet or its penetrating power, does that make the conduct reckless? Let's look at the legal definition of "reckless" in Pennsylvania. A person acts recklessly when he or she consciously disregards a substantial and unjustifiable risk. In other words, they know of a serious risk, but ignore it anyway. Where the person is located and whether other people are present can make them more or less likely to face REAP charges. The more people are present, the more likely it is that a warning shot poses a known, substantial risk. Is the shooter on the fifth floor of a ten-floor apartment building and shooting up towards the ceiling as a warning shot at risk for a REAP charge? Is he or she on a crowded city street with a metal manhole cover that can easily and likely cause a ricochet? Or is he or she the sole occupant on an 80-acre farm, attempting to ward off a trespasser who is 100 yards away?

The possibility of a REAP charge is just another reason why warning shots, in a legal sense, pose a serious and unjustifiable risk. Gun owners must be aware of the hazards behind warning shots.

V. <u>What does it mean to "reasonably" believe force is immediately necessary?</u>

Under Pennsylvania law, use of force is justifiable when a person reasonably believes that such force is "immediately necessary" to protect himself or herself against the use of unlawful force. To get this right, we need to break it down step-by-step.

What does "reasonable" mean? Further, when is something immediately necessary? Who decides whether it is or not? The answers to these questions are how the legal process decides guilt or justification. For all gun owners, these concepts are critical.

A. *How does the law determine "reasonable?"*

In determining what is reasonable, the law often uses a standard known as the "reasonable person" standard to evaluate a person's conduct. It uses a hypothetical "reasonable person." Who is a reasonable person, and how does he or she act? Ultimately, a reasonable person is whatever a jury says it is.

The legal analysis behind the reasonable person goes like this: If a person uses force or even deadly force, he or she must act like a reasonable person would have acted under the same or similar circumstances in order to be legally justified! However, if a person fails to act like a reasonable person, his or her conduct will fall below the acceptable legal standard and will not be justified. Huh? That seems very circular, right? Like saying a reasonable person is reasonable. The reasonable person standard is the law's attempt to make the concept of reasonableness an objective and measurable test. Although a lot of prosecutors (and even some trial judges) mistake the reasonable person standard as an invitation to "stand in that person's shoes" and "decide whether or not to fire," this is inappropriate as it is typically couched as a second guess with the benefit of hindsight. The law doesn't require the jury to second-guess the self-defender, but instead requires the government to disprove beyond a reasonable doubt that the self-defender was not being reasonable in his or her actions at that time.

Under this standard, the law does not focus on whether you subjectively (or personally) believed force was reasonable, but whether a "reasonable person" would have considered it reasonable, an objective standard.

If the legal system (and ultimately, again, this could be a jury) determines that a reasonable person would have believed that force was immediately necessary to prevent someone from using unlawful force against you, then you will be found legally justified in using force.

Keep in mind, however, that judges, juries, and prosecutors are simply human beings, and people can have vastly different ideas of how a reasonable person should act under any given circumstances. This is particularly true if asked to decide whether force or deadly force was immediately necessary or not.

B. *What does "immediately necessary" mean under the law?*
When does someone have a reasonable belief that force is *immediately necessary*? In Pennsylvania, it ultimately may be a jury that is tasked with determining whether someone had a reasonable belief if an action was *immediately* necessary or not.

Clearly, "immediately necessary" attempts to convey a sense of urgency for the use of force. It suggests that the harm must be imminent. Future threats will not suffice. Rather, force is reserved for when harm is "about to" take place. But again, it usually falls back to the jury to decide if this standard was met in a particular case.

As an extreme example, if someone said that he was going to drive home, get his shotgun and come back to find you and kill you, you cannot deploy deadly force at that moment because it is not *imminent*. Does this mean you should do nothing? No. Under this particular case, it would be advisable to call the police and report the threat and proceed in a state of vigilance.

Is immediate measured in seconds, or minutes? How many seconds or minutes? There is no hard or fast rule. One thing is certain, the longer the period, the harder it will be to show that it was reasonable to believe that your actions were reasonable.

Practical Legal Tip:

Throughout this book, we refer to juries making the ultimate determination of fact. There are, however, some limited occasions where a judge makes the determinations. For example, if all parties waive (give up) their right to a jury, the Court may conduct what is called a "bench trial." -*Justin*

C. *Legal presumptions: stop legal second guessing*

Under certain circumstances, a person's belief in the necessity of immediate force or deadly force will be presumed "reasonable" under Pennsylvania law. This legal presumption can be a very powerful legal tool to stop legal second guessing or "Monday morning quarterbacking" of the amount or immediacy of the force used. A legal presumption is when a jury will be instructed that if a given set of circumstances exists (*e.g.,* a person is the victim of a home invasion), the law will presume "reasonable" a person's belief in the immediate necessity of using force or deadly force, and that use of force or deadly force would, therefore, be legally justified. For more information, *see* the discussion of the Castle Doctrine in Chapter Five.

Example:

> *Harry Homeowner is asleep in his house when he hears a noise in his kitchen. Harry enters his kitchen with his .45 drawn and confronts an armed burglar. Harry fires his weapon and the burglar will burgle no more!*

In this situation, was Harry's use of deadly force in firing his gun immediately necessary, or more precisely, was Harry's belief that deadly force was immediately necessary reasonable? Did Harry, legally, have to take additional actions before firing in order to have acted reasonably?

In Harry's current situation, the law will give Harry a powerful *legal presumption* that his belief that the use of deadly force was immediately necessary was "reasonable." In Harry's example, section 505 of the Crimes Code will provide him with this presumption of "reasonableness" (as a victim of a home invasion in his dwelling). In Pennsylvania statutes, these legal presumptions read: "an actor is presumed to have a reasonable belief that deadly force is immediately necessary to protect himself against death, serious bodily injury, kidnapping or sexual intercourse compelled by force or threat if ... (fill in the appropriate circumstances)." Under these circumstances, the "reasonable belief" is chalked up in the home invasion victim's favor. There need not be any other evidence supporting a reasonable belief under these circumstances. The legal presumption of reasonableness is a powerful tool for anyone facing a criminal charge and claiming legal justification.

Be aware that a presumption may be overcome. The government can introduce evidence to rebut the presumption. While the presumption makes the government's task more difficult, it does not by any means make it impossible. Remember that anything you say can and will be used against you. A defendant's own incriminating statement is the most frequent method by which prosecutors successfully rebut presumptions.

Practical Legal Tip:

Note: a presumption is not an *absolute* ticket to victory. A prosecutor may attempt to overcome the presumption with other evidence that shows you did not act in self-defense. The absolute best way that you can ruin your presumption is by making a statement to the police. *-Justin*

D. *No presumption of reasonableness: prosecutors are allowed to second guess*

As we discussed above, under certain circumstances, the law will presume the reasonableness of a person's belief that force or deadly force is immediately necessary. However, if a person uses force or deadly force under circumstances that do not qualify for this presumption, the issue of whether a belief of the immediate necessity to use force or deadly force was or was not reasonable is left to the jury. Prosecutors are then allowed to invite the jury to second guess the reasonableness of the timing and/or degree of force used by the accused.

Accordingly, when the accused does not qualify for a legal presumption, a prosecutor has fewer hurdles in arguing that a person's use of force or deadly force was not immediately necessary. This allows for arguments in court like "the harm wasn't yet imminent," "should have retreated," "should have used lesser force," and so forth. In many circumstances (those which do not fall under the Castle Doctrine), no legal presumption of reasonable belief is afforded for uses of force or deadly force at all! In those cases, a jury will decide the issue of the reasonableness of a person's belief and, ultimately, whether or not a person is guilty of a crime.

VI. The burden of proof in criminal cases

In criminal cases, the State has the burden of proof. This means that it is the State's responsibility to present enough evidence to prove the defendant committed a crime. This burden of proof that the State bears is a standard called "beyond a reasonable doubt." It is the highest level of proof used in the American justice system. In order for a defendant to be convicted of a crime, the prosecutor must prove every single element of the crime beyond a reasonable doubt.

We are now ready to look at when Pennsylvania law allows a person to use deadly force to protect themselves and others.

CHAPTER FIVE
WHEN CAN I LEGALLY USE MY GUN: PART II
SELF-DEFENSE AND DEFENSE OF OTHERS;
UNDERSTANDING WHEN PHYSICAL FORCE AND
DEADLY PHYSICAL FORCE CAN BE LEGALLY USED
AGAINST ANOTHER PERSON

I. Introduction and overview

Understanding when a person can legally use deadly force against another is of critical importance if you are a law abiding gun owner in Pennsylvania. Although a firearm is nothing more than a tool, it is a tool that by its very nature has the ability to deliver deadly force. Most, if not all, uses of a firearm will be considered deadly force in the eyes of the law —even if it doesn't result in death— as we discussed in Chapter Four. Thus, all responsible firearms owners must know and understand when they are justified in using force and deadly force under Pennsylvania law. Remember, in order to abide by the law, you must first know and understand the law. Failure to understand the law can land an otherwise law-abiding citizen in serious legal trouble very quickly!

The primary Pennsylvania statutes dealing with self-defense and defense of others are contained in Chapter Five of the Pennsylvania Crimes Code.

> 18 Pa.C.S. §505: Use of Force in Self-Protection
> 18 Pa.C.S. §506: Use of Force for the Protection of Other Persons

The law of justified self-defense is codified in section 505 in the Pennsylvania Crimes Code. Additionally, section 505 provides that under certain circumstances, there is a legal presumption of reasonableness. Presumptions are extremely powerful when deciding if a use of force or deadly force was legally justified. Basically, in these specific situations where there is a presumption, the law will presume at the outset that you had a reasonable belief that deadly force was immediately necessary to protect yourself against death, serious bodily injury, kidnapping, or sexual intercourse compelled by force or threat (for the remainder of this chapter, we'll call that last one "rape"). In other words, the law will presume that deadly force was justified in these scenarios. Remember that a presumption is not set in stone. While the law will afford you this presumption at the outset, the presumption can be overcome by evidence.

The presumptions in section 505 are found in Pennsylvania's version of the "Castle Doctrine," even though that specific term is not mentioned in the statute. Section 506 dictates when the law affords justification for the use of force in defense of others.

In the previous chapter, several legal concepts, such as reasonableness, immediate necessity, and the categorization of force and deadly force were discussed. Those concepts have practical applications in this chapter. In this chapter, we will expand upon those topics to include when a person may be justified in using force or deadly force in self-defense, as well as those circumstances when the law specifically prohibits the use of force or deadly force.

II. Defending people with force or deadly force

A. *General self-defense justification: no presumption of reasonableness*

The primary self-defense statute in Pennsylvania is found in section 505 of the Crimes Code. Section 505 lays out the legal requirements for the justified use of force, including deadly force, for self-defense. This section establishes that a person is legally justified in using force against another "when the actor believes that such force is immediately necessary for the purpose of protecting himself against the use of unlawful force by such other person on the present occasion."

Likewise, section 505 establishes the general standard for the justified use of deadly force. Because deadly force is a type of force (it is the most extreme type of force!) a person must be justified in using force if they are to be justified in using deadly force. A person must legally be able to use force before the law will ever allow deadly force to be justified. Only under specific circumstances will deadly force be justified under Pennsylvania law. Under Pennsylvania law, deadly force is not justified unless "the actor believes that such force is necessary to protect himself against death, serious bodily injury, kidnapping or [rape]."

As discussed in the previous chapter, what a person believes is immediately necessary and whether that belief is reasonable is the difference between justification (not guilty) and conviction (guilty).

Who decides whether an actor's belief is or is not reasonable that force or deadly force is immediately necessary? Who decides if the degree of force used by someone was reasonable under a particular set of circumstances? The answer to both of these questions is the trier of fact, which is usually a jury (in a small percentage of cases, the judge serves as the trier of fact; this is known as a bench trial).

Therefore, if a person finds himself or herself facing a criminal charge and is claiming justification under the general self-defense provisions of section 505, the trier of fact (again, usually a jury) will decide if that person's belief was or was not reasonable regarding the immediate necessity of the use of force or deadly force by that person. As can be imagined, this leaves a lot of room for juries to interpret what factors are necessary to form a reasonable belief. In these situations, the trier of fact will evaluate the totality of the circumstances. As a result, these determinations are incredibly fact-dependent. There are an infinite number of factors that can have an impact on this determination.

It also leaves the door open for legal second-guessing by prosecutors as to when and how much force was used, including arguments that there was no imminent threat and as such, the force or deadly force was not really "immediately necessary." If the prosecutor convinces a jury that a person used force or deadly force when or to a degree that was not "reasonably" believed to be immediately necessary, a person's use of force or deadly force will not be legally justified, and that person will be guilty of using unlawful force or deadly force.

However, under certain circumstances, section 505 allows a person a powerful additional protection in the form of a legal presumption of reasonableness in his or her belief that the use of force or deadly force was immediately necessary.

Practical Legal Tip:

The Castle Doctrine gives you a strong advantage —a legal presumption— if you have to use deadly force against an intruder who has broken into your home. But just because you have a presumption, doesn't mean the case is closed! You can easily forfeit your presumption under the stress of the situation by making incriminating statements. -*Justin*

B. *Presumption of reasonableness under section 505*

Section 505 contains several circumstances when the law gives far more protection than is available under the general self-defense standard. Under these circumstances, the law will presume that the actor had a reasonable belief that deadly force is immediately necessary to protect himself or herself against death, serious bodily injury, kidnapping or rape. If you recall, that is the very standard for when deadly force is justified. This legal presumption, if available to an accused, is a potentially powerful legal argument and limits prosecutors in court from second-guessing either when or the amount of force used by the accused in defending himself or herself (*e.g.*, should have used non-deadly force or should have waited longer, and so forth).

C. *The "Castle Doctrine"*
1. What is the "Castle Doctrine?"

The term "Castle Doctrine" does not appear in Pennsylvania law. However, the legal concept comes from the philosophy that everybody has the right to be safe in his or her own home. Every man is the King, and every woman is the Queen, of his or her "castle."

In Pennsylvania, you generally have a duty to retreat before using deadly force if you can do so with complete safety (*see* section D). But section 505 provides that if you're not the initial aggressor, there is *no* duty to retreat at home. In other words, if you are to use deadly force in self-defense at home, you will not lose your affirmative defense just because you didn't sneak out your back door. In some states, if you can sneak out the back door safely, you must do so instead of using your firearm. In Pennsylvania, that's not the case. No king or queen is required to retreat before using force or deadly force against an intruder in his or her castle.

Additionally, if you're not the initial aggressor, there is generally no duty to retreat at your place of work. However, if the assailant is a *known co-worker* (another person whose place of work you know it to be) you *still have a duty to retreat* if it can be done with complete safety. 18 Pa.C.S. §505 (b)(2)(ii).

In Pennsylvania, other "Castle Doctrine" provisions are implemented under section 505 of the Crimes Code and take the form of powerful presumptions of reasonableness. These presumptions apply in your dwelling, residence or occupied vehicle.

As we discussed earlier, the general rule is that a person is legally justified in using deadly force if he has a:

Reasonable belief that deadly force is immediately necessary to protect himself against death, serious bodily injury, kidnapping or rape.

Under certain circumstances, the "Castle Doctrine" will provide protections beyond this general rule. Some of these protections apply when you are in your dwelling, residence, or occupied vehicle. Others —such as elimination of the duty to retreat— can apply in one's place of business or employment in some instances. It is important to remember that in Pennsylvania, Castle Doctrine protections are *not* universal. All protections do not necessarily apply in all locations. For instance, the duty to retreat can be eliminated in one's dwelling or place of work, but *not* in one's occupied vehicle. Similarly, the Castle Doctrine sometimes provides a legal presumption in one's occupied vehicle, but *not* in one's place of work.

In some "Castle Doctrine" circumstances, the law will *presume* that a person had a reasonable belief that force or deadly force was immediately necessary to prevent death, serious bodily injury, kidnapping or rape. This presumption applies to you when:

(a) A person is in the process of unlawfully and forcefully entering your dwelling, residence or occupied vehicle;

(b) A person already has unlawfully and forcefully entered your dwelling, residence or occupied vehicle;

(c) A person is attempting to unlawfully and forcefully remove you or someone else from a dwelling, residence or occupied vehicle.

As can be seen, section (a) covers conditions when someone is attempting to enter your "castle," section (b) covers situations when they *already have* entered your "castle," and section (c) covers situations when you are being unlawfully removed from your "castle." Again, a "Castle Doctrine" presumption of "reasonableness" is a powerful legal tool for any person who is accused of a crime and claiming justification. In a dwelling or residence, the presumption will be further enhanced by having no duty to retreat and will prevent prosecutors in court from second guessing when or the amount of force that was used. These presumptions are available only for a dwelling, residence or occupied vehicle.

The law will also presume that the person "breaching" the castle does so with the intention of delivering death, serious bodily injury, kidnapping or rape. Why? If somebody unlawfully and forcefully enters a dwelling, residence, or occupied vehicle, or attempts to do so, the odds are they are not there to play cards. Pennsylvania law recognizes that.

2. <u>What is a "dwelling" or "residence" under the "Castle Doctrine?"</u>

Pennsylvania law, in defining "Castle Doctrine" rights, does not use the term home, house, or property; it uses the terms "dwelling" and "residence." The presumptions are specific, limited, and do not cover an entire piece of real property. Even though an entire piece of property might not be covered, the Castle Doctrine presumptions apply to more than just a house. Chapter Five of the Pennsylvania Crimes Code defines dwelling as:

> *Any building or structure, including any attached porch, deck or patio, though moveable or temporary, or a portion thereof, which is for the time being the home or place of lodging of the actor.*

Chapter Five further defines the term "residence" as:

> *A dwelling in which a person resides, either temporarily or permanently, or visits as an invited guest.*

18 Pa.C.S. §501.

These definitions seem to include anywhere you would lay your head. Places such as apartments, trailers and hotel rooms have been specifically deemed covered under the Castle Doctrine and *include more than just the interior of the space.* Any attached porch, deck or patio is also included.

This also means that structures that are detached from the building where you sleep at night are not considered a part of your dwelling or residence. For example, Pennsylvania law does not consider your detached garage, shed, and/or barn part of your dwelling or residence. Therefore, any justified use of force or deadly force would not qualify for presumptions of reasonableness under this particular part of the law.

Keep in mind that just because "Castle Doctrine" presumptions are not available, does not mean that deadly force cannot be justified. In a detached structure such as a shed, deadly force is still justified when there is a reasonable belief that deadly force is necessary to prevent death, serious bodily injury, kidnapping or rape.

3. What is a vehicle under the "Castle Doctrine?"

Pennsylvania "Castle Doctrine" legal presumptions and protections are applicable to occupied vehicles. Notice that the presumptions only apply to an "occupied vehicle." This law doesn't afford a presumption if your car is being stolen from your driveway while you're watching through the window of your home. But if a person is attempting to "carjack" you, which is to unlawfully and with force enter your vehicle while you are in it, you will be afforded a presumption under the Castle Doctrine. Similarly, if someone attempts to unlawfully and forcefully remove you from your vehicle when you're in the vehicle, you are afforded a presumption under the Castle Doctrine.

What does Pennsylvania define as a vehicle? Under Chapter 5 of the Pennsylvania Crimes Code, a vehicle is defined as:

> *A conveyance of any kind, whether or not motorized, that is designed to transport people or property.*

18 Pa.C.S. §501.

This is a very broad definition and appears to include anything that carries people or property from one place to another, including cars, trucks, motorcycles, boats, airplanes, golf carts, bicycles, buggies, and so forth.

4. <u>Is a person legally entitled to a presumption of reasonableness if they were involved in criminal activity?</u>

In certain situations, the presumption of reasonableness does not apply. Under Pennsylvania law, a person will *not* be entitled to a presumption of reasonableness if he is engaged in criminal activity. Additionally, since the presumption of reasonableness always involves a dwelling, residence, or occupied vehicle, a person is not entitled to the presumption if they were using the dwelling, residence, or vehicle to further criminal activity. *See* 18 Pa.C.S. §505(b)(2.2)(iii).

What is criminal activity? Would a woman sitting in her car in a "No Standing" zone lose her presumption? Thankfully, no. For the purposes of the presumption of reasonableness, "criminal activity" includes conduct which is a misdemeanor or felony, is not legally justifiable, and is related to the confrontation between the person using force and the person they're using it against. *See* 18 Pa.C.S. §505(d).

5. <u>Other situations where the presumption doesn't apply</u>

The presumption of reasonableness also doesn't apply under other select circumstances. These situations go beyond criminal activity.

First, the presumption doesn't apply if the person against whom force is used has a right to be there, or is a lawful resident of the dwelling, residence, or vehicle, such as an owner or leasee. This applies to landlords & tenants ("owner[s] or leasee[s]"), roommates, and members of the family unit living under the roof at that time. This does not necessarily mean that you can't use deadly force against these people if they attempt to kill you; it just means the law will not afford you the presumption that you reasonably believed deadly force was immediately necessary. *See* 18 Pa.C.S. §505(b)(2.2)(i).

Next, the presumption doesn't apply in the context of certain custody disputes. The presumption does not apply if a parent, grandparent, or other person with lawful custody attempts to remove a child from your home. Children are precious, and most parents would do anything in their power to protect them. However, while custody disputes are undoubtedly unfortunate, the law removes the presumption in efforts to avoid them being settled with deadly force. *See* 18 Pa.C.S. §505(b)(2.2)(ii).

Finally, the presumption of reasonableness doesn't apply when force is used against a peace officer —in the course of official duties— and the person using force knew or should have known that this was the case. Sometimes, in the course of their duties, peace officers are forced to enter a home. This doesn't necessarily mean that it's permissible for a peace officer to unlawfully and forcefully enter one's home. However, the legislature has decided that the law should not presume at the outset that this situation warrants a presumption of a reasonable belief that death, serious bodily injury, kidnapping, or rape is imminent. *See* 18 Pa.C.S. §505(b)(2.2)(iv).

Remember, these situations do not necessarily remove justification. They do, however, preclude one from the heightened protections of the Castle Doctrine (namely, the presumption of reasonableness). Similarly, we discussed how a presumption could be overcome by evidence. So if a presumption does apply, one is not automatically justified. This highlights the importance of training, preparation, situational awareness, and always identifying one's target.

6. <u>A person who provokes an attack is not entitled to justification</u>

Deadly force is only justified in a small zone of circumstances. Pennsylvania law doesn't allow somebody to lure another into that zone by provoking them. Deadly force is not justified if the person using the force provoked the other guy to use of force against him, just so he could use deadly force in "self-defense" in return.

Example:

> Slick Willy can't stand his paper delivery boy, Boring Bob. Willy comes up with a plan. If only he can end up in a situation where he'd be justified in using deadly force against Bob! Willy devises a plan. Willy, who is elderly, frail and in poor health, decides that he is going to get Bob to put him in immediate danger of death or serious bodily injury. To be extra certain, he is going to get Bob into his home for the kill. Bob is boring, but he's also burly. He's about forty years of age, in good health, in great shape, and is very strong. When Bob is delivering Willy's newspaper, Willy comes to the door and meets Bob on the doorstep. Willy points to the sky and asks Bob, "Bob, what's that up there?" When Bob looks up, Willy kicks him in the groin. Bob bends over in pain. Willy approaches him again and pokes Bob in the eye. Bob is infuriated. He raises his fist and punches Willy. The punch hurts Willy very badly, sending him backwards, through his doorway, but does not knock him out. Another punch, however, may cause death or serious bodily injury given the condition of the men. Bob raises

> *his fist again and takes a step through Willy's*
> *doorway. Willy, having succeeded with his plan,*
> *pulls out a gun and shoots Bob dead.*

Would Willy be justified in his use of deadly force? No! Willy *provoked* Bob's use of force, and he did it with the intention of shooting Bob. He wanted to kill Bob, so he tried to lure him into the "zone" of justification. Deadly force is not justified under these circumstances.

7. Force not legally justified to resist arrest

Under section 505 of the Pennsylvania Crimes Code, the use of force is not justifiable to resist arrest by a known police officer. This is true even if the arrest is unlawful!

Example:

> *Jason has been pulled over for speeding and is*
> *removed from his vehicle by a uniformed police*
> *officer. For no apparent reason, the officer tells*
> *Jason that he's under arrest and tells Jason to put*
> *his hands behind his back. Jason demands an*
> *explanation, but the officer will not provide one.*
> *The officer grabs Jason to turn him around and put*
> *him in handcuffs. Jason takes a step to the side and*
> *elbows the police officer in the head.*

Even though the officer's behavior is impermissible for a mere speeding violation, and even though it appears Jason is being subjected to an illegal arrest, his legally justifiable recourse is to pursue the matter through the court system—not to use force against the officer!

8. Force is not legally justified in certain property disputes

Pennsylvania law doesn't permit the use of force against somebody who is legally trying to remove you from his or her property. This also applies to persons acting on the property owner's behalf, such as security.

Force may be justified; however, if you're using force:

- as a public officer in the performance of official duties or you're assisting an officer;
- while making a lawful arrest, or assisting in making a lawful arrest;
- while making a justified reentry onto the property after being unlawfully dispossessed; or
- you have a reasonable belief that such force is necessary to prevent death or serious bodily injury.

D. *In Pennsylvania, "Stand Your Ground" means no duty to retreat, and that's it!*

"Stand Your Ground" is a common term for laws that provide that a person has no legal duty to retreat under certain circumstances. Perhaps due to media attention, there is a common misconception that the law affords more protections than it truly does. It's important to understand the limited protections afforded under "Stand Your Ground" in Pennsylvania, as to not rely on protections that don't exist!

"Stand Your Ground" is fairly new to Pennsylvania law. It was enacted in 2011. It provides that if you are attacked in a place where you would normally have a duty to retreat, provided certain criteria are met, you "[have] the right to stand [your] ground and use force, including deadly force." As we discussed above, in Pennsylvania, there is generally a duty to retreat before using deadly force if it can be done with complete safety. Thus, the existence of no duty to retreat can be a powerful legal tool for any defendant.

Under what circumstances does "Stand Your Ground" alleviate the duty to retreat? There are more requirements than one might imagine.

In order for "Stand Your Ground" protections to apply, you must be in legal possession of a firearm, and:

a) you must have a right to be in the place where you are attacked;

b) you must reasonably believe deadly force is immediately necessary to prevent death, serious bodily injury, kidnapping, or rape; and

c) the attacker must display or otherwise use a firearm, a replica of a firearm, or any other weapon readily or apparently capable of lethal use.

All three of these conditions must be satisfied in order for the "No Duty to Retreat" provisions to apply. The first requirement is fairly straightforward. The law will not afford you the added protections of "Stand Your Ground" if you're somewhere where you have no right to be in the first place! The second requirement should also look familiar. It is the standard for justified use of deadly force. Therefore, when "Stand Your Ground" applies, the reasons for which deadly force may be used are not any more extensive than provided by Pennsylvania's general justification laws.

The last requirement clarifies exactly how narrow "Stand Your Ground" protections are. Unless the attacker has what is or appears to be a deadly weapon, "Stand Your Ground" will not apply. This requirement is extremely important, yet often overlooked. A punch in the stomach probably will not satisfy this requirement. But remember that "Stand Your Ground" merely alleviates the duty to retreat, which only exists if it can be done with complete safety. If someone is beating you with his or her fists to such an extent that deadly force is necessary to prevent death or serious bodily injury, it is unlikely that you have an opportunity to retreat with complete safety. As a result, "Stand Your Ground" protections would be unnecessary.

Practical Legal Tip:

"Stand Your Ground" is *not* as broad as the media makes it out to be. It only offers limited protections in Pennsylvania. Remember, all it does is get rid of the duty to retreat, which only exists if it can be done with complete safety! Don't forget the requirement that an attacker have what is or appears to be a deadly weapon. No deadly weapon = no "Stand Your Ground!" *-Mike*

Example:

> *Larry the Law Abiding Gun Owner is walking down a public street with a legal firearm on his hip. Unbeknownst to Larry, Teddy Luger is waiting in the bushes for Larry, and he's got a knife. As Larry, continues his stroll, Teddy jumps out of the bushes and approaches Larry. Teddy is closing in on Larry, swinging the knife in a slicing motion.*

Is Larry entitled to the protections of "Stand Your Ground?" Yes! Let's go through the requirements. 1) Larry has a right to be where he is. He is walking down the street minding his own business. 2) Larry likely has a reasonable belief that deadly force is necessary to prevent death or serious bodily injury. Teddy has launched his surprise attack and is closing in! 3) Lastly, Teddy —the attacker— is displaying or otherwise using a weapon readily or apparently capable of lethal use.

Because all three requirements are met, Larry is entitled to "Stand Your Ground" protections. What does that mean? He has no duty to retreat before using deadly force, even if he can do so with complete safety. Can Larry retreat with complete safety in this situation? The answer is, "It depends!" We need more information. How close is Teddy to Larry? What kind of physical shape are they in? If Teddy has bad knees, and can't move very well, while Larry is a professional athlete, Larry might be able to retreat with complete safety. However, in this situation, because he's entitled to the protections of "Stand Your Ground," Larry has no legal duty to retreat, even if he can do so with complete safety.

Certain things can also take you outside of the protections of "Stand Your Ground." First, you cannot be engaged in illegal activity. Like we discussed in relation to the Castle Doctrine, "illegal activity" means "conduct which is a misdemeanor or felony, is not justifiable . . . and is related to the confrontation between an actor and the person against whom force is used." Second, you cannot be in illegal possession of a firearm. Lastly, the protections do not apply if you're using force against someone that you know, or have reason to know, is a peace officer.

Remember, if a person does not qualify for "No Duty to Retreat" provisions, it does not mean that the person's use of force or deadly force was not legally justified. It simply means that a jury will evaluate whether the person's belief was "reasonable" that the use of force or deadly force was immediately necessary. If the duty to retreat is not alleviated by law, the jury must determine whether the person using deadly force could have retreated with complete safety beforehand. If the duty to retreat applies, and the jury finds that the retreat with complete safety was possible, the use of deadly force will not be justified.

Example:

> One day, looking for a shortcut through the neighborhood, Tom hops a fence (a trespass) and is walking across open property to reach the street on the other side of the property. Tom is

> *confronted by the property owner and tries to explain that he meant no harm and was just taking a shortcut. However, the property owner becomes irate and cocks his gun, aims it at Tom, and says, "I'm going to kill you!"*

Under this example, Tom is a trespasser. Because he is a trespasser and has no legal right to be at his "location," Tom will not be entitled to the "No Duty to Retreat" protections of "Stand Your Ground." Thus, a prosecutor could argue that before the use of deadly force by Tom was immediately necessary, Tom should have retreated. Remember, the duty to retreat only applies if it can be done with complete safety. So the fact that Tom did not retreat, and was not entitled to "Stand Your Ground" does not mean that Tom was not justified in defending himself. It just makes it more difficult to convince a jury of his justification.

Now let us take the example one step further:

Example:

> *Tom is scared out of his mind as he looks down the barrel of the property owner's shotgun. The two are about 20 feet apart. Tom, hearing the property owner's threat to kill him, draws his own firearm and fires two shots, killing the property owner.*

In this example, a prosecutor would be allowed to question and second-guess when and the degree of deadly force that was used. The prosecutor may argue that Tom could have, and should have retreated with complete safety. Tom does not lose his legal right to self-defense under this example, but he is not afforded the protection that the "No Duty to Retreat" provisions offer.

III. Does Pennsylvania Law Allow for Use of Force in Defense of Others?

Under Pennsylvania law, the average person has *no duty* to come to the defense of another. Even if a crime is in progress, and even if you are legally carrying a firearm, there is generally no duty to defend others. But *can* you choose to do so? Under certain circumstances, Pennsylvania law additionally permits the use of force in defense of others.

A. *When does Pennsylvania law allow for the justifiable use of force or deadly force in defense of others?*

In the last sections, we addressed the law of legal justification for the use of force or deadly force for self-defense. We now turn to when the law allows the justified use of force or deadly force to protect another person or persons.

Unlike some jurisdictions, Pennsylvania does not require that you have a special relationship with the individual you are seeking to protect. Rather, the law requires that under the facts as you reasonably believe them to be at the time of the decision to use force:

1. if you were in the same situation of the third party under attack, you would have the legal right to use the force you are going to use;
2. the third party would be legally justified in using such force to protect himself; and
3. you believe your intervention is necessary to protect the third party.

Example:

> *Gary the Good Guy heads to the convenience store for a bag of beef jerky. Manny the Manager stands behind the counter, ready to help customers, secretly hoping that his shift will pass a little more quickly. In storms Chris the Creep, with a gun raised at Manny. "Empty the cash register or I'll spread your brains across the wall!" shouts Chris. Hands in the air, Manny claims that he doesn't have access to any of the store's money. Chris becomes agitated and says "Now you've made me mad. You're dead."*

Can Gary use deadly force to protect Manny? Let's analyze the situation under the law. Under the facts that Gary believes them to be at this time, Chris is about to kill Manny. If Gary were in Manny's position, (1) would he have the right to use the force he is going to use (deadly force)? Yes. If Gary were in Manny's shoes, he would have a reasonable belief that deadly force is necessary to prevent death or serious bodily injury. Chris is pointing a gun at him, and has already threatened to kill him with it. Regardless of whether the duty to retreat would apply, there is no opportunity to retreat safely. Moving on, (2) would Manny be legally justified in using deadly force to protect himself? For the same reasons discussed above, he would. Finally, (3) Gary would have a reasonable belief that his intervention is necessary to protect Manny. Chris's words and actions indicate that he is about to kill Manny unless Gary intervenes. So, if Gary is able to end the threat that is Chris the Creep, he would be justified in doing so under Pennsylvania law.

When it comes to defense of others, the law also provides that the "protector" doesn't have any more of a duty to retreat than the person he seeks to protect. So, if the person being defended has *no* duty to retreat, the protector has no duty to retreat while defending that person.

B.   What if the situation is not as it appeared to be?

A third person and a "Good Samaritan" may not see things as they really are. It is possible to reasonably, but inaccurately, perceive the facts as they unfold. But here, the focus is on the facts and circumstances as you, the actor, reasonably believe them to be. Therefore, if you use force in defense of another as the result of a reasonable mistake, you may still be entitled to this defense.

Example:

> *Imagine that Gary is back in the convenience store with Manny. Chris storms in, and the events unfold exactly the same way. Gary shoots Chris to end the threat. As it turns out, Manny and*

> *Chris were friends. They were in on the entire thing together. The gun wasn't real, and they staged the entire thing so Chris could walk out with some cash and merchandise.*

Under the facts as Gary believed them to be, Chris was about to kill Manny, and Gary could use deadly force in defense of Manny. His perspective and knowledge of the situation are very different from the person he sought to defend. Manny was a part of the setup with Chris. Gary, however, had no reason to believe that this was staged. Considering the totality of the circumstances, it is likely that Gary's version of the facts as he believed them to be at the time, was reasonable. If a trier of fact finds that Gary's belief was reasonable, his actions will be justified.

It is also possible to have an honest, yet unreasonable belief about the facts and circumstances. If one's belief about the facts and circumstances is unreasonable, the use of force will not be justified.

Example:

> *Nicky the Knucklehead attends a rock and roll concert. The rock concert is filled with all kinds of theatrics. A miniature airplane crashes onto the stage and is consumed by flames to start the show. There are werewolves and vampires dancing on the stage, covered in blood, throughout the show. Finally, a curtain is lifted, revealing several people trapped in cages. Zombies in uniforms stand guard outside the cages. Two zombies in uniform approach the lead singer of the band, and grab him by each wrist. They start to bring him to a cage as he seemingly resists. Nicky the Knucklehead thinks that the singer is really being kidnapped, and begins to freak out. Just as the "zombies" are about to throw the lead singer into a cage, Nicky the Knucklehead shoots them dead.*

Nicky truly believed that deadly force was necessary to prevent the kidnapping of the lead singer. But would Nicky be justified in using deadly force against the zombies in this instance? No! Given the setting and the nature of the theatrical performance, Nicky could not reasonably believe that the events occurring on stage were real. Regardless of Nicky's subjective belief that the lead singer was in immediate danger of kidnapping, he would not be justified under an objectively reasonable perception of the facts.

CHAPTER SIX
WHEN CAN I LEGALLY USE MY GUN: PART III
UNDERSTANDING WHEN DEADLY FORCE
CAN BE USED AGAINST ANIMALS

I. Can I legally use deadly force against animals?
We've discussed when the law justifies the use of deadly force against an attacker. But what happens when you need to protect yourself, another person or even another animal from an attacking animal? Pennsylvania law specifically addresses the use of deadly force against certain animals in certain situations.

A. *No general "defense against animals" statute*
Various provisions of Pennsylvania law include certain protections for those who use deadly force against certain animals in a defensive manner.

B. *Affirmative defense to "Cruelty to Animals"*
Pennsylvania law criminalizes cruelty to animals in section 5511 of the Crimes Code. Specifically, section 5511 makes it a misdemeanor of the second degree to willfully and maliciously kill, maim or disfigure any domestic animal of another person or any domestic fowl of another person.

This law, however, does not affect one's ability to protect another animal from attacking animals. Section 5511 specifically does not apply to "the killing of any animal taken or found in the act of actually destroying any domestic animal or domestic fowl ..."

C. *Deadly force against dangerous dogs*
Pennsylvania law specifically addresses the protective use of deadly force against dangerous dogs. Under 3 Pa.C.S. §459-501, a person may kill any dog that is:
- pursuing, wounding or killing any domestic animal;
- wounding or killing other dogs, cats or household pets; or
- pursuing, wounding or attacking a human being.

Deadly force is permissible in these situations irrespective of whether the dog pursing, wounding, killing or attacking is licensed. In other words, regardless of whether the dog is a house pet or a stray, the conduct listed above serves as grounds for the use of deadly force.

Keep in mind that under Pennsylvania law a dog is "personal property." *Daughen v. Fox*, 539 A.2d 858, 864 (Pa. Super. 1988). In the unfortunate event that you are forced to use deadly force against another's dog, will you be liable for civil damages? The statute specifically relieves one from liability in these situations ("There shall be no liability on such persons in damages or otherwise for such killing."). After all, use of deadly force in these situations is protective and defensive in nature. The law recognizes this, and in turn, does not impose criminal or civil penalties to those who use deadly force against dogs as described above.

D. *Defense against wild animals*

Practical Legal Tip:

While many of us consider our dogs to be family members, don't forget that the law considers dogs as personal property. Because dogs are personal property, the "defense of others" laws that apply to protecting other human beings do not apply to protecting our dogs. -*Justin*

Pennsylvania law specifically anticipates the killing of "game or wildlife" in a defensive situation. However, the state of the law suggests a leery attitude toward killing game or wildlife if it otherwise violates the Game Code. Accordingly, it is unlawful to kill any game or wildlife as a means of self-protection, unless it is clearly evident from all the facts that a human was endangered to the degree that the immediate destruction of the game or wildlife is necessary. This places significant scrutiny on an individual who uses deadly force against an animal! Perhaps this is aimed at preventing rare hunters with bad intentions from unlawfully taking trophy animals, but claiming "it was coming right for us!"

Should one be involved in a defensive shooting of game or wildlife, there are mandatory reporting requirements. If you destroy the wildlife, you must report the event within 24 hours, provide for safe keeping of the wildlife where it was killed, and be available for an interview with the police. 34 Pa.C.S. §2141.

Practical Legal Tip:

Tempted to shoot a nice buck or bear out of season and claim self-defense? Don't be! Doing so will place you under a tremendous amount of scrutiny, and you'll have a lot of explaining to do. With a very high standard in place, and the penalties that come with a violation, it's not worth the risk! -*Mike*

E.   *Deadly force against animals to protect property*
Pennsylvania law expressly states: "subject to any limitations in this subchapter, nothing in this title shall be construed to prohibit any person from killing any game or wildlife:

1.   which the person may witness actually engaged in the material destruction of cultivated crops, fruit trees, vegetables, livestock, poultry or beehives;
2.   anywhere on the property under the person's control, including detached lands being cultivated for the same or similar purposes, immediately following such destruction; or

3. where the presence of the game or wildlife on any cultivated lands or fruit orchards is just cause for reasonable apprehension of additional imminent destruction."

34 Pa.C.S. §2121(a).

Although this law seems simple on its face, its protections are very narrow! First, this law only applies to certain individuals, because a "person" is very narrowly defined.

Those protected under this statute include:

A. any person cultivating, as a primary means of gaining a livelihood, any lands for general or specialized crop purposes, truck farming or fruit orchard or nursery being regularly maintained, as either the owner, lessee or a member of the family of the owner or lessee assisting with the cultivation of the land; or

B. a domiciled member of the household of the owner or lessee or an employee of the owner or lessee, regularly and continuously assisting in the cultivation of the land or other person as authorized by commission permit.

34 Pa.C.S. §2121(c).

It is also important to understand when the law demands further action before using deadly force against game or wildlife to protect property. Certain animals are deemed to be "protected" by the Game Commission. Before killing any of these protected animals, even if they are destroying property as described above, "every reasonable effort shall be made to live trap and transfer such game or wildlife." 34 Pa.C.S. §2121(b). But don't make these efforts on your own! The law provides that the "trapping and transfer shall be done in cooperation with a representative of the commission." 34 Pa.C.S. §2121(b).

The Pennsylvania Code provides that the protected status of certain animals can be removed under certain circumstances.

The Pennsylvania Code removes protection from wildlife —NOT including migratory birds, big game, threatened species and endangered species— if personal property is being destroyed or damaged. Under this section, "personal property" is separate and distinct from agricultural crops, as described in Title 34 earlier. So these protections are different than those provided for those who farm for a living. In these situations, the wildlife can only be taken by "the owner or person in charge of the personal property affected." 58 Pa. Code §141.3. The law still mandates that those taking wildlife under these circumstances do so in a lawful and humane manner. Should an individual take wildlife to protect personal property, he must turn it over to a representative of the Game Commission.

Similar applications apply when an animal that is sick or diseased and poses a threat to human safety, farm animals or pets. Under these circumstances, protected status can also be removed. Again, this does not apply to migratory birds, big game, threatened species and endangered species. Only the person in charge of the property where the threat exists, or a person under their direct supervision can take the wildlife. In these situations, the law requires that the taking be done in a "safe, expeditious and lawful manner." 58 Pa. Code §141.3.

There is an additional duty after the diseased wildlife is taken. It must be buried on site, destroyed by incineration or other proper disposal, or submitted for laboratory analysis.

For more information on the Pennsylvania Game Commission, including which animals are "protected," please visit www.pgc.state.pa.us.

F. *Dogs harassing sheep*

For Pennsylvania's more rural law abiding gun owners, a dog that harasses sheep can cause tremendous problems. Considering this potential for disaster, under certain circumstances, deadly force is permitted against dogs that harass sheep. Pennsylvania law makes it expressly legal "to shoot or kill any dog or dogs found or known to be chasing or worrying sheep, or accustomed so to do within this commonwealth ..." 3 Pa.C.S. §531. If a person uses deadly force against a sheep-harassing dog under these circumstances, he will not be liable for damages.

G. *Beware of discharge ordinances*

As a practical matter, beware of shooting animals if your local government has an ordinance preventing discharge within certain borders. Although we maintain that a complete ban violates state law, that will not prevent local law enforcement officers from enforcing these ordinances for the time being. Even though killing the animal may be lawful under the circumstances, discharging a firearm in order to do so may result in charges.

H. *Federal law defenses*

The federal law, in a comprehensive fashion, has actually had the foresight to specifically provide that a person may kill an animal protected by federal law in self-defense, such as the regulations concerning the Mexican gray wolf in 50 CFR §17.84(k)(7)(i), or the grizzly bear in 50 CFR §17.40(b)(1)(i)(B). This makes the federal law clear and comprehendible. Therefore, if you are carrying a firearm in a National Park (*see* Chapters Nine and Ten), and you find yourself face to face with a grizzly bear, you will have a legal defense for protecting yourself.

CHAPTER SEVEN

WHEN CAN I LEGALLY USE MY GUN: PART IV
UNDERSTANDING WHEN DEADLY PHYSICAL FORCE
CAN BE USED TO PROTECT PROPERTY

I. Overview of the law to protect property

Pennsylvania law justifies the use of force to protect unlawful entry, interference or trespass on property. Although the use of force may be justified to protect property, aside from a select few circumstances Pennsylvania law does not justify *deadly force* in defense of property crimes. Like the statutes addressing self-defense and defense of others, the laws addressing protection of property are found in Chapter Five of the Pennsylvania Crimes Code. Particularly, 18 Pa.C.S. §507 details "Use of force for the protection of property."

Throughout Chapter Five of the Pennsylvania Crimes Code, the term "belief" means "reasonable belief." Therefore, protection of property will be analyzed under the same "reasonable person" standard discussed in Chapters Four and Five. Additionally, the same requirement remains that a person must reasonably believe that the force or deadly force used is "immediately necessary."

II. When is someone legally justified to use "force" but not "deadly force" to protect their own property?

A. *Prevent or terminate interference with property*

The law specifically outlines when a person can use force, but not deadly force, in protection of property. Section 507 provides that the use of force is justified when one has a reasonable belief that force is immediately necessary to:

- prevent an unlawful entry or other trespass upon land;
- prevent someone from trespassing against, or unlawfully carrying away tangible moveable property;
- stop an unlawful entry or trespass on land that's already happening; or

- stop someone who's already trespassing against or unlawfully carrying away moveable tangible property.

If a person is defending his own property, he must have a reasonable belief that the property he is protecting is his or that he is lawfully possessing it. If he is defending another's land or property, he must be acting on behalf of the person who he reasonably believes possesses the land or property.

If you catch someone in the act
In plain English, if someone is unlawfully coming onto your land or taking your personal property, you are justified in using force to stop them, but not deadly force. Of course, just like instances of self-defense, you must also meet the standard of *reasonable belief in the immediate necessity of the use of force*.

Use of Force Justifiable for Protection of Property; 18 Pa.C.S. §507(a)(1)
The use of force upon or toward the person of another is justifiable when the actor believes that such force is immediately necessary to prevent or terminate an unlawful entry or other trespass upon land or a trespass against or the unlawful carrying away of tangible movable property, if such land or movable property is, or is believed by the actor to be, in his possession or in the possession of another person for whose protection he acts.

If a person is using force to protect property in this scenario, he is doing so to *prevent* the interference or taking of property. Under these circumstances, the wrong-doer's act is not complete. What if the wrong-doer has already completed the act?

B. *Recovery of property*
The second category, under section 507 is the justified use of force in *recovering* property that has been unlawfully taken from the

person or to reenter land. Under this section, use of force can also be justified to:

- get back onto land; or
- take back tangible moveable property.

> ### Justified Use of Force to Recover Your Property; 18 Pa.C.S. §507(a)(2)
>
> The use of force upon or toward the person of another is justifiable when the actor believes that such force is immediately necessary to effect an entry or reentry upon land or to retake tangible movable property, if:
>
> (i) the actor believes that he or the person by whose authority he acts or a person from whom he or such other person derives title was unlawfully dispossessed of such land or movable property and is entitled to possession; and
>
> (ii) (A) the force is used immediately or on fresh pursuit after such dispossession; or
>
> (B) the actor believes that the person against whom he uses force has no claim of right to the possession of the property and, in the case of land, the circumstances, as the actor believes them to be, are of such urgency that it would be an exceptional hardship to postpone the entry or reentry until a court order is obtained.

The person using force can do so if he reasonably believes that he is the lawful possessor, and someone else has unlawfully taken possession of the land or tangible property. Additionally, the force must be used *immediately* or in fresh pursuit after the dispossession. If not, the person can only use force if he believes the taker has no claim of right to possession of the property and if it's land, there are urgent circumstances that can't wait for the issue to be resolved in court. Again, no deadly force is allowed.

Fresh pursuit after property is taken
In the event a person's property has already been stolen, a person is only legally justified to use force to recover it *immediately after it was stolen* or in *"fresh pursuit."* A person is not allowed to use force that is not immediate, or in "fresh pursuit," to recover the property. Going to recover property later is dangerous, because beating the thief up in the process could subject you to criminal penalties and civil liability.

In addition to attempting recovery immediately after or in fresh pursuit after dispossession of property, a person must have a *reasonable belief* that the other person wasn't entitled to take it in the first place. In other words, if an ordinary, reasonable person would take the item back believing the "thief" had no right to it, then a person may be justified in doing the same thing. Keep in mind, though, this section only justifies the use of *force*. Deadly force is not justified absent special circumstances which are outlined later in this chapter.

C.   *Use of force to protect a third person's property*
Similar to the situations described above, Pennsylvania law also allows a person to use force to protect a third person's property under certain circumstances. Again, deadly force is not authorized.

A person can act on behalf of a third party, using force to protect the third party's property if he reasonably believes that force is immediately necessary to:
- prevent an unlawful entry or other trespass upon land;
- prevent someone from unlawfully trespassing against or carrying away tangible moveable property;
- stop an unlawful entry or trespass on land that's already happening; or
- stop someone who's already trespassing against or unlawfully carrying away moveable tangible property.

The person protecting the third party's property is said to be acting *for* the third party. Accordingly, the person using force must have a reasonable belief that the third party is the lawful possessor of the property.

D. *What is "possession?"*
While section 507 doesn't provide a specific definition of "possession," it does clarify a few situations that do, and do not, constitute possession.

First, if a person has parted with custody of property to another person, and the other person refuses to give it back, the person who parted with the property does *NOT* have possession anymore. However, if the property is moveable and it's still on the original person's land, it *IS* still in the original person's possession, even if the other person has physical custody of the property. So while we usually equate possession to physical custody of property, if a "taker" takes physical possession of an item from the original possessor, but hasn't left the original possessor's land yet, the original possessor still had possession, even though the taker might be holding the item!

Next, if a person has been dispossessed of land (somebody else kicked them out and took possession) the original person does *NOT* retake possession just by stepping foot on the land again. So it's not quite like a game of "tag."

Finally, if a person has a license to use or occupy real property (such as a renter), that person *DOES* have possession of the property. However, he does *NOT* have possession against the person who gave him the license to do so (such as a landlord) if the person who gave the license is acting under a claim of right.

E. *Generally, the person must say something before using force*
Under most circumstances, the law requires a person who is about to use force to first request that the other person stop interfering with his property. This could potentially avoid using force against another in the case of a mere misunderstanding. For instance, picture the luggage return at an airport. There are often multiple suitcases that appear to be exactly the same! The requirement for

a "request" before the use of force could prevent a person who innocently and accidentally grabs the wrong suitcase —which they believe to be their own— from being grabbed from behind or tackled to the ground.

While the requirement for a "request" generally applies, it does not apply under certain circumstances. First, it doesn't apply if the request would be useless. If the surrounding circumstances dictate that a request would simply be a waste of time, and would not stop the interference with the property, the requirement doesn't apply. Picture the classic "purse snatcher." A person isn't required to ask the running purse snatcher to give it up before using force to recover it. We can't expect the purse snatcher to simply comply with such a request!

Next, the requirement doesn't apply if making the request would be dangerous. The law doesn't require a person to make the request before using force if doing so would be dangerous to himself or another person. Sometimes people who take things unlawfully do so violently and aggressively. In these situations, it might be obvious that making a request for them to stop would put the requester in a dangerous position. As such, the request is not required before using force to protect the property.

Finally, the "request" requirement does not apply if substantial harm will be done to the physical condition of the property before the request can effectively be made.

F. _Use of force not justified if exclusion of the trespasser poses a risk of serious bodily injury_

Pennsylvania law does _not_ justify the use of force against a trespasser in certain situations when doing so will put the trespasser at risk of serious bodily injury. The law seems to target potential trespassers seeking shelter in an emergency. Specifically, the law reads:

> [T]he use of force to prevent or terminate a
> trespass is not justifiable under this section if
> the actor knows that the exclusion of the

trespasser will expose him to substantial danger of serious bodily injury.

When could this come into play? Perhaps a man seeking shelter from an approaching tornado tries to enter the nearest home through the back door. Under Pennsylvania law, if the owner pushes the shelter-seeking man out of the door, exposing him to be sucked up by the tornado, that force would likely not be justified.

G. *No legal presumption of reasonableness when defending property*

Pennsylvania law provides no legal presumptions of reasonableness for uses of force to protect property, whether it is preventing or terminating a trespass or interference or the recovery of property. As a result, whether force is justified to protect property is highly fact-dependent. The trier of fact (usually a jury) will be the ultimate arbiter of the reasonableness of conduct, ultimately evaluating the totality of the circumstances.

The analysis so far leads us to the question: if force may legally be used to prevent or terminate trespass or interference with property, what constitutes a trespass or interference with property?

H. *What is trespassing?*

The commonly understood meaning of trespass is "an unlawful interference with one's person, property, or rights." This definition has been expanded to refer typically to "any unauthorized intrusion or invasion of private premises or land of another." *Black's Law Dictionary, 6th ed.* This commonly understood definition of trespass is different and more expansive than the offense of criminal trespass found in section 3503 of the Crimes Code:

Buildings and Occupied Structures.
A person commits an offense if, knowing that he is not licensed or privileged to do so, he:

(i) enters, gains entry by subterfuge or surreptitiously remains in any building or occupied structure or separately secured or occupied portion thereof; or
(ii) breaks into any building or occupied structure or separately secured or occupied portion thereof.

Defiant trespasser.
(1) A person commits an offense if, knowing that he is not licensed or privileged to do so, he enters or remains in any place as to which notice against trespass is given by:
(i) actual communication to the actor;
(ii) posting in a manner prescribed by law or reasonably likely to come to the attention of intruders;
(iii) fencing or other enclosure manifestly designed to exclude intruders;
(iv) notices posted in a manner prescribed by law or reasonably likely to come to the person's attention at each entrance of school grounds that visitors are prohibited without authorization from a designated school, center or program official; or
(v) an actual communication to the actor to leave school grounds as communicated by a school, center or program official, employee or agent or a law enforcement officer.

The Pennsylvania version of criminal trespass provides three separate and distinct forms of trespass. Each of them have different requirements, but all are more specific than the traditional definition of trespass. For instance, each form requires the trespasser to have knowledge that he had no right to be in that location. The traditional definition has no such requirement.

There is a civil cause of action in Pennsylvania that more closely mirrors the traditional definition of trespass. If someone commits a trespass that meets the requirements of this civil cause of action, they can be sued in court. If the actor intends to be upon the particular piece of land in question, it is not necessary that he intend to invade the actor's interest in the exclusive possession of his land. The Supreme Court of Pennsylvania has discussed what is required of civil trespass.

> [T]he fact that a trespass results from an innocent mistake and, in that sense, is not deliberate or willful, does not relieve the trespasser of liability ... The intention which is required to make the actor liable is an intention to enter upon the particular piece of land in question irrespective of whether the actor knows or should know that he is not entitled to enter thereon.

Kopka v. Bell Tel. Co. of Pa., 91 A.2d 232, 235 (Pa. 1952) (quoting Restatement, Torts, §163, comment (b)) (additional citations omitted). So, in Pennsylvania, a person can commit an actionable trespass without necessarily committing a criminal trespass.

I. *Trespass for justification*

How then is "trespasser" defined in section 507 for purposes of defending property? Because the plain language of the section refers to "unlawful entry or other trespass" it is clear that the statute intends to follow a broader definition of trespass than just the offense of criminal trespass found in section 3503. In other words, a person may be potentially legally justified in using force against a person found trespassing on their land—even if that person has not committed the crime of criminal trespass, but only so long as the use of force is accompanied with a reasonable belief that it is immediately necessary to terminate the trespass.

Keep in mind that the law generally requires more than just a "trespass" before force is justified. Recall that the justification for use of force can be eliminated if the person entering or interfering is doing so "under a claim of right."

The verbal warning that is generally required before using force might prevent the need to use force to stop an unknowing trespasser. The requirement that the use of force be "immediately necessary" could also serve the same purpose. Without a specific definition of what "trespass" means as found in section 507, in the vast majority of cases, a jury will be the ultimate arbiter of whether or not a person had a reasonable belief that it was immediately necessary to terminate another person's unlawful entry or other trespass on the land.

J. *What is trespass against moveable tangible property?*
You have a legal right to prevent or terminate trespass against moveable tangible property, but what does this mean? There is no statutory definition of "trespass against moveable tangible property," but Pennsylvania courts have long recognized a civil cause of action for "trespass to chattels," which covers moveable tangible property. In these cases, Pennsylvania courts have found that a trespass against chattels occurs when a person intentionally takes property from another, or uses or intermeddles with a chattel in the possession of another. *Pestco, Inc. v. Associated Products, Inc.*, 880 A.2d 700, 708 (Pa. Super. 2005). This definition conforms to the traditional definition of trespass, which includes an unlawful interference with one's property. Conceivably, this would include theft, destruction, vandalism, or anything else that diminishes a person's right to their property. Whether particular conduct rises to use or intermeddling with a person's property is an issue that a trier of fact (usually a jury) decides.

K. *Is there a statutory minimum value of property before force may be legally used to protect it?*
No. There exists no statutory minimum value for property before force may be used to protect it. Section 507 does not specify that property a person seeks to protect must be of a certain minimum dollar value in order for a person to protect it. However, it is important to remember that a person must have a reasonable belief that the use of force or deadly force is immediately

necessary to protect that property before a person would be justified in using force or deadly force.

Realistically, even though a person may be in the process of taking tangible, movable property, some property may be of so little value that the use of force to protect or recover it would not be deemed reasonable by a reasonable person (which is usually determined by people on a jury).

Example:

> One day at work, Fred walks into Ricky's office and takes a half-eaten bag of chips off of Ricky's desk and walks away. Ricky, upset at having his favorite chips pilfered from his desk, jumps up and says "Hey! Give those back!" Fred gives Ricky a sarcastic "thumbs up sign" and continues to stroll and eat the chips. Ricky chases Fred down, shoves him to the ground, and starts wrestling with Fred to recover his chips. On his way to chase Fred, Ricky also passes the office kitchen where identical bags of chips are available for community consumption.

Was Ricky's use of force against Fred legally justified? Maybe. But practically speaking, it may be difficult to convince a jury of that. It may be a very hard sell to a jury that a person was beat up over a few potato chips. However, some members of a jury may value potato chips much differently, or feel strongly about the principles involved. What if a thief is stealing irreplaceable family photos? There's no monetary value to be placed there—only personal sentiment. Again, the law is silent on the subject of any monetary value of property to be defended.

The point to be made here is that some items simply may not have enough value (financial, sentimental, or otherwise) to provide a person with a *reasonable* belief that the use of force is necessary to protect or recover the item. In this example, not only do the chips have little monetary value, but there are others readily available for replacement from the kitchen. It would be hard to imagine a jury finding a person to be justified in even using force in such a situation.

Note: as discussed later in this chapter, under certain circumstances, deadly force is justified to prevent the commission of a felony in one's dwelling. If someone is destroying or interfering with one's property inside the dwelling, the value of the property may dictate whether the crime is a felony or a misdemeanor. For a detailed discussion on this topic, see the section entitled "When is someone legally justified in using 'deadly force' for the protection of property?" later in this chapter.

L. *Confinement as force*

Confinement is an acceptable type of force in protection of property. *But,* the person using confinement *must* take all reasonable measures to end the confinement as soon as he knows he can do so with safety to the property. If the person using confinement fails to do that, the confinement is *NOT* justified. So if confinement is used as force to protect property, keeping the bad guy locked up extra-long to pay him back or teach him a lesson isn't legally justified. This limitation doesn't apply if the person confined has been arrested and charged with a crime.

M. *Use of a device to protect property*

It is acceptable to use a device to protect property under certain circumstances. The justifications for use of force to protect property generally apply to use of a device, but some notable restrictions apply. Use of a device as force to protect property is justified *ONLY IF*:
- the device is not designed to cause —or known to create— a substantial risk of death or serious bodily injury;
- using that kind of device to protect property is reasonable under the circumstances as the actor reasonably believes them to be; *AND*

- the device is customarily used to protect property *OR* the actor takes reasonable care to let the probable intruders know that the device is used.

All three requirements must be met in order for the use of a device to protect property to be justified under the law. Notice that the device cannot be designed to cause or known to create a substantial risk of death or serious bodily injury. Booby traps aren't allowed! So if a person uses a spring gun tied to the door or a blow torch above the door frame (like in the movie *Home Alone*), that use of a device will not be justified to protect property. Why? A spring gun is *made* to cause death or serious bodily injury. A blow torch, while not *made* to cause death or serious bodily injury, is certainly known to cause the same.

The use of the device must also be reasonable under the circumstances. Recall that the circumstances are evaluated as the person using the device reasonably believes them to be. The person using the device must reasonably believe that the force the device is going to cause would be justified if he were to use that force in person.

Last, the device must be either customarily used to protect property *or* the person using the device must take the sufficient steps to warn probable intruders. An alarm system is likely to be considered a device customarily used to protect property even though it can potentially cause a negative reaction (such as falling backwards or having an anxiety attack). If the device is unconventional, but meets the first two requirements listed, its use can be justified if the proper precautions are taken to warn intruders that the device is used. What is an unconventional device for protecting property? Fill in the blank! Robot security guards? Generators producing loud sounds of such a low frequency that they can cause stomach sickness? These seem to be devices that are not customarily used to protect property. But remember that even if warnings are provided, the device *cannot* be made —or known to cause— death or serious bodily injury.

N. *What if you have a right to be there, but somebody won't let you in?*

We talked about keeping trespassers and wrongdoers out. What if instead the wrongdoer *won't let you in?* Pennsylvania law directly addresses "wrongful obstructors" in section 507, and provides that force can be justified to get by the "evil gatekeeper." So how and when can you get them out of your way?

First, you must reasonably believe that the wrongdoer is intentionally, or knowingly, and unjustifiably keeping you out of a place where you're lawfully entitled to go. It can't be somebody you know is likely just standing in the wrong place at the wrong time.

Also, the person using force to get past the wrongdoer must reasonably believe that the "evil gatekeeper" has no claim of right to keep the person out. Again, this implicates property disputes and potential landlord/tenant issues.

Next, force is not justified if the person being kept out knows that the person doing the obstruction has possession or custody of the land, or is keeping people out on behalf of someone in possession or custody of the land. In other words, force isn't justified against the possessor, or the possessor's bouncer! However, even in these instances, force can be justified if the person being kept out reasonably believes the circumstances are too urgent to wait for the property dispute to be resolved in court.

Finally, the force used can't be greater than would be allowed if the gatekeeper were using it to prevent trespass. In other words, this isn't a pass to go above and beyond!

All of the requirements must be met in order to use force — not deadly force— against an unlawful obstructor to get them out of the way!

III. When is someone legally justified in using "deadly force" for the protection of property?

Earlier in this chapter we noted that although deadly force is generally *not* permitted in defense of property, the law provides certain circumstaces that fall outside of this general rule. Each of these circumstances occur in a person's dwelling.

Even though the law states these circumstances justify the use of deadly force to protect property, it is apparent that these circumstances go *beyond* protecting one's interest in the property itself. These circumstances seem to protect, even if coincidentally, the safety and well-being of a person and/or loved ones.

A. *Use of deadly force to protect property in a person's dwelling*

Pennsylvania law provides a circumstance in a person's dwelling where deadly force is justified in protecting property.

Remember that under Pennsylvania law a "dwelling" is any building or structure, or a portion of a building or structure, being used as the home or lodging of the actor. This includes any attached porch, deck or patio, regardless of whether it is temporary or permanent. For a more detailed discussion on what constitutes a "dwelling," *see* Chapter Five.

First, there has to be an entry into the person's dwelling, and the person must not believe, or have any reason to believe that the entry is lawful.

Whether or not one has a "reason to believe" focuses on the surrounding circumstances, and seemingly mandates a heightened level of situational awareness. Next, the person must neither believe nor have reason to believe that any force less than deadly force would effectively terminate the entry. If a person has a belief, or has reason to believe that something short of deadly force will do, the use of deadly force will not be justified.

For instance, if the actor has reason to believe that he could physically remove the person safely (for example, a disoriented, lost elderly person), or even that the person would leave if asked, deadly force will not be justified.

Justified Use of Deadly Force to Protect Your Property; 18 Pa.C.S. §507(c)(4)

(i) The use of deadly force is justifiable under this section if:
   (A) there has been an entry into the actor's dwelling;
   (B) the actor neither believes nor has reason to believe that the entry is lawful; and
   (C) the actor neither believes nor has reason to believe that force less than deadly force would be adequate to terminate the entry.

(ii) If the conditions of justification provided in subparagraph (i) have not been met, the use of deadly force is not justifiable under this section unless the actor believes that:
   (A) the person against whom the force is used is attempting to dispossess him of his dwelling otherwise than under a claim of right to its possession; or
   (B) such force is necessary to prevent the commission of a felony in the dwelling.

B. *Use of deadly force to maintain possession of a dwelling*
The next circumstance when Pennsylvania law justifies deadly force in protection of property occurs when one tries to "dispossess" another from his dwelling. Basically, this happens when a bad guy tries to unlawfully kick somebody out of their own home and take over!

But this doesn't apply during a mere property dispute. The law specifically states that this doesn't apply if someone is trying to take possession "under a claim of right."

C. *Use of deadly force to prevent the commission of a felony in a dwelling*

Last, Pennsylvania law justifies the use of deadly force to protect property if it is necessary to prevent the commission of a felony in one's dwelling.

While there are numerous felonies outlined in the Crimes Code, some common felonies in Pennsylvania include Murder, Voluntary Manslaughter, Aggravated Assault, Arson Endangering Persons, Arson Endangering Property, certain forms of Criminal Mischief, certain Thefts, Robbery, Burglary, Kidnapping and Rape.

Note: under these last circumstances, there is some overlap with the laws of self-defense and defense of others. Remember, deadly force is justified under Pennsylvania law when one has a reasonable belief that it is immediately necessary to prevent death, serious bodily injury, kidnapping or intercourse by force or threat. For a more detailed discussion, see Chapter Four.

In order to know when a felony is being committed in one's dwelling, one must understand what crimes are felonies, and how the Pennsylvania Crimes Code defines these specific crimes. Remember, the justification tied directly to "felonies" applies only if deadly force is necessary to prevent the commission of a felony in one's dwelling. While discussion of each and every felony in the Crimes Code is beyond the scope of this chapter, below are the definitions of various crimes that are felonies under Pennsylvania law.

1. *Arson Endangering Persons*, 18 Pa.C.S. §3301(a):

A person commits a felony of the first degree if he intentionally starts a fire or causes an explosion, or if he aids, counsels, pays or agrees to pay another to cause a fire or explosion, whether on his own property or on that of another, and if:

- he thereby recklessly places another person in danger of death or bodily injury, including but not limited to a firefighter, police officer or other person actively engaged in fighting the fire; or

- he commits the act with the purpose of destroying or damaging an inhabited building or occupied structure of another.

2. *Burglary,* 18 Pa.C.S. §3502:

A person commits the offense of burglary if, with the intent to commit a crime therein, the person:

- enters a building or occupied structure, or separately secured or occupied portion thereof that is adapted for overnight accommodations in which at the time of the offense any person is present;
- enters a building or occupied structure, or separately secured or occupied portion thereof that is adapted for overnight accommodations in which at the time of the offense no person is present;
- enters a building or occupied structure, or separately secured or occupied portion thereof that is not adapted for overnight accommodations in which at the time of the offense any person is present; or
- enters a building or occupied structure, or separately secured or occupied portion thereof that is not adapted for overnight accommodations in which at the time of the offense no person is present.

Defense. It is a defense to prosecution for burglary if any of the following are true at the time of the commission of the offense:

- The building or structure was abandoned.
- The premises are open to the public.
- The actor is licensed or privileged to enter.

3. *Certain Thefts*, 18 Pa.C.S. §3921 *et seq.*

Pennsylvania law contains several different forms of theft. These can be found in Chapter 39 of the Pennsylvania Crimes Code. It is very important to understand that *not all thefts are felonies.* In fact, whether a theft is a felony often hinges upon *what is being stolen*. Generally, theft of an item with a value of $2,000 or more is a felony. Theft of specific items —such as firearms— is a felony regardless of monetary value. While there are other forms of theft beyond those defined below, Theft by Unlawful Taking or Disposition and Theft by Extortion are most pertinent to this chapter, because they are most capable of being committed in one's dwelling.

Theft by Unlawful Taking or Disposition, **18 Pa.C.S. §3921**

(a) Movable property.—A person is guilty of theft if he unlawfully takes, or exercises unlawful control over, movable property of another with intent to deprive him thereof.

(b) Immovable property.—A person is guilty of theft if he unlawfully transfers, or exercises unlawful control over, immovable property of another or any interest therein with intent to benefit himself or another not entitled thereto.

Theft by Extortion, **18 Pa.C.S. § 3923**

(a) A person is guilty of theft if he intentionally obtains or withholds property of another by threatening to:
(1) commit another criminal offense;
(2) accuse anyone of a criminal offense;
(3) expose any secret tending to subject any person to hatred, contempt or ridicule;
(4) take or withhold action as an official, or cause an official to take or withhold action;
(5) bring about or continue a strike, boycott or other collective unofficial action, if the property is not demanded or received for the benefit of the group in whose interest the actor purports to act;

(6) testify or provide information or withhold testimony or information with respect to the legal claim or defense of another; or

(7) inflict any other harm which would not benefit the actor.

(b) Defenses.—It is a defense to prosecution based on paragraphs (a)(2), (a)(3) or (a)(4) of this section that the property obtained by threat of accusation, exposure, lawsuit or other invocation of official action was honestly claimed as restitution or indemnification for harm done in the circumstances to which such accusation, exposure, lawsuit or other official action relates, or as compensation for property or lawful services.

4. *Robbery*, 18 Pa.C.S. §3701:

A person is guilty of robbery if, in the course of committing a theft, he:

- inflicts serious bodily injury upon another;
- threatens another with or intentionally puts him in fear of immediate serious bodily injury;
- commits or threatens immediately to commit any felony of the first or second degree;
- inflicts bodily injury upon another or threatens another with or intentionally puts him in fear of immediate bodily injury;
- physically takes or removes property from the person of another by force however slight.

An act shall be deemed "in the course of committing a theft" if it occurs in an attempt to commit theft or in flight after the attempt or commission.

5. *Criminal Mischief,* 18 *Pa.C.S.* §3304:

It is vital to note that like theft, whether Criminal Mischief is a felony specifically turns on the value of the property involved. Criminal mischief is not a felony *unless* "the actor intentionally causes pecuniary loss in excess of $5,000." The Supreme Court of

Pennsylvania has specifically addressed this issue in the context of section 507 and the use of deadly force to protect property. In *Commonwealth v. Horner*, an intruder entered the home with a baseball bat, knocked a television set to the floor and yelled "You're all going to get it now!" The intruder was shot immediately thereafter. The Supreme Court of Pennsylvania found that "as a matter of law, the members of the [household] were not justified in using deadly force" reasoning "the only crime [the intruder] may have committed was criminal mischief, and that crime is not a felony unless pecuniary loss in excess of $5,000 ..." *Commonwealth v. Horner*, 442 A.2d 682, 687 (Pa. 1982).

This further emphasizes that only under *very limited circumstances* is deadly force justified in defense of property. The Pennsylvania Crimes Code defines Criminal Mischief as follows;

A person is guilty of Criminal Mischief if he:

- damages tangible property of another intentionally, recklessly, or by negligence in the employment of fire, explosives, or other dangerous means listed in 18 Pa.C.S. §3302(a) (relating to causing or risking catastrophe);
- intentionally or recklessly tampers with tangible property of another so as to endanger person or property;
- intentionally or recklessly causes another to suffer pecuniary loss by deception or threat;
- intentionally defaces or otherwise damages tangible public property or tangible property of another with graffiti by use of any aerosol spray-paint can, broad-tipped indelible marker or similar marking device;
- intentionally damages real or personal property of another; or
- intentionally defaces personal, private or public property by discharging a paintball gun or paintball marker at that property.

IV. How can I assist law enforcement?

A. *Acting under a police officer's direction*

Almost without fail, as attorneys we are regularly asked about whether you can make a citizen's arrest, and how you can best assist law enforcement in dicey situations. As every legal situation is unique, here we'll just provide a brief summary of the general law, as well as reference some of the statutes governing the use of citizen's arrests and how to assist authorities.

Take note that thrusting yourself into the middle of a crime can be a tremendous risk to your personal safety. Additionally, there is always the chance that you will be scrutinized and subject to legal action, even if your actions are lawful. In taking action, it is important that you understand the risks involved and are certain that you are willing to take those risks.

Under 18 Pa.C.S. §508(b)(2), when a peace officer directs an individual to assist him, that person is justified in using any force he reasonably believes to be necessary to effect the arrest. He is also justified in using any force he reasonably believes to be necessary to defend himself or another from bodily harm while making the arrest. *Note: the use of deadly force is limited, and will be discussed later in this chapter.*

Section 508 details when a law enforcement officer is able to use force against a suspect. In order to enable officers to use all available resources at their disposal (such as an ordinary citizen), the statute is expanded to include individuals acting at an officer's direction.

You may wonder whether one can lose their justification if the officer is directing you to make an unlawful arrest. The law does not require a person to know all of the facts and circumstances, or to be a legal expert for that matter. Accordingly, unless the person *knows* that the arrest is unlawful, his conduct will be justified.

B. _Not acting under a police officer's direction_

There is no specific statute detailing when a person may legally make a citizen's arrest. However, the Supreme Court of Pennsylvania has upheld the longstanding principle that "[a] private person in fresh pursuit of one who has committed a felony may arrest without a warrant." _Kopko v. Miller_, 892 A.2d 766, 774 (Pa. 2006) (quoting _Commonwealth v. Chermansky_, 242 A.2d 237, 239 (Pa. 1968)). So when can force be used in such an arrest? This question is answered in 18 Pa.C.S. §508(b):

Private person's use of force in making arrest.—

>(1) A private person who makes, or assists another private person in making a lawful arrest is justified in the use of any force which he would be justified in using if he were summoned or directed by a peace officer to make such arrest, except that he is justified in the use of deadly force only when he believes that such force is necessary to prevent death or serious bodily injury to himself or another.

>_(2) Intentionally omitted_

>(3) A private person who assists another private person in effecting an unlawful arrest, or who, not being summoned, assists a peace officer in effecting an unlawful arrest, is justified in using any force which he would be justified in using if the arrest were lawful, if:

>>(i) he believes the arrest is lawful; and

>>(ii) the arrest would be lawful if the facts were as he believes them to be.

This statute allows an ordinary person to use force when making or assisting in making an arrest, as it does not require the person to be in a peace officer's presence! Instead, the protections and justifications afforded at the direction of an officer are maintained as long as he would be justified in using that force at the direction of an officer. Keep in mind that the use of _deadly force_ is limited!

C. *When can a person use deadly force in assisting law enforcement?*

In order to be legally justified in using deadly force to help law enforcement, a person must comply with the requirements of 18 Pa.C.S. §508(a)(1). When acting under the direction of a peace officer, deadly force is justified *only if there exists a reasonable belief:*

> that such force is necessary to prevent death or serious bodily injury to himself or such other person, or when he believes both that:
>
> (i) such force is necessary to prevent the arrest from being defeated by resistance or escape; and
>
> (ii) the person to be arrested has committed or attempted a forcible felony or is attempting to escape and possesses a deadly weapon, or otherwise indicates that he will endanger human life or inflict serious bodily injury unless arrested without delay.

D. *When can a person use deadly force during an arrest when a law enforcement officer is not present?*

If a person is *not* acting under the direction of a peace officer, justification for the use of deadly force is even more limited. In these situations, deadly force is justified *only if* that person reasonably believes that such force is necessary to prevent death or serious bodily injury to himself or another. This seems no more expansive than the general justifications provided for self-defense and defense of others.

E. *Detaining potential thieves: "shopkeeper's privilege"*

The law has long recognized limited rights of store owners to briefly detain people suspected of stealing. This is commonly known as the "shopkeeper's privilege" or the "retailer's privilege." Pennsylvania law codifies the shop keeper's privilege in 18 Pa.C.S. §3929(d), as a part of the Retail Theft statute. Common scenarios include when a loss prevention official for the store will take a person into some type of custody while they investigate whether an item was stolen from their business.

Retail Theft (Detention);
18 Pa.C.S. §3929(d)

Detention. A peace officer, merchant or merchant's employee or an agent under contract with a merchant, who has probable cause to believe that retail theft has occurred or is occurring on or about a store or other retail mercantile establishment and who has probable cause to believe that a specific person has committed or is committing the retail theft may detain the suspect in a reasonable manner for a reasonable time on or off the premises for all or any of the following purposes: to require the suspect to identify himself, to verify such identification, to determine whether such suspect has in his possession unpurchased merchandise taken from the mercantile establishment and, if so, to recover such merchandise, to inform a peace officer, or to institute criminal proceedings against the suspect. Such detention shall not impose civil or criminal liability upon the peace officer, merchant, employee, or agent so detaining.

V. What crimes can I be charged with when my use of deadly force is not justified?

We've reached the end of our discussion on when you may be justified to use a weapon in defense of your person or property. Now it's time to give a brief summary of where you'll find yourself in legal trouble if you don't meet the elements of justification as we've described throughout this book. The following tables list some of the crimes involving the use of deadly force or a firearm and where relevant provisions may be found in the Pennsylvania Crimes Code.

Crimes Involving Deadly Force or a Firearm:

1. Murder: *see* 18 Pa.C.S. §2502
2. Voluntary Manslaughter: *see* 18 Pa.C.S. §2503
3. Involuntary Manslaughter: *see* 18 Pa.C.S. §2504
4. Simple Assault: *see* Pa.C.S. §2701
   a. Includes pointing a gun at another
5. Aggravated Assault: *see* Pa.C.S. §2702
6. Recklessly Endangering Another Person: *see* 18 Pa.C.S. §2705
7. Terroristic Threats: *see* 18 Pa.C.S. §2706
   a. Includes pointing a gun at another

What Do I Do Immediately After I Use My Firearm?

1. Make sure that the threat is contained or neutralized;
2. Return your firearm to safekeeping;
3. Call 911 and tell them you (or another person) have been the victim of a crime. Give the operator your location and description. Avoid giving any unnecessary information, and avoid telling them you shot someone. It may be wise to suggest an ambulance is needed. Then hang up with 911;
4. Call the U.S. Law Shield Emergency Hotline and follow the instructions your program attorney gives you;
5. Wait for police and do not touch any evidence;
6. Be careful of police questions and always be ready to invoke your right to silence and your right to counsel at any time.

CHAPTER EIGHT
LAW OF CONCEALED CARRY: PART I
THE PERMIT QUALIFICATIONS, REQUIREMENTS, APPEALS, AND REGULATIONS

Pennsylvania has an extensive history of protecting its citizens' right to bear arms. As discussed at the outset of this book, the right to bear arms provision of the Pennsylvania Constitution predates, and even influenced the Second Amendment of the United States Constitution. *Open carry* is generally permitted with or without a License to Carry Firearms (LTCF) outside of Philadelphia. However, Pennsylvania law requires individuals to have a LTCF in order to carry a firearm (1) concealed on or about their person, (2) in a vehicle, or (3) in Philadelphia, whether openly or concealed. Because a LTCF is required to carry a concealed firearm, many colloquially refer to it as a "concealed carry license."

To obtain a LTCF, a person must meet certain qualifications, submit an application to the local sheriff and pay fees. Remember that Pennsylvania defines the term "firearm" very narrowly. Accordingly, a LTCF applies to handguns, short-barreled rifles and short-barreled shotguns. It doesn't impact the lawful carry of standard long guns or other kinds of weapons. This chapter deals exclusively with the process associated with obtaining a License to Carry Firearms in Pennsylvania. For more on the rights and protections associated with holding a License to Carry Firearms, *see* Chapter Nine.

I.   Pennsylvania concealed carry law
The Pennsylvania laws establishing a "concealed carry" licensing scheme date back to the 1930's. Today, Pennsylvania has the second most license holders in the nation. With over one million license holders, more than 10% of Pennsylvanians have a License to Carry Firearms! *See Concealed Carry Permit Holders Across the United States* by John R. Lott, Ph.D.

Under 18 Pa.C.S. §6109, county sheriffs are the issuing authority for a LTCF. *Note: under 18 Pa.C.S. §6109, residents of a city of the first class (only Philadelphia) must apply with the chief of police of that city. Everybody else applies through their local sheriff. Even though Philadelphia residents must apply through the chief of police, for the purpose of this chapter, we will simply refer to the issuing authority as the "sheriff."*

Pennsylvania is a "shall issue" state. Applicants are not required to demonstrate some kind of substantial need for a LTCF, and a sheriff cannot deny an applicant a LTCF without a legal reason to do so.

But it wasn't always that way! In its early years, the Pennsylvania laws governing the issuance of a License to Carry Firearms in Pennsylvania used to read:

> [T]he sheriff of a county may, upon the application of any person, issue a license to such person to carry a firearm...if it appears that the applicant has good reason to fear an injury to his person or property, or has any other proper reason for carrying a firearm, and that he is a suitable person to be so licensed.

The word "may" gave sheriffs the authority to deny applicants who were otherwise entirely qualified under the law! Although this gave sheriffs a great deal of discretion, most sheriffs —in practice— granted all applicants who met the legal requirements. Some sheriffs, however, did not. In *Gardner v. Jenkins,* the Commonwealth Court upheld the sheriff's ability to deny applicants who met the requirements, holding that issuance was "not mandatory, but discretionary." 541 A.2d 406, 408 (Pa. Cmwlth. 1988).

Thankfully, the Pennsylvania legislature swiftly took action in response to this case. Today, that law reads:

> *A License to Carry Firearms ... shall be issued if, after an investigation not to exceed 45 days, it appears that the applicant is an individual concerning whom no good cause exists to deny the license.*

The law also lists specific reasons why an applicant would be ineligible for a LTCF. With these rules in place, Pennsylvania became —and remains today— a "shall issue" state.

Section 6109 of the Pennsylvania Crimes Code contains the law on how a License to Carry Firearms is administered in Pennsylvania. Throughout this chapter, we will discuss the process associated with applying for and keeping a Pennsylvania License to Carry Firearms.

II. Applying for a LTCF

A. *The application process*

In this section, we will discuss the LTCF application process. We will also discuss the qualifications necessary to obtain a LTCF, as well as potential disqualifications. Unlike many states, Pennsylvania imposes no legal mandate on applicants to take educational courses, take exams, or complete a shooting qualification. Rather, so long as there is no legal reason to deny an applicant, the applicant is afforded his or her license upon completing the application process and paying the required fee.

Who is eligible for a LTCF? Anybody who is at least 21 years of age and is not legally *disqualified* from obtaining a LTCF is eligible. In other words, everybody who is at least 21 years old is eligible unless something specifically renders them ineligible.

The process begins by filling out an application and submitting it to the sheriff. Upon receipt, the sheriff will conduct an investigation. During this phase, the sheriff will:

1. investigate the applicant's record of criminal conviction;

2. investigate whether or not the applicant is under indictment for or has ever been convicted of a crime punishable by imprisonment exceeding one year;

3. investigate whether the applicant's character and reputation are such that the applicant will not be likely to act in a manner dangerous to public safety;

4. investigate whether the applicant would be precluded from receiving a license under subsection (e)(1) or section 6105(h)(relating to persons not to possess, use, manufacture, control, sell or transfer firearms); and

5. conduct a criminal background, juvenile delinquency and mental health check following the procedures set forth in section 6111 (relating to sale or transfer of firearms), receive a unique approval number for that inquiry and record the date and number on the application.

These investigations can uncover reasons why an applicant is legally ineligible to receive a LTCF. In reality, running an applicant's information through the Pennsylvania Instant Check System (PICS) accounts for a substantial portion of the investigation. The PICS utilizes information gathered by Pennsylvania State Police to determine whether or not an individual is disqualified under the law. For many applicants, the PICS check takes only minutes to complete.

Under 18 Pa.C.S. §6109, a LTCF shall *not be* issued to any of the following:

i. An individual whose character and reputation is such that the individual would be likely to act in a manner dangerous to public safety.

ii. An individual who has been convicted of an offense under The Controlled Substance, Drug, Device and Cosmetic Act.

iii. An individual convicted of a crime enumerated in section 6105.

These include:

- Section 908 (relating to prohibited offensive weapons).
- Section 911 (relating to corrupt organizations).
- Section 912 (relating to possession of weapon on school property).
- Section 2502 (relating to murder).
- Section 2503 (relating to voluntary manslaughter).
- Section 2504 (relating to involuntary manslaughter) if the offense is based on the reckless use of a firearm.
- Section 2702 (relating to aggravated assault).
- Section 2703 (relating to assault by prisoner).
- Section 2704 (relating to assault by life prisoner).
- Section 2709.1 (relating to stalking).
- Section 2716 (relating to weapons of mass destruction).
- Section 2901 (relating to kidnapping).
- Section 2902 (relating to unlawful restraint).
- Section 2910 (relating to luring a child into a motor vehicle or structure).
- Section 3121 (relating to rape).
- Section 3123 (relating to involuntary deviate sexual intercourse).
- Section 3125 (relating to aggravated indecent assault).
- Section 3301 (relating to arson and related offenses).
- Section 3302 (relating to causing or risking catastrophe).
- Section 3502 (relating to burglary).
- Section 3503 (relating to criminal trespass) if the offense is graded a felony of the second degree or higher.
- Section 3701 (relating to robbery).
- Section 3702 (relating to robbery of motor vehicle).
- Section 3921 (relating to theft by unlawful taking or disposition) upon conviction of the second felony offense.
- Section 3923 (relating to theft by extortion) when the offense is accompanied by threats of violence.
- Section 3925 (relating to receiving stolen property) upon conviction of the second felony offense.

- Section 4906 (relating to false reports to law enforcement authorities) if the fictitious report involved the theft of a firearm as provided in section 4906(c)(2).
- Section 4912 (relating to impersonating a public servant) if the person is impersonating a law enforcement officer.
- Section 4952 (relating to intimidation of witnesses or victims).
- Section 4953 (relating to retaliation against witness, victim or party).
- Section 5121 (relating to escape).
- Section 5122 (relating to weapons or implements for escape).
- Section 5501(3) (relating to riot).
- Section 5515 (relating to prohibiting of paramilitary training).
- Section 5516 (relating to facsimile weapons of mass destruction).
- Section 6110.1 (relating to possession of firearm by minor).
- Section 6301 (relating to corruption of minors).
- Section 6302 (relating to sale or lease of weapons and explosives).
    iv. An individual who, within the past ten years, has been adjudicated delinquent for a crime enumerated in section 6105 (listed above) or for an offense under The Controlled Substance, Drug, Device and Cosmetic Act.
    v. An individual who is not of sound mind or who has ever been committed to a mental institution.
    vi. An individual who is addicted to or is an unlawful user of marijuana or a stimulant, depressant or narcotic drug.
    vii. An individual who is a habitual drunkard.
    viii. An individual who is charged with or has been convicted of a crime punishable by imprisonment for a term exceeding one year except as provided for in Section 6123 (relating to waiver of disability or pardons).

ix. A resident of another state who does not possess a current license or permit or similar document to carry a firearm issued by that state if a license is provided for by the laws of that state, as published annually in the Federal Register by the Bureau of Alcohol, Tobacco and Firearms of the Department of the Treasury under 18 U.S.C. §921(a)(19) (relating to definitions).

x. An alien who is illegally in the United States.

xi. An individual who has been discharged from the armed forces of the United States under dishonorable conditions.

xii. An individual who is a fugitive from justice. This subparagraph does not apply to an individual whose fugitive status is based upon nonmoving or moving summary offense under Title 75 (relating to vehicles).

xiii. An individual who is otherwise prohibited from possessing, using, manufacturing, controlling, purchasing, selling or transferring a firearm as provided by section 6105.

xiv. An individual who is prohibited from possessing or acquiring a firearm under the statutes of the United States.

Practical Legal Tip:

A law abiding gun owner who doesn't live in Pennsylvania can get a non-resident License to Carry Firearms. But Pennsylvania law requires that they have a license to carry in their home state in order to qualify. As a practical matter, this usually means that our friends and family who live in New York, New Jersey and Maryland are not eligible. -*Mike*

By law, the sheriff's investigation can take no longer than 45 days. The sheriff *must* issue a LTCF to the applicant if the investigation provides no good cause to deny the license. In other words, there is no burden on the applicant to show good cause why he should be granted the license, or why he needs the license. Rather, the sheriff has to have good cause to *deny* the applicant. The applicant need not show that he has a special reason why he would like to —or needs to— carry a firearm.

Note: there is a portion of the application requiring the applicant to disclose a "reason" for obtaining a LTCF. The choices include "self-defense, employment, hunting and fishing, target shooting, gun collecting or 'other,'" with a portion to fill in the blank. An applicant is not required to provide any further proof of this reason, or establish that the reason amounts to a "need." The section dealing with the applicant's "reason" generally proves insignificant during the application process.

B. <u>*An individual whose character and reputation is such that the individual would be likely to act in a manner dangerous to public safety*</u>

Aside from these specific reasons provided by the law, the sheriff can deny an applicant whose character and reputation are such that the applicant would likely act in a manner dangerous to public safety. This is the only part of the process that allows the sheriff to use discretion, rather than clear cut legal prohibiting factors. Most applications require the applicant to provide two references who are not family members for the investigation. In practice, not all sheriffs even contact these references during their investigation. In fact, there is a current trend to eliminate this reference question among sheriffs in Pennsylvania.

The law provides sheriffs with this little bit of discretion in the LTCF application process. Unfortunately, there is no bright line test for making this determination. While there is no specific list of character traits or conduct that should cause a sheriff to deny an applicant, case law suggests that a sheriff may deny an application based on factors other than the individual's criminal history record. *See generally*, *Moats v. Pennsylvania State Police*, 782 A.2d 1102, 1105 (Pa. Cmwlth. 2001); *Morley v. City of Phila. Licenses & Inspections Unit*, 844 A.2d 637, 638 (Pa. Cmwlth. 2004).

C. *What is a "habitual drunkard?"*

There is no modern case law dealing with what exactly constitutes a "habitual drunkard." However, some very old case law may provide us with some guidance. In 1851, the Supreme Court of Pennsylvania held that:

> *A man may be [a] habitual drunkard, and yet be sober for days and weeks together. The only rule is, has he a fixed habit of drunkenness? Was he habituated to intemperance whenever the opportunity offered? We agree that a man who is intoxicated or drunk one-half his time is [a] habitual drunkard, and should be pronounced such.*

Ludwick v. Commonwealth, 18 Pa. 172, 175 (1851).

D. *An individual who has been convicted of an offense under The Controlled Substance, Drug, Device and Cosmetic Act*

The Controlled Substance, Drug, Device and Cosmetic Act refers to the laws found in Title 35, beginning at 35 P.S. §780-101. These laws encompass numerous offenses involving the unlawful possession of drugs and drug paraphernalia. Because Pennsylvania law renders a person with *any* conviction under The Controlled Substance, Drug, Device and Cosmetic Act ineligible for a LTCF, it is very important to know which crimes are included in this prohibition. Keep in mind that some of these crimes carry minor punishments. As a result, some applicants fail to recognize that such a conviction renders them ineligible for a LTCF. If in doubt about *any* previous conviction, consult with counsel before submitting an application.

E.   *Crime punishable by imprisonment exceeding one year*

A common, and somewhat confusing disqualifier is found in section 6109(e)(1)(viii):

> An individual who is charged with or has been convicted of a crime punishable by imprisonment for a term exceeding one year except as provided for in section 6123 (relating to waiver of disability or pardons).

Although this particular disqualifier seems self-explanatory, that is far from the case. In short, "one year" doesn't always mean one year. The Uniform Firearms Act provides a definition for "crime punishable by imprisonment exceeding one year" in 18 Pa.C.S. §6102. The definition reads:

> "Crime punishable by imprisonment exceeding one year." The term does not include any of the following:
>
> (1) Federal or State offenses pertaining to antitrust, unfair trade practices, restraints on trade or regulation of business.
>
> (2) State offenses classified as misdemeanors and punishable by a term of imprisonment not to exceed two years.

So "crime punishable by imprisonment exceeding one year" *doesn't literally mean* every crime capable of sending a person to prison for more than one year. For example, in Pennsylvania, misdemeanors of the second degree ("M2") are punishable by "imprisonment not exceeding two years." By those standards, it would appear that an M2 would be punishable by imprisonment exceeding one year. However, because state misdemeanors carrying a maximum sentence of two years *don't count* as crimes punishable by imprisonment exceeding one year, an M2 conviction will not necessarily render a person ineligible for a LTCF.

It is important to note that the law looks to the *maximum sentence*. It doesn't matter if a person doesn't serve the maximum sentence, or doesn't serve any time at all. The law looks to what *could have been*. In other words, all that matters is the sentence the crime could have carried in the worst-case scenario.

Keep in mind that there are many disqualifiers other than crimes "punishable by imprisonment exceeding one year." For instance, as discussed in this chapter, convictions under The Controlled Substance, Drug, Device and Cosmetic Act will render a person ineligible *regardless of the maximum sentence.* It is NEVER a good idea to submit an application if unsure about an answer. When in doubt, seek counsel.

Practical Legal Tip:

Don't forget that non-violent offenses can also render a person ineligible for a License to Carry Firearms. Even a second offense DUI-Highest Rate can make a person ineligible for a LTCF. Don't be mistaken — not only those convicted of violent crimes are legally ineligible for a LTCF. *-Justin*

F. *What if I completed Accelerated Rehabilitative Disposition ("ARD")? Can I get a LTCF?*

In Pennsylvania, sometimes criminal charges are resolved through Accelerated Rehabilitative Disposition ("ARD") rather than a plea deal or trial. ARD is a pretrial diversionary program available for first time offenders under certain conditions. It is similar to being subject to probation. Successful completion of the ARD program is not a criminal conviction. As a result, ARD will not automatically disqualify a person from getting a LTCF. Recall, however, that a sheriff can deny an applicant based on "character and reputation." Because the "character and reputation" determination is not limited to criminal convictions, some sheriffs have been known to look at the conduct involved with an incident that led to ARD.

G. *If you don't disclose, you can be charged with a crime!*
Every LTCF application contains a standard statement that must be signed and dated by the applicant. This requirement is set forth in section 6109, which also provides the language to be contained in the statement. Part of the statement reads:

> *I hereby certify that the statements contained herein are true and correct to the best of my knowledge and belief. I understand that, if I knowingly make any false statements herein, I am subject to penalties prescribed by law.*

If you are not sure about how you should answer one of the questions, hold off and find out! Consult with counsel before "taking a stab at it" or filling it out to "see what happens." Pennsylvania prosecutors are very aggressive in prosecuting those who fail to disclose disqualifying information for the crime of false swearing (misdemeanor). Remember, just because you have passed a PICS check in purchasing a firearm does not necessarily mean you are presently eligible for a LTCF.

III. LTCF Denials
Those who are denied a LTCF must be informed by the sheriff in writing. By law, this notice is to cite the specific reasons for denial, and must be sent to the applicant by certified mail at the address listed in the application. If an applicant is denied his or her LTCF, the law provides a right to appeal the decision.

1. Appealing denials based on the PICS
Denials based on the PICS must be challenged with the Pennsylvania State Police (PSP) within 30 days of the date of denial. Within 20 days of receiving the challenge, PSP must provide the challenger with the basis for denial and give the challenger the opportunity to provide additional information for the purposes of the review. Within 60 days of the challenge, PSP must issue a final

decision, including all information that formed the basis for its decision.

In the event that PSP denies the challenge, the challenger can appeal the decision to the Attorney General. The challenger has 30 days to appeal PSP's denial of a challenge. The Attorney General must conduct a hearing, and will make a decision based entirely on its own findings. In other words, the Attorney General doesn't have to give any special weight or any deference to PSP's decision. At this hearing, the burden is on the Commonwealth to prove that the denial was valid.

Finally, if the Attorney General affirms PSP's determination, the challenger can appeal the Attorney General's decision to the Commonwealth Court.

2. Appealing denials based on "character and reputation"
When denials are based on the applicant's "character and reputation" rather than a disqualifying factor uncovered by the PICS, the decision comes straight from the sheriff. The law imposes a duty on the sheriff to determine whether an applicant's "character and reputation are such that the applicant will not be likely to act in a manner dangerous to public safety." Because this determination doesn't come from PSP —as a PICS denial would— the process is different than challenging a PICS denial. Instead, a denial based on "character and reputation" must be appealed directly to the applicant's local Court of Common Pleas. In Philadelphia, appeals of denials are heard first by the Licensing & Inspections Review Board. If the Board rules against the applicant, the applicant can appeal the Board's decision to the Court of Common Pleas.

IV. Revocation of a LTCF
1. When can a LTCF be revoked?
Under section 6109, a LTCF can be revoked by the issuing authority (the sheriff) "for good cause." The statute goes on to mandate that

a LTCF be revoked if the license holder becomes disqualified (*see* the disqualifiers earlier in section II. A. of this chapter).

When revoking a license, the sheriff is required by law to send the license holder notice of revocation and provide a specific reason for revocation. The sheriff must send this notice to the licensee by certified mail, and additionally provide the Pennsylvania State Police with notice that the individual's LTCF is no longer valid. Upon receipt of the notice of revocation, the license holder has five days to surrender the revoked license to the issuing authority (sheriff who revoked the license).

2. Appealing a revocation

Sometimes, a LTCF is improperly revoked. The law provides a specific avenue for relief in these instances. Those who wish to appeal the revocation of their LTCF can do so by filing an appeal with the local Court of Common Pleas. The Court of Common Pleas will conduct a hearing and make its own determination from scratch. Similar to the Attorney General in a PICS appeal, the court will make a decision entirely on its own findings. The sheriff's decision is not given any weight, or deference. On the contrary, at these hearings *the burden of proof is on the sheriff.* That means that the sheriff has to prove that there exists "good cause" for the revocation in order for it to stand. The person bringing the appeal need not prove that the revocation was improper.

In the event that the Court of Common Pleas affirms the revocation, the former license holder can appeal this decision to the Commonwealth Court of Pennsylvania.

3. You have a duty to tell on yourself!

Rooted in the Fifth Amendment right against self-incrimination, in most situations that can lead to punishment, there is no duty to tell on yourself. But things are different when you have a LTCF. When you submit your application, you consensually accept a duty to tell on yourself in certain situations! Earlier we discussed the standard statement that each applicant must sign and date. Along with the certification that the information provided is true and correct, the statement includes a duty to tell on yourself should you become ineligible. It reads:

> If I am issued a license and knowingly become ineligible to legally possess or acquire firearms, I will promptly notify the sheriff of the county in which I reside or, if I reside in a city of the first class, the chief of police of that city.

In other words, if you become ineligible, the law doesn't allow you to keep your license just because your local sheriff is under informed, makes a mistake, accidentally overlooks the disqualification, or simply hasn't gotten around to formally revoking your license.

That concludes our discussion on the procedures associated with applying for and keeping a LTCF. Now that we understand who is eligible for a LTCF and how an eligible person can obtain one, Chapter Nine will cover the rights and protections afforded to those with a valid LTCF.

CHAPTER NINE
LAW OF CONCEALED CARRY: PART II
WHAT, HOW, AND WHERE YOU CAN
LEGALLY CARRY WITH A LTCF

I.   What is allowed with a LTCF?

In the previous chapter, we discussed the process and procedures associated with applying for and maintaining a License to Carry Firearms (LTCF) in Pennsylvania. As we stated, generally, open carry is permitted with or without a LTCF outside of Philadelphia. However, under Pennsylvania law, one must have a valid LTCF in order to carry a firearm (1) concealed on or about their person, (2) in a vehicle, or (3) in Philadelphia, whether openly or concealed.

In this chapter, we will discuss what kind of firearms are covered under a LTCF, when a LTCF is required and where firearms are prohibited even with a valid LTCF. We will also dispel some common myths associated with carrying firearms in Pennsylvania.

A.   *What kind of firearms are covered under a LTCF?*

In Pennsylvania, a LTCF only applies to handguns, short-barreled rifles and short-barreled shotguns. Conventional shotguns and rifles are not covered under a LTCF.

The Pennsylvania Uniform Firearms Act (PA UFA) defines a firearm as:

- Any pistol or revolver with a barrel length less than 15 inches;
- Any shotgun with a barrel length less than 18 inches;
- Any rifle with a barrel length less than 16 inches; or
- Any pistol, revolver, rifle or shotgun with an overall length of less than 26 inches.

The PA UFA dictates that the barrel length of a firearm is determined by measuring from the muzzle of the barrel to the face of the closed action, bolt or cylinder (whichever is applicable).

B. *When is a LTCF required?*

In 18 Pa.C.S. §6106, we find:

> [A]ny person who carries a firearm in any vehicle or any person who carries a firearm concealed on or about his person, except in his place of abode or fixed place of business, without a valid and lawfully issued [License to Carry Firearms] commits a felony of the third degree.

As we have previously noted, this law prohibits carrying a firearm concealed or in a vehicle without a LTCF. Notice that at the outset, this law does not apply to a person's "place of abode" (home) or "fixed place of business." As a result, carrying a concealed firearm in these locations without a LTCF is not a crime in and of itself.

But what is a "fixed place of business?" At first glance, it would appear that a LTCF is simply not required to carry a concealed firearm at work. However, the Superior Court of Pennsylvania has interpreted this far more narrowly. In *Commonwealth v. Carr*, the Superior Court held that the exception for those carrying a firearm in their "fixed place of business" is "limited to those persons who have a controlling, proprietary, or possessory interest in their place of business." 483 A.2d 542, 544 (Pa. Super. 1984). In other words, those who are merely employees are not exempt from the requirement for an LTCF at work. Rather, one must have some kind of ownership or control over his "place of business" in order for the exemption to apply.

II. Where can a LTCF holder legally carry a concealed handgun?

A LTCF is valid throughout the Commonwealth. Therefore, those with a Pennsylvania License to Carry Firearms can legally carry a firearm on their person and in a vehicle in every city in Pennsylvania, including Philadelphia. However, there are certain specific locations in which carrying a firearm is prohibited in Pennsylvania, even if licensed to carry firearms. This can get confusing, because one must account not only for state law, but federal law as well. Some places that are off-limits may seem surprising. Similarly, some places that are *not* off-limits may seem surprising. It is important to distinguish law from flaw and stay away from the locations that legally prohibit firearms. It is in this area that gun owners who wish to follow the law can turn into accidental criminals.

A. *Prohibited places for LTCF holders*

Under Pennsylvania law, there are places where persons are prohibited from carrying a firearm whether or not that person is a LTCF holder. There are also some prominent locations that prohibit firearms under federal law. These federal limitations apply not only in Pennsylvania, but in all 50 states and the District of Columbia. In this chapter, we will discuss the different places where firearms are legally prohibited.

1. Prohibited places under Pennsylvania law
a. *Court facilities*

Law-abiding gun owners must be aware of the restrictions imposed upon possession of firearms in "court facilities." Under Pennsylvania law, it is a crime to knowingly have a firearm in a court facility, or to knowingly cause a firearm to be present in a court facility. The law additionally provides a separate offense for possession or transport of a firearm into a courtroom with the intent that the firearm be used to commit a crime. For law-abiding gun owners, the latter provision is of little concern.

In order to understand the law, one must understand how the law defines a "court facility." The statute indicates that the term "court facility" is not so broad as to include the entire court building. The statutory definition includes various courtrooms, judge's chambers, witness rooms, jury deliberation rooms, attorney conference rooms, prisoner holding cells, offices of court clerks, the district attorney, the sheriff and probation and parole officers, and *any adjoining corridors*.

> ### 18 Pa.C.S. §913.
> ### Possession of firearm or other dangerous weapon in court facility
>
> (a) Offense defined.—A person commits an offense if he:
> (1) knowingly possesses a firearm or other dangerous weapon in a court facility or knowingly causes a firearm or other dangerous weapon to be present in a court facility; or
> (2) knowingly possesses a firearm or other dangerous weapon in a court facility with the intent that the firearm or other dangerous weapon be used in the commission of a crime or knowingly causes a firearm or other dangerous weapon to be present in a court facility with the intent that the firearm or other dangerous weapon be used in the commission of a crime.

What is an adjoining corridor? According to the Commonwealth Court of Pennsylvania, "[a]n adjoining corridor is a passageway that is adjacent to a court facility, *i.e.*, a passageway that has common bounding lines with a court facility." *Minich v. Cnty. of Jefferson*, 869 A.2d 1141, 1143 (Pa. Cmwlth. 2005) (*citing* Webster's Third New International Dictionary 26-27 (1993)) (internal quotations omitted). The Commonwealth Court ultimately concluded that the first floor hallway of the courthouse in question *was* an adjoining corridor because it connected with the "District Court, the Prothonotary's Office/Clerk of Courts and the Office of the Register and Recorder/Clerk of Orphan's Court, all of which are court facilities." *Id.* at 1144.

Along with this restriction, however, the statute provides some protection for law-abiding gun owners in courthouses. First, the statute mandates that courthouses post notices "conspicuously at each public entrance to each courthouse or other building containing a court facility and each court facility." If the courthouse fails to post a compliant notice, those who enter with a firearm can only be convicted under the statute if they actually knew that they were violating the law. The statute also mandates that courthouses provide lockers or storage facilities for gun owners to check their firearms as they enter the courthouse. Those who do so must be issued a receipt.

It is important to note that in this restriction the term "firearm" includes "[a]ny weapon, including a starter gun, which will or is designed to expel a projectile or projectiles by the action of an explosion, expansion of gas or escape of gas." 18 Pa.C. S. §913(f).

Practical Legal Tip:

If you choose to bring your firearm to a courthouse, use caution. Alert the security member in a calm and polite fashion. Using language such as "I have a license to carry and would like to check my firearm" will likely work out better than "Hey! I've got a gun!" -*Mike*

This definition is broader than the definition provided by the Pennsylvania Uniform Firearms Act, which generally only covers handguns, short-barreled rifles and short-barreled shotguns. Accordingly, conventional rifles and shotguns are subject to the court facility ban.

b.   *Detention facilities & correctional facilities*
In Pennsylvania, it's a crime to "unlawfully [introduce] within a detention facility [or] correctional institution . . . any weapon, tool, implement, or other thing which may be used for escape." 18 Pa.C.S. §5122. Section 5122 makes it a crime to unlawfully provide these listed items to an inmate, which should be of little concern to law-abiding gun owners.

Additionally, more stringent prohibitions are provided in Title 61 of the Pennsylvania Crimes Code. Under 61 Pa.C.S. §5902, it is illegal to bring any weapons into a correctional institution, any connected buildings, or onto any land that Pennsylvania uses for inmates. Accordingly, firearms are legally prohibited in prisons, jails, detention facilities, or any place that is used to process, hold, or house arrested persons or prisons.

c. Mental hospitals

Under 18 Pa.C.S. §5122, it is also illegal to unlawfully introduce a weapon, tool, implement, or other thing which may be used for escape into a mental hospital. The law does not specify an exemption for those with a License to Carry Firearms.

However, because 61 Pa.C.S. §5902 does not have a counterpart for mental hospitals, there is not a clear, stringent prohibition on licensed individuals carrying firearms in mental hospitals. There is presently no case law interpreting "unlawful introduction" to include the lawful possession of a firearm.

According to the statute, "the word 'unlawfully' means surreptitiously or contrary to law, regulation or order of the detaining authority." At the very least, this seems to suggest that each individual mental hospital —as a detaining authority— is given the force of law with respect to firearm prohibition. While the language may seem permeable, this will remain an unsettled area of law until the court interprets it definitively.

Additional firearm restrictions can be found in 50 P.S. §4605 (The Mental Health Act). It reads:

> It shall be unlawful for anyone to directly or indirectly, sell, give or furnish to any person admitted, committed or detained in a facility, any weapon or other instrument which may be used to inflict injury unless the instrument is a tool of the activity in which the person has permission to engage.

Most obviously, this law prohibits handing guns over to persons committed to a mental hospital. But the term "indirectly furnish" is somewhat ambiguous, and leaves the opportunity for loose interpretation.

Perhaps 18 Pa.C.S. §5122 might not seem air tight because of the inclusion of the term "unlawful," and 50 P.S. §4605 leaves ambiguity in prohibiting direct or indirect giving or furnishing of weapons. The fact is that this is an unsettled area of law for which a concrete "yes" or "no" answer does not exist. In these cases, it is best to err on the side of caution, unless you are prepared to become the subject of a test case. Until there is further clarification from either the Pennsylvania courts or the legislature, mental hospitals should be treated as off-limits.

d. School Buildings, School Grounds or School Transportation

Pennsylvania law prohibits possession of a firearm "in the buildings of, on the grounds of, or in any conveyance providing transportation to or from" any elementary or secondary school (K-12). Although this restriction applies to public schools, it is *not limited* to public schools. It includes schools that are "publicly-funded," private schools "licensed by the Department of Education" and any "parochial school." In Pennsylvania, this covers just about any school from Kindergarten all the way through high school. In other words, this includes all school grounds except universities.

There is ongoing confusion because the law provides a specific defense if "the weapon is possessed and used in conjunction with a lawful supervised school activity or course or is possessed for other lawful purpose." The confusion persists because what exactly qualifies under "other lawful purpose" is not entirely clear. The statute does not specifically define "other lawful purpose" and there is no definitive case law interpreting the term. As a result, whether "other lawful purpose" includes a LTCF holder who carries for self-defense remains uncertain. At the very least, it is clear that some prosecutors are willing to bring charges against LTCF holders under this statute.

As discussed above, when the law remains unsettled, it is best to err on the side of caution. Although a person charged with a crime under these circumstances may have a viable, articulable defense, those unwilling to be the subject of a test case would be best suited treating these locations as if firearms are prohibited.

B. *Automobiles, watercraft, and other places*
　　1. May a person carry a concealed handgun in an automobile?
Yes. A LTCF holder in Pennsylvania can legally carry a concealed handgun in their vehicle. Those without a LTCF are generally prohibited from having a handgun in their vehicle, unless one of the 16 exceptions of 18 Pa.C.S. §6106(b) applies.

　　2. May a person legally carry a concealed handgun in a commercial vehicle?
Yes. One question that is often asked is whether a person who operates a commercial shipping vehicle (such as a semi-truck or similar) is entitled to follow the same rules and regulations governing ordinary LTCF holders in Pennsylvania. The answer to this question is simple: Yes, they are. This is because there are no specific Pennsylvania or federal regulations regarding carrying in a commercial shipping vehicle beyond those regulations that may be imposed by the operator's employer. This may be a breach of company policy, but not the law and is not a crime. Obviously, if a commercial driver crosses into another state, that person is then subject to the laws of that state.

　　3. May a person with a LTCF carry a concealed handgun on a boat or watercraft in Pennsylvania?
Yes. Although the Pennsylvania Fish and Boat Commission prohibits the "carry or use of firearms on Commission owned or controlled properties," an exception is provided for those who have a valid LTCF or fall under one of the exceptions provided under 18 Pa.C.S. §6106.

4. <u>May a person with a LTCF carry a concealed handgun in a state or municipal park?</u>

Yes. Pennsylvania law allows those with a LTCF to carry in state parks. Pennsylvania law allows the regulation of state parks through the Pennsylvania Code, which generally prohibits the carry of firearms in parks. However, under 18 Pa.C.S. §6109 (m.2), those with a License to Carry Firearms may carry concealed or in a vehicle regardless of these prohibitions.

A local municipality is preempted by state law from prohibiting the possession of firearms and is, therefore, not authorized to prevent the legal carrying thereof. The Commonwealth Court of Pennsylvania recently struck down a city ordinance preventing the carry of firearms in municipal parks. *Dillon v. City of Erie*, 83 A.3d 467 (Pa. Cmwlth. 2014). It is important to note, however, that some municipalities still have illegal ordinances prohibiting carry in municipal parks anyway. Most notably, both Philadelphia and Harrisburg have ordinances preventing carry in municipal parks. While any person prosecuted under these illegal ordinances would have a tremendous argument that the ordinance is void and unenforceable, this may not prevent the prosecution in and of itself.

Note: U.S. Law Shield of Pennsylvania challenged an illegal "Parks" ordinance in U.S. Law Shield of Pennsylvania, LLC et al. v. City of Harrisburg, et al. In that case, the Court of Common Pleas preliminarily enjoined the City of Harrisburg from enforcing the parks ordinance. This litigation is ongoing, and the Court of Common Pleas has yet to reach a final holding on the merits.

5. <u>Can a LTCF holder carry in a restaurant?</u>

Pennsylvania law does not prohibit an individual from carrying a firearm in a restaurant that sells alcohol or even in a bar. In fact, in Pennsylvania it is not even illegal to drink alcohol while lawfully carrying a firearm. It is important to note the peculiarity of Pennsylvania's approach, because it is the minority approach. Many states, even those with minimal gun control laws, prohibit carrying firearms in bars, restaurants that serve alcohol, or at the very least, prohibit those who are carrying from drinking alcohol themselves. This is not so in Pennsylvania. It is important to remember that just because something is legal, doesn't automatically make it a good idea. It is absolutely crucial to exercise extreme caution and be responsible with firearms around alcohol.

6. Can a person have their gun in a hotel?

There is no Pennsylvania law prohibiting firearms in hotels or places of temporary lodging.

7. Can a person have their gun in a casino?

There is no Pennsylvania law generally prohibiting the possession of a firearm in a casino. There is an administrative regulation prohibiting the carry of dangerous weapons in a licensed facility. 58 Pa.Code §465a.13. However, the law makes clear that it "does not apply to the possession of firearms carried in accordance with [the Pennsylvania Uniform Firearms Act]."

Although there is no general prohibition of the lawful possession of firearms in a casino under Pennsylvania law, individual establishments maintain the right to set their own policies regarding the possession of firearms on their private premises.

C. *Federal Property*

A LTCF and its rights are a product of state law and convey no rights to the LTCF holder that have been recognized under federal law. However, in certain instances, the federal government recognizes these state rights on certain federal property.

1. Federal Buildings: firearms are prohibited

> **Firearms Prohibited in Federal Facilities;**
> **18 U.S.C. §930(a)**
>
> ...whoever knowingly possesses or causes to be present a firearm or other dangerous weapon in a federal facility (other than a federal court facility), or attempts to do so, shall be fined under this title or imprisoned not more than 1 year...

Under this statute, a "federal facility" refers to any building or part of a building that is owned or leased by the federal government and is a place where federal employees are regularly present for the purpose of performing their official duties. *See* 18 U.S.C. §930(g)(1). However, this statute does not apply to "the lawful performance of official duties by an officer, agent, or employee of the United States, a State, or a political subdivision thereof, who is authorized by law to engage in or supervise the prevention, detection, investigation, or prosecution of any violation of law," nor does it apply to federal officials or members of the armed forces who are permitted to possess such a firearm by law, or the lawful carrying of a firearm incident to hunting or "other lawful purposes." 18 U.S.C. §930(d). This statute does not govern the possession of a firearm in a federal court facility.

2. National Parks

Those with a valid LTCF may legally carry in National Parks but not buildings within the park, such as ranger stations because these are federal buildings. Under federal law, for firearms purposes, all federal parks are subject to the concealed carry laws of the state in which the park is located. *See* 16 U.S.C. §1a-7b. A LTCF holder may, therefore, carry a handgun concealed in a federal park, but not in federal buildings in the park.

The law specifically reads:

> a person may possess, carry, and transport concealed, loaded, and operable firearms within a national park area in accordance with the laws of the state in which the national park area, or that portion thereof, is located, except as otherwise prohibited by applicable Federal law.

36 CFR §2.4.

Because the law directly notes that this exception to any prohibitions applies to "concealed" firearms, LTCF holders are not permitted to open carry in National Parks.

3. VA Hospitals: firearms prohibited

Firearms Prohibited at Veterans Affairs Hospitals; 38 CFR §1.218(a)(13)
No person while on property shall carry firearms, other dangerous or deadly weapons, or explosives, either openly or concealed, except for official purposes.

One place where many law-abiding LTCF holders fall victim is at the VA Hospital. Although Pennsylvania law does not prohibit firearms in hospitals, and only references "mental hospitals," the VA Hospital system is governed by federal law which prohibits the carrying of any firearm while on VA property. This includes the parking lot, and any other area which is the property of the VA.

Under federal law, 38 CFR §1.218(a)(13) states that "no person while on property shall carry firearms, other dangerous or deadly weapons, or explosives, either openly or concealed, except for official purposes." The "official purposes" specified refer specifically to the VA Hospital Police. This area gets good people in trouble because the Department of Veterans Affairs has its own set of laws and guidelines and is not controlled strictly by the Gun Control Act and the general provisions regarding the prohibition of firearms on federal property. The VA law is much more restrictive, and many veterans have found themselves in trouble when they valet-park their vehicle and the valet discovers a concealed handgun in the console or concealed in the door storage area. How rigidly this law is enforced is determined by the individual hospital administrators as described in 38 CFR §1.218(a), however, regardless of how strictly the law is enforced firearms are still prohibited under the law and the VA police are very aggressive in enforcing them.

4. United States Post Offices: firearms prohibited

Firearms Prohibited at Post Offices; 39 CFR §232.1(l)
Notwithstanding the provisions of any other law, rule or regulation, no person while on postal property may carry firearms, other dangerous or deadly weapons, or explosives, either openly or concealed, or store the same on postal property, except for official purposes.

Under this regulation, firearms or other deadly weapons are prohibited on *postal property* which includes not only the building, but all property surrounding the building where a post office is located. This includes the parking lot (*e.g.*, a person's vehicle where a firearm may be stored), as well as the sidewalks and walkways. Like the VA Hospital, United States Post Offices are another exception to the rule. In 2013, there was a decision by a United States District Court addressing this issue in Colorado which allowed a license holder to bring his firearm into the parking lot of the Avon, Colorado Post Office. However, in 2015, that case was reversed on appeal, by the U.S. Tenth Circuit Court of Appeals. In 2016, the U.S. Supreme Court refused to review the Tenth Circuit's reversal. It should be noted that the U.S. Tenth Circuit does not include Pennsylvania, and therefore had no legal bearing on the prohibition against possessing firearms on United States Post Office property in Pennsylvania.

5. <u>Military bases and installations: firearms generally prohibited</u>

Military bases and installations are treated much like the VA Hospital and U.S. Post Offices in that they have, and are governed by, a separate set of rules and regulations with respect to firearms on the premises of an installation or base and are generally prohibited. Military installations are governed by the federal law under Title 32 of the Code of Federal Regulations. Moreover, the sections covering the laws governing and relating to military bases and installations are exceedingly numerous. There are, in fact, sections which are dedicated to only certain bases such as 32 CFR §552.98 which only governs the possessing, carrying, concealing, and transporting of firearms on Fort Stewart/Hunter Army Airfield.

D. *Can municipalities restrict firearms rights?*
   1. <u>Can cities or other governmental agencies enact firearms laws or regulations regarding the carrying of a concealed handgun by LTCF holders that are more restrictive than state laws?</u>

No, because municipalities are restricted by the Pennsylvania General Assembly from passing ordinances further restricting the carry of firearms. 18 Pa.C.S. §6120. Under this section, municipalities and other local governments cannot regulate the carry of firearms in any manner. This includes regulating any location that isn't prohibited under state law. As previously discussed, open carry is prohibited in Philadelphia without a valid LTCF. However, this prohibition is a function of state law, and not by way of municipal ordinance. *See* Chapter One for a complete discussion.

   2. <u>General preemption laws not specific to LTCF holders</u>

The preemption law found in 18 Pa.C.S. §6120 prohibits municipalities and local governments from regulating the "ownership, possession, transfer or transportation of firearms" with respect to any person—not just LTCF holders.

Keep in mind that despite this prohibition, many local governments have illegal ordinances and regulations on the books. Until these issues are resolved in the court system, be warned that local governments might continue to enforce their illegal ordinances.

E.   *How big of a handgun can a LTCF holder legally carry?*
A Pennsylvania License to Carry Firearms is subject to the Pennsylvania definition of a "firearm." This definition includes:

> any pistol or revolver with a barrel length less than 15 inches, any shotgun with a barrel length less than 18 inches or any rifle with a barrel length less than 16 inches, or any pistol, revolver, rifle or shotgun with an overall length of less than 26 inches. The barrel length of a firearm shall be determined by measuring from the muzzle of the barrel to the face of the closed action, bolt or cylinder, whichever is applicable.

In short, this includes handguns, short-barreled rifles and short-barreled shotguns.

Short-barreled rifles and short-barreled shotguns are subject to the National Firearms Act ("NFA") and must be properly registered with the Bureau of Alcohol, Tobacco, Firearms and Explosives ("BATFE"). Unless and until a person registers an item subject to the NFA, and receives a valid tax stamp for that item, possession is illegal under federal and state law.

Additionally, as we mentioned in Chapter Two, federal law dictates that any firearm which has any barrel with a bore of more than one-half inch in diameter (.50 caliber) is a "destructive device" and is subject to the NFA (except for certain shotguns). Possession of any such firearm without the proper paperwork associated with NFA firearms is illegal whether a person is a LTCF holder or not. For more information on destructive devices and the NFA, *see* Chapter Fourteen.

III. Interactions with Law Enforcement Officers

A. *Do I have to tell a law enforcement officer if I am legally carrying a firearm?*

Pennsylvania law does not require a person to volunteer the fact that he is carrying a firearm. While some states impose a legal duty upon armed citizens to inform law enforcement officers of that fact (for example, Ohio, Oklahoma, and many more), Pennsylvania law has no such requirement.

Although not required, a person carrying a firearm is *not prohibited* from informing a law enforcement officer that he or she is carrying. There is simply no legal requirement to do so.

B. *Do I have to provide my LTCF if a law enforcement officer asks to see it?*

Yes. The Pennsylvania Crimes Code requires a LTCF holder to produce his or her license upon lawful demand by a law enforcement officer. 18 Pa.C.S. §6122. Failure to produce a LTCF at the time of arrest or at the preliminary hearing creates a rebuttable presumption that the person does not have a license. So it's extremely important for Pennsylvania LTCF holders to carry their LTCF (or equivalent that is honored in Pennsylvania) in their physical possession at all times when carrying. Similarly, if one is carrying under one of the exceptions listed in 18 Pa.C.S. §6106(b), he must provide proof of qualification for an exception upon lawful demand.

C. *Can a police officer legally take a LTCF holder's handgun away?*

This is an area of Pennsylvania law that remains unsettled at this time. There is no Pennsylvania law that specifically grants law enforcement officers the right to temporarily seize a LTCF holder's firearm during an encounter.

The Fourth Amendment of the United States Constitution protects citizens from unreasonable searches and seizures. The key component of this protection stems from the word *unreasonable*. The Supreme Court of the United States has deemed some searches and temporary seizures to be reasonable under certain circumstances in the interest of the safety of the officer. *See generally, Terry v. Ohio, 392 U.S. 1 (1968).* Similarly, the Supreme Court of the United States has found that "[w]hat is at most a mere inconvenience cannot prevail when balanced against legitimate concerns for the officer's safety." *Pennsylvania v. Mimms*, 434 U.S. 106, 111 (1977).

Therefore, although Pennsylvania law does not expressly provide for law enforcement officers to temporarily seize a firearm during an encounter, many law enforcement officers rely on this broader concept in order to do so.

As a practical matter, an officer who chooses to temporarily confiscate a firearm is unlikely to change his mind based upon an attempted constitutional lecture. Remember, the primary goal when interacting with a law enforcement officer should always be to stay safe and to go home (not to prison). In many situations, taking action such as filing a complaint with the department, or even filing a lawsuit, will provide more fruitful results than engaging in a heated argument with the officer on the scene.

D. *What are passengers with a LTCF in a vehicle legally obligated to do when the driver is stopped by law enforcement?*

Because Pennsylvania law does not require a citizen to immediately disclose that he or she is armed, there is no requirement for a passenger to inform a law enforcement officer that he or she is armed. However, as discussed earlier, a LTCF holder must present his or her LTCF upon lawful demand by a law enforcement officer.

Practical Legal Tip:

During interactions with law enforcement officers, a law-abiding gun owner should have three main goals: (1) don't do anything that would cause you to get shot, (2) lawyer up, and (3) get home safely to your family. -*Justin*

IV. Reciprocity

A. *Can I carry a concealed handgun in other states if I have a Pennsylvania LTCF?*

Yes, at the time of the writing of this chapter the following states recognize a Pennsylvania LTCF:

Alabama	Alaska	Arizona	Arkansas	Colorado*
Florida*	Georgia	Idaho	Indiana	Iowa
Kansas	Kentucky	Louisiana	Michigan*	Mississippi
Missouri	Montana	New Hampshire	North Carolina	North Dakota
Ohio**	Oklahoma	South Dakota	Tennessee	Texas
Utah	Vermont	Virginia	West Virginia	Wisconsin
Wyoming				

*Indicates only recognizes a Pennsylvania LTCF for Pennsylvania residents
**Indicates only recognizes a Pennsylvania LTCF while temporarily visiting

Reciprocity either exists between Pennsylvania and these states or they have unilaterally decided to recognize a Pennsylvania LTCF. Every state has the authority to determine whether or not their state will recognize a carry license or permit issued by another state. Reciprocity is where states enter into an agreement with each other, in this case, to recognize each other's carry licenses. However, states are not required to have reciprocity with one another nor are they required to recognize another state's carry license.

There are many states that issue their own licenses, but refuse to recognize a carry license from another state. Conversely, there are states that choose to recognize some or all other states' carry licenses. Pennsylvania gives the Pennsylvania Attorney General the authority to negotiate reciprocity agreements with other states or to issue proclamations which will unilaterally recognize other states' carry licenses. There are some states that recognize a Pennsylvania LTCF, but Pennsylvania does not recognize their license. As of the date of writing, a Pennsylvania LTCF is recognized by 31 other states.

Although Pennsylvania no longer has reciprocity with Maine, Maine is a constitutional carry state. Carrying a firearm, concealed or otherwise, is not prohibited for the following individuals, so long as they are not otherwise legally prohibited from possessing a firearm:
- individuals over the age of 21
- individuals 18 years of age or older and under 21 years of age and is on active duty in the Armed Forces of the United States or the National Guard
- honorably discharged veterans of the Armed Forces of the United States or the National Guard

See 25 M.R.S. §2001-A.

Those who do not hold a valid license honored by Maine may face restrictions upon carrying in certain locations. See, e.g. 26 M.R.S. §600.

When it comes to reciprocity issues, it is always best to check with a lawyer prior to travel as these agreements are subject to change.

B. *What out-of-state handgun licenses does Pennsylvania recognize?*

As of the date of the writing of this chapter, Pennsylvania recognizes handgun licenses issued by the following states:

Alaska	Arizona*	Arkansas	Colorado	Florida*
Georgia	Indiana	Iowa	Kansas	Kentucky
Louisiana	Michigan	Mississippi*	Missouri	Montana
New Hampshire	North Carolina	North Dakota**	Ohio	Oklahoma
South Dakota	Tennessee	Texas	Utah*	Virginia
West Virginia*	Wisconsin	Wyoming		

Indicates Pennsylvania only recognizes a license held by a resident of that state
**Pennsylvania only recognizes a North Dakota Class I Permits*

An out-of-state concealed carry license holder must follow Pennsylvania law while in Pennsylvania just like a Pennsylvania LTCF holder must follow the laws of the state he or she is located in when traveling. For example, a Florida Concealed Weapons and Firearms License will allow a person to carry a concealed handgun, knife, electric weapon, billy club, and tear-gas gun while in Florida. A person with a Florida license will not be able to use his or her Florida Concealed Weapons and Firearms License to carry a billy club (black jack) as such a weapon is prohibited in Pennsylvania per section 908 of the Pennsylvania Crimes Code.

C. *What state's laws apply to me when using my Pennsylvania LTCF in another state?*

Anytime a Pennsylvania LTCF holder is in another state, even if that state recognizes a Pennsylvania LTCF, the law of the state where the person is currently located will be the law which governs that person's firearms possession and use. If a person is traveling to another state, they must abide by that state's laws, just like a non-resident of Pennsylvania visiting Pennsylvania must follow Pennsylvania law. Most common laws Pennsylvanians should be aware of are the places that are off-limits to LTCF holders, as most of the time they vary from state to state. For example, while there is no crime in a LTCF holder entering a bar while carrying in

Pennsylvania, carrying in a bar in Texas or Oklahoma will get a person carrying a quick trip to jail.

D. *Can persons who are not Pennsylvania residents obtain a Pennsylvania LTCF?*

Yes. Under 18 Pa.C.S. §6109, Pennsylvania residency is not required in order to be eligible to obtain a Pennsylvania LTCF. However, section 6109 does explicitly disqualify non-residents who do not possess a current license or permit to carry a firearm in their state of residence. For example, a Texan without a License To Carry a handgun issued by the Texas Department of Public Safety cannot receive a Pennsylvania LTCF. However, if that Texan does have a Texas License to Carry, he or she is eligible for a Pennsylvania LTCF.

CHAPTER TEN

POSSESSING, CARRYING, AND TRANSPORTING FIREARMS WITHOUT A LTCF

This chapter deals with when and where a person may possess, carry, or transport a firearm if they do not hold a Pennsylvania License to Carry Firearms (LTCF) or a concealed carry permit honored in Pennsylvania. One salient fact about Pennsylvania firearms law is that when it comes to transportation of firearms, the law treats long guns differently from handguns. As a result, under Pennsylvania law, one must have a LTCF in order to transport a handgun unless an exception applies. On the other hand, a LTCF is generally unnecessary to transport an unloaded long gun.

As discussed in Chapter Nine, open carry is generally legal in Pennsylvania with or without a LTCF. However, because a LTCF is generally necessary to transport a handgun in a vehicle, a person without a LTCF will face practical issues unless walking is his or her preferred mode of travel.

The laws discussed in this chapter are found primarily in Pennsylvania Crimes Code, Title 18, Chapter 61, entitled "Firearms and Other Dangerous Articles." This chapter of the Crimes Code governs how firearms can be possessed and carried in Pennsylvania, and it also contains various exceptions to any such rules. Because handguns and long guns are treated differently under Pennsylvania law, this chapter will examine each separately.

I. Possession of firearms in Pennsylvania without a LTCF

Pennsylvania law does not require a person to have any kind of license in order to merely possess a gun. Some states require a person to get a special permit to purchase a firearm (*e.g.* New Jersey). In Pennsylvania, this is not the case. So long as the proper procedures are followed, a person who is legally eligible to possess a firearm may purchase one in Pennsylvania. Similarly, if a person moves from another state to Pennsylvania, he or she can continue to possess their firearm(s) so long as he or she is not legally disqualified from possessing firearms. Note: crossing state lines with most weapons covered under the National Firearms Act (NFA) requires a separate procedure. For more on the NFA, *see* Chapter Fourteen.

There is no requirement that a person register firearms in Pennsylvania. Quite the opposite, Pennsylvania law specifically declares that the state does not have the authority to require registration of firearms.

As set forth in 18 Pa.C.S. §6111.4:

> *Notwithstanding any section of this chapter to the contrary, nothing in this chapter shall be construed to allow any government or law enforcement agency or any agent thereof to create, maintain or operate any registry of firearm ownership within this Commonwealth. For the purposes of this section only, the term "firearm" shall include any weapon that is designed to or may readily be converted to expel any projectile by the action of an explosive or the frame or receiver of any such weapon.*

This law was enacted in June of 1995. In 2004, the Supreme Court of Pennsylvania was presented an issue as to the scope of §6111.4. *Allegheny Cnty. Sportsmen's League v. Rendell*, 860 A.2d 10 (Pa. 2004). Under Pennsylvania law, in-state handgun transfers must go through a Federal Firearms Licensee or the sheriff's office, barring certain exceptions (for more on transfers, *see* Chapter Three). Ultimately, Pennsylvania State Police (PSP) maintain the records of such transfers. Consequently, the plaintiffs sued for injunctive relief, asserting that the maintenance of such records violated §6111.4. The Court held that PSP's maintenance of these records did not violate §6111.4 because the records did not constitute a "registry of firearm ownership." Rather, the records only reflect certain sales and transfers of handguns. *Id.* at 17.

In the Commonwealth Court, Judge Friedman wrote a concurring and dissenting opinion, which strongly disagreed with the Court's ultimate holding. Judge Friedman reasoned that "the words [of the statute] are clear and free from ambiguity" and "a database of handgun sales is a 'registry of firearm ownership.'" *Allegheny Sportsmen's League v. Ridge*, 790 A.2d 350, 362-63 (Pa. Commw. Ct. 2002) *aff'd sub nom. Allegheny Cnty. Sportsmen's League v. Rendell*, 860 A.2d 10 (Pa. 2004).

Regardless of whether the record of handgun transfers acts as a de facto registry, there is no requirement that a person register firearms in Pennsylvania.

II. Carrying a firearm in Pennsylvania without a LTCF

A. *May be carried openly in public*

Pennsylvania law does not require a person to have a LTCF in order to carry a long gun or handgun. The law only requires a LTCF for one to carry a "firearm" as defined by the Pennsylvania Uniform Firearms Act: (1) concealed on or about their person (2) in a vehicle or (3) in Philadelphia, whether openly or concealed.

Outside of Philadelphia, as long as a person is not legally prohibited from possessing firearms there is no law preventing him or her from carrying a gun open and conspicuously. This is true whether dealing with a handgun or a long gun.

Many ask whether they can be charged with "brandishing" for open carrying. In Pennsylvania, there is no such crime as "brandishing." One may be charged with simple assault, however, for attempting "by physical menace to put another in fear of imminent serious bodily injury." 18 Pa.C.S. §2701. Pennsylvania courts have never found the open carry of a firearm in and of itself to meet the elements necessary for simple assault.

B. *Carrying at one's place of abode or fixed place of business*
Pennsylvania law does not require a LTCF to carry a firearm —even if concealed— in one's "place of abode" or "fixed place of business."

What is a "place of abode?" The Supreme Court of Pennsylvania has held that a "'place of abode' is the actual house or apartment of a person. It does not include common areas to which a person has a right of access but which are shared with others who have a similar right of access." *Commonwealth v. Ortiz*, 738 A.2d 403, 405 (Pa. 1999). In that case, the Defendant did not have a LTCF, and carried a concealed handgun in an enclosed backyard of an apartment building. *Id.* at 404. Based upon this decision, we know that the term "place of abode" is construed very narrowly. While a person need not own his "place of abode," the Supreme Court of Pennsylvania's interpretation tells us that it is limited to a person's house or apartment.

The term "place of business" has also been interpreted very narrowly in Pennsylvania. While it may seem to mean that the exception applies while one is at work, the Superior Court of Pennsylvania has held that it only applies if one has "ownership or control over the 'fixed place of business.'" *Commonwealth v. Carr*, 483 A.2d 542, 543 (Pa. Super. 1984). In that case, the Defendant — a gas station employee— carried a concealed handgun while at work. The Superior Court found that the "gasoline service station clearly was the fixed place of business of the proprietor" and not the place of business of the Defendant. *Id.* The court reasoned that the Defendant had no controlling, proprietary, or possessory interest in the service station. *Id.*

C. *Carrying under an exception*
As briefly mentioned earlier in this chapter, there are exceptions to the general rule that one may not carry a firearm concealed or in a vehicle without a LTCF. In fact, there are 16 of them. Most of the exceptions that cover carrying a concealed handgun, however, do not apply to the common public. The most common exceptions

that may apply to carrying concealed include the "recently-expired LTCF" exception and the "statutory reciprocity" exception. A full list of the exceptions and a discussion of some of the most common exceptions can be found below, in section III of this chapter.

D. *Carrying long guns concealed*

Because Pennsylvania law does not specifically prohibit carrying concealed long guns, it is not illegal. However, as will be discussed below, *loaded long guns are prohibited in vehicles whether or not one has a LTCF.*

III. Transportation of firearms in Pennsylvania without a LTCF

A. *Long guns*

In Chapter Nine, we discussed how the transportation of handguns in a vehicle in Pennsylvania is generally illegal without a LTCF. Transportation of long guns in a vehicle, however, is different. There is no Pennsylvania law that generally prohibits the transportation of long guns in a vehicle, or that requires a LTCF in order to do so. As a result, transportation of *unloaded* long guns is generally legal.

Like most general rules, this one has its exceptions. First, Pennsylvania law makes it illegal to transport any loaded long gun. This prohibition applies even to those with *a valid LTCF*!

> ### Carrying Loaded Weapons Other than Firearms; 18 Pa.C.S. §6106.1
>
> (a) General rule.-- Except as provided in Title 34 (relating to game), no person shall carry a loaded pistol, revolver, shotgun or rifle, other than a firearm as defined in section 6102 (relating to definitions), in any vehicle. The provisions of this section shall not apply to persons excepted from the requirement of a license to carry firearms under section 6106(b)(1), (2), (5) or (6) (relating to firearms not to be carried without a license) nor shall the provisions of this section be construed to permit persons to carry firearms in a vehicle where such conduct is prohibited by section 6106.

What does "loaded" mean? Under Pennsylvania law, it sometimes depends upon the type of firearm. All firearms are considered "loaded" if there is a round in the chamber that is capable of being fired. If a firearm has a non-detachable magazine, it is loaded if the magazine contains a live round. Likewise, if a firearm has a cylinder, it is loaded if there is a live round in any chamber of the cylinder.

If a firearm has a detachable magazine, Pennsylvania law provides a broader definition of "loaded." A firearm with a detachable magazine is loaded if the magazine contains live rounds, and it is set in the well of the firearm, *or* if the magazine contains live rounds and is in the same container as the firearm. Just because the magazine is detached does *not* mean that it is "unloaded!" The full text of the statute reads as follows:

> *"Loaded." A firearm is loaded if the firing chamber, the nondetachable magazine or, in the case of a revolver, any of the chambers of the cylinder contain ammunition capable of being fired. In the case of a firearm which utilizes a detachable magazine, the term shall mean a magazine suitable for use in said firearm which*

magazine contains such ammunition and has been inserted in the firearm or is in the same container or, where the container has multiple compartments, the same compartment thereof as the firearm. If the magazine is inserted into a pouch, holder, holster or other protective device that provides for a complete and secure enclosure of the ammunition, then the pouch, holder, holster or other protective device shall be deemed to be a separate compartment.

18 Pa.C.S. §6102

Although the prohibition *does* apply to those with a valid LTCF, it does not apply to:

- Constables, sheriffs, prison or jail wardens, or their deputies, policemen of this Commonwealth or its political subdivisions, or other law-enforcement officers;
- Members of the army, navy, marine corps, air force or coast guard of the United States or of the National Guard or organized reserves when on duty;
- Officers or employees of the United States duly authorized to carry a concealed firearm; and
- Agents, messengers and other employees of common carriers, banks, or business firms, whose duties require them to protect moneys, valuables and other property in the discharge of such duties.

Notice that the prohibition applies to any "loaded pistol, revolver, shotgun or rifle, other than a firearm as defined in [section 6102 of the Uniform Firearms Act]." Due to Pennsylvania's definition of the term "firearm," this prohibition covers conventional shotguns and rifles as defined in Title I of the Gun Control Act of 1968 ("GCA"). However, the definition does not cover short-barreled rifles (SBR) and short-barreled shotguns (SBS) covered under Title II of the GCA. Accordingly, those with a valid LTCF may legally carry a loaded, properly registered SBR or SBS in a vehicle.

Long guns in a vehicle in Philadelphia
There is a common concern regarding the transport of unloaded long guns, in a car, in Philadelphia.

In 18 Pa.C.S. §6108 we find:
> *No person shall carry a firearm, rifle or shotgun at any time upon the public streets or upon any public property in a city of the first class unless:*
> *(1) such person is licensed to carry a firearm; or*
> *(2) such person is exempt from licensing under section 6106(b) of this title (relating to firearms not to be carried without a license).*

Many interpret this to mean that open carry is illegal in Philadelphia without a LTCF. Some, however, have contended that this applies to long guns being transported in a vehicle. While the latter interpretation may be strained, it is at the very least worthy of discussion.

First and most importantly, there are no published, and therefore precedent carrying, decisions in the Pennsylvania Superior Court or the Pennsylvania Supreme Court on this issue. Therefore, we must look to what is in the Uniform Firearms Act. As discussed above, generally, transport of an unloaded long gun in a vehicle is legal, with or without a License to Carry Firearms.

Transporting a "firearm" requires a LTCF barring a few exceptions (for further discussion about handguns, short-barreled rifles and short-barreled shotguns, *see* later in this chapter).

Transporting a loaded long gun is prohibited by §6106.1 regardless of your LTCF status (*see* discussion above). The question becomes whether transport of an unloaded long gun in your car, using public streets in Philadelphia, would violate §6108.

In §6106, the License to Carry Firearms is specifically addressed. Here, the legislature specifically prohibits carrying "a firearm in any vehicle" or "concealed on or about [one's] person" barring some exceptions. While obtaining a LTCF serves as an exception, it does not serve as the *sole* exception. The legislature specifically recognized that in order for certain activities to be possible (for example, purchasing a firearm and bringing it home) other exceptions were necessary. While §6108 references §6106(b), only certain protections afforded under §6106(b) pertain to long guns. For example, the protections pertaining to law enforcement, hunting and federal law (18 U.S.C. §926A) do NOT technically apply to long guns under §6106.

If you take this position, some absurd results may come about such as:

- Could the legislature have intended to restrict the transport of long guns by law enforcement under §6108?
- Does this mean that Philadelphia outright rejects its citizens' the opportunity to take in their vehicles, on the streets, long guns to go hunting elsewhere within the state?
- Does it mean that Philadelphia outwardly rejects 926A, a federal law, but only as it applies to long guns?

To interpret carry "upon the public streets or upon any public property" to include transport in motor vehicles on the streets, would effectively mean exactly all of the above.

Also, there is some very limited guidance from our appellate courts in a related discussion on the other provision of section 6108. There is case law discussing the factors considered in determining whether something is "public property" under §6108. *Commonwealth v. Goosby*, 380 A.2d 802 (Pa. Super. 1977). In that case, the court found that a man on a sidewalk used by the general public was "upon public property" for purposes of the statute. The court looked at the character of the use of the property, who had access to the property, and whether or not private individuals have greater dominion over the property than the general public. *Id.* at 806. An analogous argument can be made that the inside of one's vehicle has very different characteristics than those listed by the court. The public doesn't have access to the inside of one's vehicle as they would outside on the public streets or public property. Typically, (we would expect) an individual has greater dominion over his own vehicle than the random public. These appear to be the factors the court has considered in that context and they appear to be persuasive in this context. Like any law, when there is no clear-cut answer supported by case law (or clearly defined by statute), it is vital to use caution.

B. *Handguns*
    1. Handguns in vehicles
As discussed in Chapter Nine, a valid LTCF (or other honored license) is generally permitted to have a "firearm" (handgun, short-barreled rifle, or short-barreled shotgun) in a vehicle. Under certain specific circumstances, the law allows one without a LTCF to have a firearm in their vehicle. In fact, 18 Pa.C.S. §6106 provides 16 exceptions to the general rule.

> ### Firearms Not to be Carried Without a License; 18 Pa.C.S. §6106
>
> Except as provided in paragraph (2), any person who carries a firearm in any vehicle or any person who carries a firearm concealed on or about his person, except in his place of abode or fixed place of business, without a valid and lawfully issued license under this chapter commits a felony of the third degree.

First, what is a "vehicle" in this context?
In this chapter, the legislature didn't provide us with a concrete definition. Furthermore, to date, the court has not interpreted what constitutes a "vehicle" under the statute. Perhaps providing guidance (and equally as important, perhaps not) the justification section in Title 18 defines a vehicle as:

> *A conveyance of any kind, whether or not motorized, that*
> *is designed to transport people or property.*

18 Pa.C.S. §501.

This has no direct bearing on §6106, but it gives us insight as to what the legislature may have had in mind.

Further, the Vehicle Code defines the term "vehicle" as:

> Every device in, upon or by which any person or property is or may be transported or drawn upon a highway, except devices used exclusively upon rails or tracks. The term does not include a self-propelled wheel chair or an electrical mobility device operated by and designed for the exclusive use of a person with a mobility-related disability.

75 Pa.C.S. §102.

Again, this definition is clearly not authoritative with regards to §6101. Either way, these seem to include just about every conceivable mode of transportation.

Does that mean motorcycles? Based on either definition, a motorcycle would apply. It is important to note that section 6106 addresses carrying firearms in any vehicle *or* concealed on or about one's person. In other words, the law applies to carrying firearms in a vehicle even if it is completely open and conspicuous. Furthermore, the statute specifically mentions "any vehicle." Not car, not automobile, but vehicle, which includes a motorcycle in the remainder of Pennsylvania's statutory definitions. Accordingly, without a License to Carry Firearms, one may only transport a firearm on a motorcycle if one of the exceptions applies.

What about motor homes? This gets increasingly tricky. Again, devoid of any clarification from the legislature or interpretation from the court, it is best to err on the side of caution. Do motor homes transport people? Absolutely. Based upon the other definitions of vehicle provided, it seems like a motor home would neatly meet the criteria.

There may be one issue with the definition applying to motor homes, however. The Supreme Court has held that the Second Amendment guarantees the right of citizens to possess guns —*at least in the home*— for self-defense purposes. *District of Columbia v. Heller*, 554 U.S. 570 (2008). As a result, can Pennsylvania possibly prevent citizens from keeping firearms in their motor homes without a license? Perhaps. Other states require licensing procedures in order to keep firearms in the home, although there remains ongoing litigation challenging some of these requirements.

It may be helpful to draw distinctions. Maybe there can be no black and white rule when it comes to motor homes. Perhaps, like many other legal issues, it depends. A motor home serves many different purposes. If a motor home is not used as a primary residence, but is used predominantly for travel, it seems likely that it would be considered a vehicle under this section. Additionally, in such an instance, it appears less likely that the restriction would crumble under constitutional scrutiny. If the motor home *is* the primary residence, is planted in a lot, hooked up to utilities, has no wheels or wheels on blocks, and doesn't move, it would appear less reasonable to consider that motor home a "vehicle" under the statute. Even if the motor home is in fact the primary residence, it is likely that any time it is in motion, it will be considered a vehicle. So while a completely stationary motor home that is a primary residence *may* fall outside the lines, there is a very strong basis for §6106 to apply to motor homes otherwise. Perhaps motor homes can be a vehicle in certain contexts, and a dwelling or residence is others. Until binding authority provides a clear answer, absent a License to Carry Firearms, the most cautious approach would be to keep your firearms out of the motor home unless an exception applies.

Next, what are the exceptions? The requirement that one have a valid LTCF to have a handgun in the vehicle does not apply to:

(1) Constables, sheriffs, prison or jail wardens, or their deputies, policemen of this Commonwealth or its political subdivisions, or other law-enforcement officers.

(2) Members of the army, navy, marine corps, air force or coast guard of the United States or of the National Guard or organized reserves when on duty.

(3) The regularly enrolled members of any organization duly organized to purchase or receive such firearms from the United States or from this Commonwealth.

(4) Any persons engaged in target shooting with a firearm, if such persons are at or are going to or from their places of assembly or target practice and if, while going to or from their places of assembly or target practice, the firearm is not loaded.

(5) Officers or employees of the United States duly authorized to carry a concealed firearm.

(6) Agents, messengers and other employees of common carriers, banks, or business firms, whose duties require them to protect moneys, valuables and other property in the discharge of such duties.

(7) Any person engaged in the business of manufacturing, repairing, or dealing in firearms, or the agent or representative of any such person, having in his possession, using or carrying a firearm in the usual or ordinary course of such business.

(8) Any person while carrying a firearm which is not loaded and is in a secure wrapper from the place of purchase to his home or place of business, or to a place of repair, sale or appraisal or back to his home or place of business, or in moving from one place of abode or business to another or from his home to a vacation or recreational home or dwelling or back, or to recover stolen property under Section 6111.1(b)(4) (relating to Pennsylvania State Police), or to a place of instruction intended to teach the safe handling, use or maintenance of firearms or back or to a location to which the person has been directed to relinquish firearms under 23 Pa.C.S. §6108 (relating to relief)

or back upon return of the relinquished firearm or to a licensed dealer's place of business for relinquishment pursuant to 23 Pa.C.S. §6108.2 (relating to relinquishment for consignment sale, lawful transfer or safekeeping) or back upon return of the relinquished firearm or to a location for safekeeping pursuant to 23 Pa.C.S. §6108.3 (relating to relinquishment to third party for safekeeping) or back upon return of the relinquished firearm.

(9) Persons licensed to hunt, take furbearers or fish in this Commonwealth, if such persons are actually hunting, taking furbearers or fishing as permitted by such license, or are going to the places where they desire to hunt, take furbearers or fish or returning from such places.*

(10) Persons training dogs, if such persons are actually training dogs during the regular training season.*

(11) Any person while carrying a firearm in any vehicle, which person possesses a valid and lawfully issued license for that firearm which has been issued under the laws of the United States or any other state.

(12) A person who has a lawfully issued License to Carry Firearms pursuant to Section 6109 (relating to licenses) and that said license expired within six months prior to the date of arrest and that the individual is otherwise eligible for renewal of the license.

(13) Any person who is otherwise eligible to possess a firearm under this chapter and who is operating a motor vehicle which is registered in the person's name or the name of a spouse or parent and which contains a firearm for which a valid license has been issued pursuant to Section 6109 to the spouse or parent owning the firearm.

(14) A person lawfully engaged in the interstate transportation of a firearm as defined under 18 U.S.C. §921(a)(3) (relating to definitions) in compliance with 18 U.S.C. §926A (relating to interstate transportation of firearms).

(15) Any person who possesses a valid and lawfully issued license or permit to carry a firearm which has been issued under the laws of another state, regardless of whether a

reciprocity agreement exists between the Commonwealth and the state under Section 6109(k), provided:

> (i) The state provides a reciprocal privilege for individuals licensed to carry firearms under Section 6109.
> (ii) The Attorney General has determined that the firearm laws of the state are similar to the firearm laws of this Commonwealth.

(16) Any person holding a license in accordance with section 6109(f)(3).

*Before any exception shall be granted under exceptions (9) or (10) to any person 18 years of age or older licensed to hunt, trap or fish or who has been issued a permit relating to hunting dogs, such person shall, at the time of securing his hunting, furtaking or fishing license or any time after such license has been issued, secure a sportsman's firearm permit from the county treasurer.

Some of these exceptions apply specifically to law enforcement officers, members of the service, dealers, and others as a result of employment status. Those exceptions are beyond the scope of this book. However, let's discuss some of the more common exceptions that may apply to the average law-abiding gun owner.

2. Target shooting

A person does not need a LTCF to own a handgun in Pennsylvania. If a person owns a handgun, it's probably a good idea to train with that handgun! But can you transport a handgun to and from the range without a LTCF? Yes. The law prohibiting handguns in vehicles without a LTCF does not apply to persons engaged in target shooting while going to and from target practice or their place of assembly. It is important to note that the exception requires the firearm to be *unloaded* while traveling to or from a place of assembly or target practice.

As discussed earlier in this chapter, unloaded means there are *no live rounds* in the cylinder or detachable magazine. In the case of a handgun with a detachable magazine, the magazine contains no live rounds if it is set in the well of the firearm. If the magazine is detached from the firearm and contains live rounds, it must not be in same container as the firearm. However, if the container has multiple compartments, a magazine containing live rounds must be in a different compartment than the firearm. If the magazine is in a pouch, holder, holster or other protective device that provides for a complete and secure enclosure of the ammunition, then the pouch, holder, holster or other protective device is considered a separate compartment. Remember, just because the magazine is detached does *not* mean that it is "unloaded!"

The law does not define "place of assembly" and there is no case law providing guidance as to what it means. This would seemingly include a place for a group of shooters to meet before heading directly to the range. However, without a definition or an interpretation from Pennsylvania courts, it is impossible to provide a specific applicable example. As with any law that is ambiguous, it is vital to be extra cautious not to run afoul. You don't want to be the test case!

3. Place of purchase

If a person buys a new handgun, they are probably not planning on staying at the place of purchase forever! For those without a LTCF, Pennsylvania law accounts for this.

As long as the firearm is unloaded and stored in a "secure wrapper," the law allows travel from the place of purchase to the home or place of business. It is important to remember that Pennsylvania construes the term "place of business" very narrowly. For more on this topic, *see* section II of this Chapter.

It is equally as important to note that there is no authoritative case law interpreting the term "secure wrapper" and the statute does not provide a definition. In a non-precedential decision (not binding on other courts) the Superior Court of Pennsylvania affirmed a trial court decision that briefly discussed the term "secure wrapper." In *Commonwealth v. Saita*, the jury did not find that the Defendant's firearm was "not loaded, was in a secure wrapper, and was being carried between Defendant's home and place of business." *See* WL 7078221, (Pa. Super. Nov. 12, 2015). The Defendant did not have a valid LTCF. In the trial court opinion, the court noted that the Defendant admitted that the firearm was "in a holster on his waistband and not in a secure wrapper." *Id.* at 5. The trial court also noted that the Defendant "carried [the firearm] as he conducted his business from his tow truck and ultimately into the Processing Center located in the Courthouse, not from his place of purchase to his home or place of business, etc." *Id.* At the very least, this opinion puts law-abiding gun owners on notice that a holster on one's person does not clearly fall into the class of "secure wrappers."

4.   Place of repair, sale or appraisal

Similar to the "place of purchase" exception, the law allows those without a LTCF to transport a firearm to a place of repair, sale or appraisal and back to his home or place of business within the state. However, like the "place of purchase" exception, the firearm must be unloaded and stored in a secure wrapper.

Keep in mind that the term "place of abode" has been interpreted very narrowly in Pennsylvania. For a more in depth discussion about this, *see* section II in this chapter.

5.   Between places of business

Most people don't live or work at the same place forever, and some people have more than one place of business or place of abode. With that in mind, Pennsylvania law provides an exception for those without a LTCF who are "moving from one place of abode or business to another" within the state. This exception also requires that the firearm be kept unloaded and stored in a secure wrapper. Remember the narrow definitions of "place of abode" and "place of business!"

6. Vacation or recreational dwellings

The law allows those without a LTCF to transport a firearm from his home to a vacation or recreational home or dwelling or back within the state. Under this exception, those without a LTCF can continue to protect themselves in their temporary dwelling while on vacation. This exception, like many others, requires the firearm to be unloaded and stored in a secure wrapper.

7. Place of instruction

Earlier we discussed the "target shooting" exception. Similarly, there is an exception for those without a LTCF going to or from a place of instruction intended to teach the safe handling, use or maintenance of firearms. "Place of instruction" includes any hunting club, rifle club, rifle range, pistol range, shooting range, the premises of a licensed firearms dealer or a lawful gun show or meet. The firearm must be unloaded and stored in a secure wrapper.

8. Hunting, fishing and dog training

The prohibitions of carrying concealed or in a vehicle without a LTCF do not apply to "persons licensed to hunt, take furbearers or fish in this Commonwealth, if such persons are actually hunting, taking furbearers or fishing as permitted by such license" or traveling to and from a location to participate in such activities. There is another exception for "persons training dogs, if such persons are actually training dogs during the regular training season." Each of these exceptions requires the person have a valid sportsman's firearm permit from the county treasurer.

9. Out of state license holders

Pennsylvania honors carry licenses from many, but not all other states. Even if a person's license to carry is not honored in Pennsylvania, one may carry a firearm in any vehicle with a "valid and lawfully issued license for that firearm which has been issued under the laws of the United States or any other state." In other words, if a person's license to carry is not honored in Pennsylvania, it will still allow the person to carry a firearm in a vehicle in

Pennsylvania. If the license is not honored in Pennsylvania, that person must not get out of the vehicle with a concealed firearm on his or her person!

10. <u>The recently expired LTCF</u>
The law provides an exception that essentially acts as a grace period for a recently expired LTCF. This exception applies to those who have been validly issued a LTCF that has expired "within six months prior to the date of arrest ..." The exception also requires that the person be "otherwise eligible for renewal" of the LTCF. In other words, if something has changed since the LTCF was issued and the person is disqualified from receiving a LTCF under 18 Pa.C.S. §6109, this exception will not apply.

11. <u>Certain family members</u>
One exception deals with car sharing situations among certain relatives. The exception covers any person who is:
- otherwise eligible to possess a firearm;
- is operating a vehicle that is registered in their own name, or in the name of a spouse or parent;
- the vehicle contains a firearm owned by the person's spouse or parent; and
- the spouse or parent who owns the firearm has a valid LTCF.

Imagine a spouse or parent leaves a firearm in their own vehicle, or in their spouse or child's vehicle. Then, the spouse or child — who does not have a LTCF, but is legally eligible to possess such a firearm— drives the vehicle, and the firearm is still there. Although the spouse or child without a LTCF would generally be prohibited from having a firearm in the vehicle, the exception will apply.

Keep in mind that the firearm in the vehicle must be the kind of firearm that is covered under a valid LTCF. Additionally, it is important to note that the "parent/child" relationship is only covered *one way.* An eligible child would be covered if the gun belonged to their parent (who is a LTCF holder), but a parent without a LTCF would *not* be covered if the gun belonged to their child.

12. Interstate travel under 18 U.S.C. §926A

A major protection afforded to traveling law-abiding gun owners comes from the Firearm Owners Protection Act, 18 U.S.C. §926A, nicknamed the "Safe Passage" provision. This will be discussed in detail later in this chapter. Although Pennsylvania law cannot trump this federal protection, the legislature decided to explicitly acknowledge that those abiding by the federal protections of section 926A are not subject to punishment under 18 Pa.C.S. §6106.

13. Statutory reciprocity

This protection applies to certain persons who have an out-of-state license to carry that is not explicitly honored by Pennsylvania via reciprocity agreement (for more on reciprocity agreements, *see* Chapter Nine). The exception applies to those with a valid license to carry under the laws of another state, provided:

- the state provides a reciprocal privilege for individuals licensed to carry firearms under section 18 Pa.C.S. §6109; and
- the Pennsylvania Attorney General has determined that the firearm laws of the state are similar to the firearm laws of this Commonwealth.

Most recently, we have seen this exception come into play with those licensed to carry in Ohio. Although there is no valid reciprocity agreement between Pennsylvania and Ohio, Ohio honors valid licenses from any state for non-resident visitors, Pennsylvania included. Additionally, the Pennsylvania Attorney General has determined that the firearm laws of the state are similar to the firearm laws of this Commonwealth. Accordingly, the Pennsylvania Attorney General's website indicates that Ohio and Pennsylvania have "statutory reciprocity."

IV. Traveling across state lines with firearms

Many people vacation and travel outside of Pennsylvania. Naturally, no Pennsylvanian wants to travel unarmed if they can help it, but, unfortunately, not every state shares the same views on gun ownership and gun rights as we do in the Keystone State. This is especially true in the northeast corner (many of the states that border Pennsylvania, such as New York, New Jersey and Maryland) and the west coast of the United States. How then does a person pass through states that have restrictive firearms laws or those different from Pennsylvania? For example, how does a person legally pass *through* a state that prohibits the possession of a handgun without a license from that state? The answer: safe-passage legislation.

A. *Federal law: qualifying for firearms "Safe Passage"*

Traveling across state lines with a firearm means that a person may need to use the provisions of the federal law known as the "Safe Passage" provision. Federal law allows individuals who are legally in possession of firearms in their state (the starting point of traveling) to travel through states that are not as friendly. This protection is only available under federal law to transport such firearms across state lines for lawful purposes, as long as they comply with the requirements of the Firearm Owners Protection Act, 18 U.S.C. §926A, nicknamed the "Safe Passage" provision. The first requirement to qualify for the Federal "Safe Passage" provision is that throughout the duration of the trip through the anti-firearm state, the firearm must be unloaded and locked in the trunk, or if the vehicle has no trunk, locked in a container that is out of reach or not readily accessible from the passenger compartment. The ammunition also must be locked in the trunk or a container. Note that for the storage of both firearms and ammunition, the glove box and center console compartment are specifically not allowed under the statute.

B. *"Safe Passage" requires legal start to legal finish*

To get protection under federal law, a gun owner's journey must start and end in states where the traveler's possession of the firearm is legal; for instance, a person traveling with their Glock 17 starting in Pennsylvania and ending in Vermont. Even though a person must drive through New York or Massachusetts to get to Vermont, as long as the person qualifies under the "Safe Passage" provision, then they may legally pass through. However, if the start point was Pennsylvania and the end point was New York (a place where the handgun would be illegal), there is no protection under the federal law. Safe-passage requires legal start and legal finish.

Although traveling across state lines naturally invokes federal law, it is important to remember that whenever a person finally completes their journey and reaches their destination state, the laws of that state control the possession, carrying, and use of the firearm. Federal law does not make it legal or provide any protection for possession of a firearm that is illegal under the laws of the destination state (*i.e.*, the end state of your travels).

C. *What is the definition of "traveling" for "Safe Passage" provisions?*

The final requirement for protection under the federal law is that individuals MUST be "traveling" while in the firearm hostile state. The legal definition of "traveling" is both murky and narrow. The "Safe Passage" provision protection has been held in courts to be limited to situations that strictly relate to traveling and nothing more. Traveling is a term that is not defined in the federal statute; however, it has received treatment in the courts that is indicative of what one can expect. Generally speaking, if a person stops somewhere for too long they cease to be "traveling" and, therefore, lose their protection under the "Safe Passage" provision. How long this time limit is has not been determined either statutorily or by case law with any definitiveness.

While stopping for gas or restroom breaks might not disqualify a person from the "traveling" protection, this issue has not been directly resolved by the courts. As is true with any unsettled area of law, one can never be too cautious. Using too little caution can lead to becoming a test case.

Ostensibly, any stop for an activity not directly related to traveling could be considered a destination and thus you would lose the legal protection. For example, in Chicago anyone in the city for more than 24 hours is not considered to be traveling under local policy. In an actual case, stopping for a brief nap in a bank parking lot in New Jersey caused a Texan driving back home from Maine to lose the "traveling" protection. He received 5 years in prison for possession of weapons that are illegal under New Jersey law. Of course, if the driver would have made it to Hershey, Pennsylvania, he would have been safe. The moral of the story is to travel through these gun-unfriendly states as fast as you can (without breaking the speed limit, of course)!

D. *Protection under federal law does not mean protection from prosecution in unfriendly states*

To make matters even worse for firearms travelers, even if a person qualifies for protection under the federal "Safe Passage" provision, New Jersey and New York seem quite proud to treat this protection as an affirmative defense. This means that someone can be arrested even though he or she met all of the requirements of the federal statute. Then, they would have to go to court to assert this defense. In other words, while a person could beat the rap, they will not beat the ride! This becomes even more troublesome in the instance of someone who is legally flying with their firearm, and then due to flight complications, must land in New Jersey or New York, as travelers in this position have been arrested or threatened with arrest.

Once again, the "Safe Passage" provision only applies while a person is traveling; as soon as they arrive at their destination and cease their travels, the laws of that state control a person's actions. Remember: check all applicable state firearms laws before you leave for your destination!

V. Air travel with a firearm

A. *How do I legally travel with a firearm as a passenger on a commercial airline?*

It is legal to travel with firearms on commercial airlines so long as the firearms transported are unloaded and in a locked, hard-sided container as checked baggage. Under federal law, the container must be completely inaccessible to passengers. Further, under U.S. Homeland Security rules, firearms, ammunition and firearm parts, including firearm frames, receivers, clips, and magazines, are prohibited in carry-on baggage. The Transportation Safety Administration (TSA) also requires that "realistic replicas of firearms are also prohibited in carry-on bags and must be packed in checked baggage. Rifle scopes are permitted in carry-on and checked bags." It is important for law-abiding gun owners to inspect their baggage several times to ensure that it contains no prohibited items before traveling!

1. Firearms must be inaccessible

Federal law makes it a crime subject to fine, imprisonment for up to 10 years, or both, if a person "when on, or attempting to get on, an aircraft in, or intended for operation in, air transportation or intrastate air transportation, has on or about the individual or the property of the individual a concealed dangerous weapon that is or would be accessible to the individual in flight." 49 U.S.C. §46505(b). Additionally, under 49 U.S.C. §46303(a) "[a]n individual who, when on, or attempting to board, an aircraft in, or intended for operation in, air transportation or intrastate air transportation, has on or about the individual or the property of the individual a concealed dangerous weapon that is or would be accessible to the individual in flight is liable to the United States Government for a civil penalty of not more than $10,000 for each violation."

2. Firearms must be checked in baggage

The following guidelines are put out by the TSA for traveling with firearms on airlines: "To avoid issues that could impact your travel and/or result in law enforcement action, here are some guidelines to assist you in packing your firearms and ammunition:

- All firearms must be declared to the airline during the ticket counter check-in process.

- The term firearm includes: (Please *see*, for instance, United States Code, Title 18, Part 1, Chapter 44 for information about firearm definitions.)
- Any weapon (including a starter gun) which will, or is designed to, or may readily be converted to expel a projectile by the action of an explosive.
- The frame or receiver of any such weapon.
- Any firearm muffler or firearm silencer.
- Any destructive device.
- The firearm must be unloaded.
- As defined by 49 CFR §1540.5, 'A loaded firearm means a firearm that has a live round of ammunition, or any component thereof, in the chamber or cylinder or in a magazine inserted in the firearm.'
- The firearm must be in a hard-sided container that is locked. A locked container is defined as one that completely secures the firearm from being accessed. Locked cases that can be pulled open with little effort cannot be brought aboard the aircraft.
- If firearms are not properly declared or packaged, TSA will provide the checked bag to law enforcement for resolution with the airline. If the issue is resolved, law enforcement will release the bag to TSA so screening may be completed.
- TSA must resolve all alarms in checked baggage. If a locked container containing a firearm alarms, TSA will contact the airline, who will make a reasonable attempt to contact the owner and advise the passenger to go to the screening location. If contact is not made, the container will not be placed on the aircraft.
- If a locked container alarms during screening and is not marked as containing a declared firearm, TSA will cut the lock in order to resolve the alarm.
- Travelers should remain in the area designated by the aircraft operator or TSA representative to take the key back after the container is cleared for transportation.

- Travelers must securely pack any ammunition in fiber (such as cardboard), wood or metal boxes or other packaging specifically designed to carry small amounts of ammunition.
- Firearm magazines and ammunition clips, whether loaded or empty, must be securely boxed or included within a hard-sided case containing an unloaded firearm.
- Small arms ammunition, including ammunition not exceeding .75 caliber for a rifle or pistol and shotgun shells of any gauge, may be carried in the same hard-sided case as the firearm, as long as it follows the packing guidelines described above.
- TSA prohibits black powder or percussion caps used with black-powder.
- Rifle scopes are not prohibited in carry-on bags and do not need to be in the hard-sided, locked checked bag." *See* www.tsa.gov.

B. *May I have a firearm while operating or as a passenger in a private aircraft flying just in Pennsylvania?*

Generally, yes. There is nothing to suggest that a private aircraft is treated unlike any other motorized vehicle under Pennsylvania law. For more information concerning firearms in vehicles, *see* our earlier discussion in this chapter.

C. *May I have a firearm in a private aircraft that takes off from Pennsylvania and lands in another state?*

In situations where a private aircraft is taking off from one state and landing in another, the law will simply view this as traveling interstate with firearms. Where no other statutes apply to the person's flight, the person will be subject to the provisions of 18 U.S.C. §926A regarding the interstate transportation of a firearm: "any person who is not otherwise prohibited by this chapter from transporting, shipping, or receiving a firearm shall be entitled to transport a firearm for any lawful purpose from any place where he may lawfully possess and carry such firearm to any other place where he may lawfully possess and carry such firearm if, during such transportation the firearm is unloaded, and neither the firearm nor any ammunition being transported is readily accessible or is directly accessible from the passenger compartment of such transporting vehicle."

This statute allows a person to transport firearms between states subject to the following conditions: that the person can lawfully possess the firearm at his or her points of departure and arrival, and that the firearm remains unloaded and inaccessible during the trip. However, what if the person is a LTCF holder and wants to carry concealed between states? Fortunately, 18 U.S.C. §927 states that Section 926A does not pre-empt applicable state law. Thus, if a person can lawfully carry a concealed weapon in the state in which he or she boards the aircraft and in the state in which he or she lands, the LTCF holder is not subject to the unloaded and inaccessible restrictions of section 926A.

For operations of private aircraft within one state, a person will only be subject to the laws of the state within which he or she is operating. The person will need to review that state's statutes to determine whether they impose any restrictions on possession of firearms within non-secure areas of airports. The person will also need to be familiar with the airports he or she will be visiting to determine whether each airport has any restrictions (*e.g.*, policies prohibiting the carry of firearms, *etc.*).

VI. <u>Understanding gun-free school zone laws</u>
Pennsylvania law prohibits possession of a firearm (including handguns and long guns) "in the buildings of, on the grounds of, or in any conveyance providing transportation to or from any elementary or secondary publicly-funded educational institution, any elementary or secondary private school licensed by the Department of Education or any elementary or secondary parochial school." In other words, this includes all school grounds except universities.

The law provides a specific defense *if* "the weapon is possessed and used in conjunction with a lawful supervised school activity or course or is possessed for other lawful purpose." What exactly qualifies under "other lawful purpose" is not entirely clear. One could argue that self-defense is a lawful purpose, but the courts have yet to interpret the statute that way.

A. *Federal "Gun Free School Zone" law: 18 U.S.C. §922(q)*
The prohibition under Pennsylvania law, for the most part, renders the federal "Gun Free School Zone" law moot. Even if federal law would permit one to have a firearm on school grounds, *Pennsylvania law would still prohibit firearms under most circumstances.*

The text of the federal "Gun Free School Zone" law is found in 18 U.S.C. §922(q), and creates its own independent criminal offense. This law states that it is a federal crime for a person to possess a firearm that has moved through interstate commerce (this includes virtually all firearms), on the grounds of or within 1,000 feet of a public, parochial, or private school. Under this federal law, the mere possession of a firearm by the occupant of a motor vehicle while driving past a school or dropping off a child, is a federal crime.

However, federal law provides seven exceptions:
1. *Exception one*: if the possession is on private property which is not part of the school grounds. This means that a person living within 1,000 feet of a school can keep a firearm in their house.
2. *Exception two*: if the individual possessing the firearm is licensed to do so by the state in which the school zone is located or a political subdivision of the state, and the law of the state or political subdivision requires that, before an individual obtains such a license, the law enforcement authorities of the state or political subdivision verify that the individual is qualified under law to receive the license. This means that a LTCF holder may legally carry a

concealed firearm into a "gun free school zone." However, there is one important note about the statute: a person can only lawfully carry in a school zone located in the state that issued the firearms license. Therefore, if a person has a Pennsylvania LTCF they can only carry through Pennsylvania school zones. If that Pennsylvania LTCF holder is traveling through another state, the exception under federal law does not apply to them, and they are in violation of this law. It also means that a Pennsylvania resident, who holds a non-resident non-Pennsylvania concealed carry license or permit, does not benefit from this exception and is in violation of the law if they take a firearm into a school zone.

3. *Exception three*: if the firearm is not loaded, and is in a locked container, or a locked firearms rack that is on a motor vehicle. This means that if a firearm is unloaded and carried in a locked case, or other type of locked container, such as a glove box or trunk, there is no violation of the federal law.

4. *Exception four*: if the firearm is carried by an individual for use in a program approved by a school in the school zone. This exception covers school-sponsored shooting activities, such as an ROTC program.

5. *Exception five*: if the firearm is carried by an individual in accordance with a contract entered into between a school in the school zone and the individual or an employer of the individual. This means that school security guards can carry firearms while on the job.

6. *Exception six*: if the firearm is carried by a law enforcement officer acting in his or her official capacity. This exception covers police officers while on-duty only. It does not appear to cover them while they are off-duty, even if they are required by state law to carry while off-duty.

7. *Exception seven*: if the firearm is unloaded and is in the possession of an individual while traversing school property for the purpose of gaining access to public or private lands open to hunting, if the entry on school

premises is authorized by school authorities. This means that if a hunter must cross school property to get to a lawful hunting ground, they must have the permission of the school, and the firearm must be unloaded.

Remember that even if one falls under one of these exceptions, possession of a firearm on school grounds is *still a crime under Pennsylvania law* unless possessed and used in conjunction with a lawful supervised school activity or course, or is possessed for "another lawful purpose." As discussed above, it is not entirely clear what constitutes "another lawful purpose."

B. *Is a person legally permitted to possess a firearm at a college or university?*

Legally speaking, there is no general firearms prohibition that applies to colleges and universities in Pennsylvania. Rather, the law allows each institution to decide what kind of rules to implement. However, in light of recent Supreme Court holdings regarding the Second Amendment, many of Pennsylvania's state universities have lifted the complete bans they once had in place. Instead, these universities have updated their policies to permit those with a License to Carry Firearms to carry, at least in some places, on campus.

In general, the universities have placed numerous restrictions on where on campus one can carry. As a result, gun owners will generally be extremely limited on campuses, which invites us to question whether it is worth the trouble, or even practical to do so. Either way, there is no general prohibition of carrying firearms on a college or university campus in Pennsylvania.

VII. "No Gun" signs & policies on private property

Dealing with "No Gun" signs and "No Gun" policies on private property is the same in Pennsylvania whether one has a LTCF or not.

There are certain places where firearms are legally prohibited regardless of whether you have a License to Carry Firearms. These locations are discussed in detail in Chapter Nine. In these locations, the "No Gun" signs put you on notice of the law, and whether one has a LTCF or not, he or she must obey the law.

Then there are private establishments. We're talking about private businesses that aren't off-limits under state or federal law. For instance, a coffee shop (there is no Pennsylvania or federal law prohibiting firearms in coffee shops).

Some private businesses have "No Gun" signs at the door. Some of them are so small, oddly placed, and unnoticeable. Others are prominently displayed and more likely to be seen by entering customers. As a practical matter, many law-abiding gun owners take their business elsewhere when they see these signs. It is certainly their right to do so. But what is the legal impact of these signs and policies?

There are generally two sources of legal authority giving force to private businesses that prohibit firearms on their property.

The first source comes from state statutes that expressly give "No Gun" signs on private property the force of law. Some states have laws that make entry in and of itself —if a "No Gun" sign is posted at a private business— a crime. In these states, if a customer chooses to ignore the "No Gun" sign at the coffee shop, he is simply breaking the law.

In Pennsylvania, we have no such law. There is no statute specifically granting those "No Gun" signs posted by private businesses the force of law. The legislature has not specifically deemed entering an establishment with a posted "No Gun" policy a criminal act.

There is, however, a second source of legal authority allowing private businesses to prohibit firearms on their property: the laws of trespass. At the outset, one thing is clear. Whether or not a "No Gun" sign is posted, a private property owner has the right to have his or her own policies. This includes policies that exclude firearms from his or her premises. Whether or not the owner can really achieve that goal by simply having a policy is an entirely different matter, but that is for a different conversation. Other businesses might even have a policy expressly prohibiting open carry.

Businesses may also have policies prohibiting firearms or open carry that are *not* posted. Businesses are entitled to have these policies, and those who wish to enter or remain on the premises must abide by these policies.

If a gun owner is confronted with a request or order to leave due to a "No Gun" policy, he or she must do so. Failure to leave would make him or her a defiant trespasser. Even if the location is generally open to the public, notification of the "No Gun" policy provides notice that one's invitee status (his legal invitation to be on private property) is revoked and that those carrying guns are not welcome. In other words, the private business, because of its policy, does not give individuals the privilege to shop there while armed. If a gun owner stays there knowing he has no right to do so, he is trespassing.

The situation becomes less clear when a business owner is so frightened of a person's gun that he immediately calls the police. For obvious reasons, this is more common with open carry than with concealed carry. Can the gun-owning customer be charged as a trespasser even though nobody has asked him to leave? In this particular situation, probably not.

Let's take a look at the letter of the law for both Criminal Trespass and Defiant Trespass:

> Criminal trespass.
> (a) Buildings and occupied structures.–
> (1) A person commits an offense if, knowing that he is not licensed or privileged to do so, he:

(i) enters, gains entry by subterfuge or surreptitiously remains in any building or occupied structure or separately secured or occupied portion thereof.

18 Pa.C.S. §3503(a).

If nobody has informed the gun owner of the policy and asked him to leave, he may not know that he was not licensed or privileged to enter or stay on the premises.

What about businesses with signs? Do business owners who post signage make entrance contingent upon the customer leaving their firearms behind? Does a "No Gun" sign convey that message to the customer? If so, it seems there is an argument to be made that when a gun owner *sees* a "No Gun" sign at the entrance of a business, he knows he is not privileged to enter the building with his gun. But it is certainly not clear cut.

Moving forward, we have defiant trespass:

Defiant trespasser.–

(1) A person commits an offense if, knowing that he is not licensed or privileged to do so, he enters or remains in any place as to which notice against trespass is given by:

(i) actual communication to the actor;

(ii) posting in a manner prescribed by law or reasonably likely to come to the attention of intruders.

18 Pa.C.S. §3503(b).

Similarly, an argument can be made that a gun owner who overtly ignores a "No Gun" sign knows that he is not privileged to enter the premises. This particular law mentions signage. However, this seems to be aimed at signs giving "notice against trespass ... reasonably likely to come to the attention of intruders." "Notice against trespass" appears to be tailored toward signs that say things such as, well... "no trespassing." "No trespassing" signs send the clear message that persons are not permitted in an area without permission. "No Gun" signs certainly send a clear message that the owner has a policy against firearms on the premises.

Again, the question is whether the customer's privilege to enter, and therefore ability to spend money, is contingent upon abiding by the policy. If so, is an armed customer an "intruder?" The law doesn't define the term "intruder," but if the gun owner enters despite direct notification of the policy, quite possibly.

The law also lists specific defenses.

> (c) Defenses.—It is a defense to prosecution under this section that:
>
> (1) a building or occupied structure involved in an offense under subsection (a) of this section was abandoned;
>
> (2) the premises were at the time open to members of the public and the actor complied with all lawful conditions imposed on access to or remaining in the premises; or
>
> (3) the actor reasonably believed that the owner of the premises, or other person empowered to license access thereto, would have licensed him to enter or remain.

18 Pa.C.S. §3503(c).

The focus here will be on (c)(2). When we're talking about places that are generally open for business, they are open to members of the public. But how does one comply with "all lawful conditions imposed on access?" Does that mean as long as one comes in through the customer's entrance, rather than a private back door or broken window, that he qualifies for this defense? Or is being "gun-free" a condition on access? Is one's entry contingent upon leaving their guns at home or in their car? This is yet another tough question, to which there are no definitive answers in the developed case law in Pennsylvania. There is no case law specifically dealing with this issue, and there seems to be at least an articulable argument on either side.

The official comment to the statutes makes an effort to clarify:

> The offense is limited to situations where the objective circumstances show an unwanted intrusion by the actor; not every entry on lands of another is a trespass. Neither the inadvertent trespasser nor the trespasser who reasonably believes that the owner would have licensed him to enter the premises will be penalized.

Perhaps an unsuspecting gun owner's saving grace is the phrase "knowing that he is not licensed or privileged to do so." As this is an element of the offense, the prosecutor (government) will have the burden to prove *beyond a reasonable doubt* that the customer saw the sign or otherwise knew about the anti-gun policy in place. This is a very high burden to meet. Unless a gun owner openly admits that he saw and ignored the sign, this burden might prove extremely difficult to meet.

All in all, there is no case law that deals directly with trespass charges and "No Gun" signs. Accordingly, there have been no criminal prosecutions that have led to appellate court decisions on the issue. But just because something has never happened before doesn't necessarily mean it's *never* going to happen. As is true when it comes to *any* area of the law that is not clearly settled, it is vital to be aware of all the arguments that exist.

CHAPTER ELEVEN
RESTORATION OF FIREARMS RIGHTS:
THE LAW OF PARDONS AND EXPUNGEMENTS

I. Is it possible to restore a person's right to bear arms?

What happens after a person has been convicted of a crime? Is it possible to later clear his or her name and/or criminal record? If possible, what is the process for removing a conviction and restoring a person's right to purchase and possess firearms?

This chapter will explain how a person under very limited circumstances may be able to have arrest records, criminal charges, and even criminal convictions expunged and/or pardoned. We wish to offer words of caution at the very beginning of this chapter as total success both at the federal and state level in this arena may be rare.

Further, each state has different rules concerning these issues and there is a completely different set of rules under federal law. Although we will be examining mostly federal law in this area as well as Pennsylvania state law, it is important to note that a Pennsylvania based pardon will only be effective on Pennsylvania convictions, not on other states' convictions. For example, if one were to have a conviction for a domestic violence offense in the state of Maryland, one cannot apply for a Pennsylvania pardon to "clear" that Maryland conviction. Also, interestingly enough, a pardon issued by the President of the United States does not "clear" a state conviction. Article II, Section 2, Clause 1 of the Constitution of the United States, provides: "The President . . . shall have Power to grant Reprieves and Pardons for Offenses against the United States, except in Cases of Impeachment." Thus, the President's authority to grant clemency is limited to federal offenses and offenses prosecuted by the United States Attorney for the District of Columbia in the name of the United States in the D.C. Superior Court. However, per 18 U.S.C. §921(a)(20), if one is granted a Gubernatorial pardon for a conviction for a crime, any federal prohibition related to that crime is removed.

Before we begin a meaningful discussion, it is important to explain two terms and concepts: clemency/pardon and expungement.

A. *What is clemency?*

Clemency is the action the government, usually the chief executive (*e.g.,* the President of the United States on the federal level or a governor on the state level), takes in forgiving or pardoning a crime or canceling the penalty of a crime either wholly or in part. Clemency can include full pardons after a conviction, full pardons after completion of deferred adjudication community supervision, conditional pardons, pardons based on innocence, commutations of a sentence, emergency medical reprieves, and family medical reprieves. Clemency can be granted at both the federal and state levels.

B. *What is expungement?*

Expungement is the physical act of destroying or purging government criminal records. This is unlike sealing which is simply hiding the records from the public. Under certain circumstances, a person may have their criminal record either expunged or sealed.

Practical Legal Tip:

Restoring firearms rights through a pardon is far from impossible. But it's important to understand that the process takes a very long time —several years— and there are never any guarantees. - *Justin*

II. <u>Federal law</u>
A. *Presidential Pardon*

Under Article II, Section 2 of the United States Constitution, the President of the United States has the power "to grant reprieves and pardons for offenses against the United States, except in cases of impeachment." The President's power to pardon offenses has also been interpreted to include the power to grant conditional pardons, commutations of sentence, conditional commutations of sentence, remission of fines and forfeitures, respites, and amnesties. However, the President's clemency authority only extends to federal offenses; the President cannot grant clemency for a state crime.

1. <u>How does a person petition for federal clemency or a pardon?</u>

Under federal law, a person requesting executive clemency must petition the President of the United States and submit the petition to the Office of the Pardon Attorney in the Department of Justice. The Office of the Pardon Attorney can provide petitions and other required forms necessary to complete the application for clemency. *See* 28 CFR §1.1. Petition forms for commutation of sentence may also be obtained from the wardens of federal penal institutions. In addition, a petitioner applying for executive clemency with respect to military offenses should submit his or her petition directly to the Secretary of the military branch that had original jurisdiction over the court-martial trial and conviction of the petitioner.

The Code of Federal Regulations (CFR) requires an applicant to wait five years after the date of the release of the petitioner from confinement, or in a case where no prison sentence was imposed, an applicant is required to wait five years after the date of conviction prior to submitting a petition for clemency. The regulation further states, "[G]enerally, no petition should be submitted by a person who is on probation, parole, or supervised release." 28 CFR §1.2. With that in mind, the President can grant clemency at any time, whether an individual has made a formal petition or not. For example, President Gerald Ford granted a full and unconditional pardon to former President Richard Nixon prior to any indictment or charges being filed related to his involvement in Watergate.

2. <u>What should a petition for clemency include?</u>

Petitions for executive clemency should include the information required in the form prescribed by the United States Attorney General. This includes information:

a. that specifically states the purpose for which clemency is sought, as well as attach any and all relevant documentary evidence that will support how clemency will support that purpose;

b. that discloses any arrests or convictions subsequent to the federal crime for which clemency is sought;

c. that discloses all delinquent credit obligations (whether disputed or not), all civil lawsuits to which the applicant is a party (whether plaintiff or defendant), and all unpaid tax obligations (whether local, state, or federal);

d. that includes three character affidavits from persons not related to the applicant by blood or marriage.

In addition, acceptance of a Presidential Pardon generally carries with it an admission of guilt. For that reason, a petitioner should include in his or her petition a statement of the petitioner's acceptance of responsibility, an expression of remorse, and atonement for the offense. All of the requirements are contained in 28 CFR §§1.1-1.11.

3. <u>What happens after a petition for executive clemency is submitted?</u>

All petitions for federal clemency are reviewed by the Office of the Pardon Attorney in the Department of Justice. A non-binding recommendation on an application is made to the President. Federal regulations also provide for guidelines and requirements to notify victims of the crimes, if any, for which clemency is sought. The President will either grant or deny a pardon. There are no hearings held on the petition, and there is no appeal of the President's decision.

4.   What is the effect of a Presidential Pardon?

A pardon is the forgiveness of a crime and the cancellation of the penalty associated with that crime. While a Presidential Pardon will restore various rights lost as a result of the pardoned offense, it will not expunge the record of your conviction. This means that even if a person is granted a pardon, the person must still disclose their conviction on any form where such information is required, although the person may also disclose the fact that the offense for which they were convicted was pardoned. The best course of action in order to minimize headaches, as a practical matter, is to disclose the conviction on the ATF FORM 4473 but explain that a Presidential Pardon was granted. The same holds true on the PSP Form SP 4-113 for handgun transfers in Pennsylvania.

B.   *Expungement of federal convictions*

1.   No law exists for general federal expungement

Congress has not provided federal legislation that offers any comprehensive authority or procedure for expunging criminal offenses. Recall that a federal court cannot expunge a state court record.

There exist only statues that allow expungement in certain cases for possession of small amounts of controlled substances (*see* Section IIB(2)) and interestingly, a procedure to expunge DNA samples of certain members of the military wrongfully convicted. Because there is no statutory guidance, federal courts have literally made up the rules and procedures themselves, often coming to different conclusions.

Some federal court circuits have stated that they have no power to expunge records. However, other federal courts have indicated that they do have the power to expunge. Specifically, Courts of Appeals in the First, Third (where Pennsylvania sits), Sixth, Eighth, and Ninth Circuits have cited *Kokkonen v. Guardian Life Ins. Co. of*

Am., 511 U.S. 375 (1994) in declining to recognize ancillary jurisdiction over expungement motions on equitable grounds, as have district courts in the Eleventh Circuit. Conversely, appellate authority in the Second, Fourth, Fifth, Seventh, Tenth, and D.C. Circuits continues to recognize jurisdiction for expungement motions pursuant to the courts' inherent powers. This issue remains legally murky.

2. <u>Expungement for drug possession: statutory authority</u>
Under a federal law entitled "special probation and expungement procedures for drug possessors," certain persons are allowed to request a federal court to issue an expungement order from all public records. 18 U.S.C. §3607. Congress intended this order to restore the person to the status he or she "occupied before such arrest or institution of criminal proceedings." 18 U.S.C. §3607(c).

In order to qualify for the expungement, you must have been under the age of 21 when you were convicted, you must have no prior drug offenses, and your conviction must have been for simple possession of a small amount of a controlled substance.

3. <u>How does a person have firearms rights restored under federal law?</u>
Under the Gun Control Act of 1968, a person who has received a Presidential pardon is not considered convicted of a crime preventing the purchase and possession of firearms subject to all other federal laws. *See* 18 U.S.C. §§921(a)(20) and (a)(33). In addition, persons who had a conviction expunged or set aside or who have had their civil rights restored are not considered to have been convicted for purposes of the GCA "unless the pardon, expungement, or restoration of civil rights expressly provides the person may not ship, transport, possess, or receive firearms." 18 U.S.C. §§921(a)(20) and (a)(33).

The GCA also provides the United States Attorney General with the authority to grant relief from firearms disabilities where the Attorney General determines that the person is not likely to act in a manner dangerous to the public safety and where granting relief would not be contrary to the public interest. 18 U.S.C. §925(c). The Attorney General has delegated this authority to the ATF. Unfortunately, Congress has failed since Fiscal Year 1992 to appropriate funds that would allow the ATF to spend money to investigate or act upon applications from individuals seeking relief from federal firearms disabilities. However, as of the date of the writing of this chapter, there is a current version of the appropriations bill that would allow the ATF to implement Federal Firearms Relief again for the first time since 1992. The ATF has stated that if the appropriations bill is implemented, it does not currently have an action plan in place to address the forecasted river of applications it will receive. This means that until the ATF's funding and ability to investigate has been restored, a person's best—and most likely—option to have their firearms rights restored is through a Presidential pardon in the case of a federal conviction.

III. Pennsylvania law

A. *Clemency by the Governor and Board of Pardons*

The power to grant Gubernatorial clemency is found in the Pennsylvania Constitution. Unlike the Presidential pardon process where the President of the United States can act unilaterally and without even a request to act, a Pennsylvania Gubernatorial based act of pardon must go through a distinct process. As is written in the Pennsylvania Constitution in Article IV, Section 9(a) "no pardon shall be granted, nor sentence commuted, except on the recommendation in writing of a majority of the Board of Pardons ... after full hearing in open session, upon due public notice." The Governor is not required or bound to accept the recommendation of the Board. However, the Governor cannot act lawfully on a request for clemency (including pardon) without the recommendation of the Board of Pardons. The rate of merit reviews, public hearings, and grants of pardon can fluctuate, depending on the administration. *See* Board of Pardons website: www.bop.pa.gov/Statistics/Pages/Statistics-by-Year.aspx.

1. <u>What effect does a Pennsylvania Pardon have?</u>

Per the Pennsylvania Board of Pardons publications, "A pardon constitutes total forgiveness by the state, makes the crime as if it never happened and allows a job applicant to deny he was ever convicted of the crime without worry of any sanction. It is recommended though, that such a denial be explained to be based on the existence of a pardon from the Governor."

A Pennsylvania Gubernatorial Pardon for a Pennsylvania conviction for a disabling crime on the federal level will restore both federal and state rights to bear arms. As per 18 U.S.C. §921(a)(20):

> What constitutes a conviction of such a crime shall be determined in accordance with the law of the jurisdiction in which the proceedings were held. Any conviction which has been expunged, or set aside or for which a person has been pardoned or has had civil rights restored shall not be considered a conviction for purposes of this chapter, unless such pardon, expungement, or restoration of civil rights expressly provides that the person may not ship, transport, possess, or receive firearms.

A grant of a Gubernatorial pardon does not expunge one's record. Instead, it makes it possible to have the records subject to the pardon expunged. So without the separate act of applying for an expungement in Pennsylvania, the crimes for which one was granted a pardon will still show up on background checks, but it will say "Pardoned." Therefore, it is always best to apply to have the records expunged when one is granted a pardon from the Governor.

2. <u>Who is on the Board of Pardons?</u>

Per the Pennsylvania Constitution (Article IV, §9(b)), the Board must consist of the following people: "the Lieutenant Governor who shall be chairman, the Attorney General and three members appointed by the Governor with the consent of a majority of the members elected to the Senate for terms of six years. The three members appointed by the Governor shall be residents of Pennsylvania. One shall be a crime victim, one a corrections expert and the third a doctor of medicine, psychiatrist or psychologist."

3. **Who is eligible for executive clemency in Pennsylvania?**

Technically, any form of conviction (probation without verdict, a plea of *nolo contendere*, or a guilty plea or verdict) for any crime in Pennsylvania is eligible for a pardon. However, if someone has been impeached, that person's impeachment cannot be expunged, set aside, sealed or pardoned by the Governor. Unlike the federal five-year wait period outlined above, there is no required wait to apply for pardon in Pennsylvania. As a practical matter, it is generally best to wait until you can demonstrate a sufficient period of non-recidivism and that you have been appropriately involved in the community prior to filing.

4. **What factors does the Board consider?**

There is no statutory or constitutional guidance as far as static factors that the members of the Board must or can consider in forming their vote. If there is a victim of a crime, the victim will be notified. As a matter of practical concern, the position of any victim will weigh heavily on the Board's consideration. However, it will not be an automatic veto if the victim is against the pardon.

According to the Board of Pardon's website, they offer the following insight:

Factors Considered in Pardon Applications

1. How much time has elapsed since the commission of the crime(s)? Obviously, this factor, coupled with being crime free after the offense, is one of the best indicators of whether the applicant has been successfully rehabilitated. Further, the more serious, or numerous, the crime(s), the greater the period of successful rehabilitation that the applicant should be able to demonstrate.

2. Has the applicant complied with all court requirements? The applicant should be able to

demonstrate successful completion of all court-imposed requirements such as probation, parole, and payment of all fines and costs. If unsure of the latter, applicants should check with the County Clerk of Courts, and get receipts for any recent payments.

3. Has the applicant made positive changes to his/her life since the offense(s)? Successful rehabilitation may also be demonstrated by positive changes since the offense(s) in applicant's career, education, family or through community or volunteer service, particularly in areas that relate to the offense(s).

4. What is the specific need for clemency? The applicant should identify a specific need for clemency, *e.g.*, a particular job that applicant cannot get, or some particular activity that he/she cannot participate in without clemency as opposed to the more general answers of "employment purposes" or "to put this behind me" that applicants frequently use. Except in extraordinary circumstances, the Board does not view a pardon as an appropriate means of restoring any disability that has been imposed pursuant to a state law, *e.g.*, suspension of driver's license, revocation of professional or business licensure, *etc.* Rather, the Board generally defers to the General Assembly and the means of restoration provided for in the law in question.

5. What is the impact on the victim(s) of the offense(s)? The Board's regulations require that victims or next of kin be notified and given the opportunity to appear at the hearing or make a confidential submission in writing. Applicants should be aware that victims or next of kin may be present and, in any event, will have their viewpoint considered by the Board.

5. <u>How does a person seek executive clemency in Pennsylvania?</u>

There is an application process, a fee, an interview with investigators, and perhaps a hearing before the Board of Pardons. The interview process can be either relatively easy or quite intrusive and detailed. Not all cases will get a public hearing. Any hearing before the Board of Pardons is decidedly informal. The witnesses are not sworn. There is no cross-examination. It is not supposed to be an adversarial process.

The most important thing to note about the process of Executive Clemency in Pennsylvania is that it takes time. A lot of time. Due to the increase in the sheer number of applications coupled with the increase of employment related background checks has caused a greater than three year wait period between application and action by the Board. For better detail and up to date information on the process please consider visiting: www.bop.state.pa.us /portal/server.pt/community/process/19509.

B. *Pennsylvania expungement*

Beyond the scope of this book is the world of Pennsylvania expungements. There are processes in place to remove and expunge convictions for summary and traffic related offenses. *See* 18 Pa.C.S. §9122(b). It is beyond the scope of this book as summary criminal convictions are not federal or state disabling events in terms of someone's firearms rights. Also beyond the scope of this book is an expungement for offenses that were handled through the Accelerated Rehabilitative Disposition (ARD) program whether handled at the minor judiciary level (a Magisterial District Judge) or at the Court of Common Pleas level. *See* Pennsylvania Rules of Criminal Procedure Rule 320. However, it is important to note that successful completion of the ARD program for certain types of offenses cannot properly lead to expungement under Pennsylvania law (18 Pa.C.S. §9122(b.1)). Specifically, ARD outcomes for the following crimes cannot be expunged:

1. 18 Pa.C.S. §3121 (relating to rape)
2. 18 Pa.C.S. §3122.1 (relating to statutory sexual assault)
3. 18 Pa.C.S. §3123 (relating to involuntary deviate sexual intercourse)
4. 18 Pa.C.S. §3124.1 (relating to sexual assault)
5. 18 Pa.C.S. §3125 (relating to aggravated indecent assault)
6. 18 Pa.C.S. §3126 (relating to indecent assault)
7. 18 Pa.C.S. §3127 (relating to indecent exposure)
8. 18 Pa.C.S. §5902(b) (relating to prostitution and related offenses)
9. 18 Pa.C.S. §5903 (relating to obscene and other sexual materials and performances)

If there is a conviction of a Pennsylvania criminal offense, expungement via Pennsylvania courts is generally not an option. Outside of summary offenses, judicially ordered expungements are only available if "(1) An individual who is the subject of the information reaches 70 years of age and has been free of arrest or prosecution for ten years following final release from confinement or supervision," or "(2) An individual who is the subject of the information has been dead for three years." 18 Pa.C.S. §9122(b). Therefore, the only option for those who are not dead or who are under 70 is through the Pennsylvania Board of Pardons and action by the Governor as described in detail earlier.

C. *The unusual case of Pennsylvania DUI convictions and the right to bear arms in Pennsylvania*

Pursuant to 18 Pa.C.S. §6105(c)(3), "A person who has been convicted of driving under the influence of alcohol or controlled substance as provided in 75 Pa.C.S. §3802 (relating to driving under influence of alcohol or controlled substance) or the former 75 Pa.C.S. §3731, on three or more separate occasions within a five-year period... shall [be restricted]... [from] transfer[ing] or purchas[ing] firearms after the third conviction." If someone is disqualified under this provision, that person may apply to the Court of Common Pleas in the place of the person's current residence to lift this restriction after a period of ten years, not including any time spent in incarceration, has passed since the applicant's most recent conviction.

Practical Legal Tip:

Expungements can be available for more serious crimes *only after* they have been pardoned. Remember, pardons and expungements are two separate and distinct processes. While a pardon can restore your rights, only an expungement can clear your record. After receiving a pardon, one can petition for an expungement, which will get rid of any records of the pardoned offense(s). *-Mike*

CHAPTER TWELVE
I'M BEING SUED FOR WHAT?
CIVIL LIABILITY IF YOU HAVE USED YOUR GUN

I. What does it mean to be sued?

The term "lawsuit" refers to one party's assertion in a written filing with a court that another party has violated the law. In the context of firearms, typically the party suing has been injured and wants a ruling or judgment from the court to that effect that most likely will entitle the person suing to receive money.

A. *What is a civil claim or lawsuit?*

A civil "lawsuit" or "suit" refers to the actual filing of written paperwork with a court (1) asserting that another party violated the law, and (2) seeking some type of redress. A "claim" can exist without the filing of a lawsuit. A claim is simply the belief or assertion that another party has violated the law. Many parties have claims they never assert, or sometimes parties informally assert the claim in hopes of resolving the disputes without the filing of a lawsuit. Also, another term commonly used is "tort" or "tort claim." A tort is a civil claim arising out of a wrongful act, not including a breach of contract or trust, that results in injury to another's person, property, reputation, or the like. The claims described below are all tort claims.

B. *Difference between "civil claims" and "criminal charges"*

To start with the basics, there are two different aspects of the legal system that gun owners may face after the use of a firearm: criminal and civil. There are several names and descriptive terms used for each (*e.g.*, civil lawsuit, criminal actions, civil claims, criminal proceedings, *etc.*), but regardless of the terms, the same breakdown applies. Most cases are either criminal or civil. There is another subgroup of proceedings called administrative actions. Those actions are not covered by this chapter.

With that said, the three primary differences between a criminal action and a civil proceeding are: (1) who or what is bringing the action or lawsuit, (2) what they are seeking, and (3) what is the burden of proof? These differences are fairly straightforward:

1. State versus individual bringing claims

In a criminal case, the party bringing the action is the "sovereign," meaning the United States or the Commonwealth of Pennsylvania believes that a person violated their laws. Even if an individual calls the police, fills out a criminal complaint, or even asks the district attorney to file charges, the party who actually brings a criminal action is the commonwealth, county, *etc.*, not the individual.

However, a civil action may be filed by any individual, business or other entity (partnership, LLC, trust, *etc.*). The entity bringing the claim is called the "plaintiff." Even governmental entities can bring civil claims; *e.g.*, if you negligently shoot a county propane tank causing a fire, the county can sue you civilly for those damages. The typical gun case, though, will involve an individual filing a lawsuit against another individual for damages caused by the firearm. If the incident occurs at a place of business, the plaintiff may also sue the business claiming that it is in some way at fault for the incident. The party being sued is typically called the "defendant."

2. Relief sought/awarded

In a criminal case, the entity prosecuting the case is usually seeking to imprison or fine you. Most crimes are punishable by "X" number or days/months/years in prison or jail, and a fine not to exceed "X" dollars.

By contrast, the plaintiff in the civil case is almost always seeking a monetary award. Several other types of relief are available (declaratory, injunctive, specific performance), but for the most part, gun cases will involve the plaintiff seeking monetary damages.

3. Burden of proof

In a criminal case, the standard is "beyond a reasonable doubt." The trier of fact (usually a jury) must find that no reasonable person could conclude any other way. This is a very high threshold and is difficult to meet. In civil cases, however, a plaintiff must prove a person is liable for damages by a "preponderance of the evidence" standard. A preponderance of the evidence is a much lower standard than the criminal standard of beyond a reasonable doubt. It generally means that the party with the greater weight of credible evidence wins that issue. The preponderance of the evidence has been described as more than half, that is, if the evidence demonstrates that something "more likely occurred than not," this meets the burden of proof. Whereas in a criminal case, if there exists any "reasonable doubt," the burden of proof is not met and there must be an acquittal. It does not mean the party with the most exhibits or greater number of witnesses will prevail. One highly credible witness can prevail over the testimony of a dozen biased, shady witnesses.

Example:

> John mistakes a utility meter reader for a burglar due to his disheveled appearance, tool bag, and because he looks to be snooping around John's house but not trying to gain entry and is in no way posing a threat to John who is safe and away. John fires a shot and injures the meter reader.

Possible criminal liability under these facts: the Commonwealth of Pennsylvania could bring criminal charges against John for a number of crimes (aggravated assault, attempted murder, reckless endangerment of another person, and so forth). The Commonwealth would be seeking to imprison or fine John for his conduct, and it would be required to prove that John committed the crime at issue "beyond a reasonable doubt."

Possible civil liability: the meter reader could also file a civil lawsuit against John alleging that John was at least negligent or committed the torts of assault and battery. The meter reader would seek monetary damages and be required to prove his claims by a "preponderance of the evidence."

C. *Impact of result in one court upon the other*

1. Can a result in a criminal trial be used in a civil trial?

In Pennsylvania, the answer is "it depends." In this context, the courts look to the legal doctrines of *res judicata* and collateral estoppel. These two legal doctrines govern the impact of a ruling or judgment in one case upon a separate case involving the same set of facts and circumstances. For the present discussion, if a person is found guilty of a crime in a criminal proceeding because that court uses a standard of "beyond a reasonable doubt," which is higher than the civil requirement of "preponderance of the evidence," the finding of the criminal court may be used for purposes of establishing civil liability. The way the Supreme Court of Pennsylvania has stated it, if the defendant "has had his day in court and has failed to instill even a reasonable doubt in the collective mind of his then jury" then "[n]o valid reason exists why he should be given a chance to try his luck with another jury." *Hurtt v. Stirone*, 206 A.2d 624, 626-27 (Pa. 1965). Entire chapters in law books have been written on these topics, so, suffice to say, this section is a brief overview of these laws.

A criminal trial resulting in acquittal, however, may be treated differently. Just because a jury has found that the high burden of "beyond a reasonable doubt" was not met does not necessarily mean that the lesser standard of "preponderance of the evidence" (or more likely than not) has not been met. As a result, "Pennsylvania has consistently followed the rule that the criminal judgment is not admissible as evidence to prove that the defendant did not do the act complained ... of ..." *Pennsylvania Tpk. Comm'n v. U.S. Fid. & Guar. Co.*, 194 A.2d 423, 426 (Pa. 1963) (citations omitted).

In Pennsylvania, "convictions and guilty pleas are admissible under the Pennsylvania Rules of Evidence only where used against the guilty party." *LeDonne v. W.C.A.B. (Graciano Corp.),* 936 A.2d 124, 129 (Pa. Cmwlth. 2007).

The criminal concept of *nolo contendere* or "no contest," however, often generates confusion in this area. In a criminal case, a plea of *nolo contendere* or no contest means that the defendant does not admit guilt but does not contest that a jury could find against him or her guilty beyond a reasonable doubt. The plea, however, still results in a judgment that is the equivalent to a finding of guilt of the crime in terms of prior record score and former felon not to possess purposes. However, and importantly, the Pennsylvania Rules of Evidence prohibit the use of a plea of *nolo contendere* as evidence in a subsequent criminal or civil proceeding. Pa.R.E. 410(a)(2). A plea of *nolo contendere* can be used, however, in an administrative proceeding. *See generally, Eisenberg v. Com., Dep't of Pub. Welfare,* 516 A.2d 333 (Pa. 1986).

Example:

> *Phil and Jeremy become involved in a road rage incident and an altercation follows. Phil shoots Jeremy, wounding him. When all is sorted out, Phil is found guilty of aggravated assault and receives punishment from the court (remember, criminal trials use the "beyond a reasonable doubt" standard).*

If Jeremy later sues Phil from the injuries he sustained when Phil shot him, Jeremy, in his civil action, will very likely be allowed to use the finding of guilt in the criminal case (because it used the higher standard of reasonable doubt) to establish his burden in the civil case (the lower preponderance of the evidence standard) that he is owed damages or money in the civil case. This is an example of collateral estoppel. Phil will not be permitted to re-litigate his liability in the civil case.

Both doctrines are based on the concept that a party to a legal proceeding should not be able to endlessly litigate issues that have already been decided by the legal system. At its most basic level, it means that a party to a legal proceeding who receives a final ruling on a particular issue, win or lose, cannot attempt to have another trial court or even the same court decide the same issue.

Note about appeals: this is a different concept than an appeal, or asking the court in the first proceeding to reconsider its ruling, or grant a new trial. An appeal is a request to a higher court to review the decision of a lower court. Likewise, in any given case, the parties will have numerous opportunities to ask the current court to reconsider its rulings, or even ask for a new trial after a trial is completed. Collateral estoppel and *res judicata* come into play after a final judgment that is no longer subject to appeal or revision by the trial court.

Example:
> *Michele is sued for accidentally shooting Nancy. Nancy wins a judgment of $350 against Michele, much less than Nancy believed she was damaged.*

In that case, Nancy can appeal the decision, or even ask the trial court for a new trial. However, Nancy cannot file another, or new, lawsuit regarding the same incident and attempt to recover more in the second case because of the doctrine of *res judicata*. In order for the doctrine to apply, the facts, circumstances and issues must be the same.

Example:
> *James fires his hunting rifle from his deer blind, hitting Peter with one round. Peter files a civil suit against James and loses at trial. The court awards Peter no damages. Peter appeals and loses the appeal also.*

Peter is legally barred from recovering in another lawsuit against James involving the same incident. However, Peter is not barred from filing suit against James for damages arising out of another set of facts and circumstances, for example, if the two are involved in a car wreck on a different day.

2. Civil case result impact on criminal case

Suppose you lose a civil suit and a judgment is entered against you arising out of a shooting incident. Can that judgment be used to establish that you committed a crime? No. The burden of proof is much higher in the criminal context than the civil case. The plaintiff proved his civil case by a "preponderance of the evidence." This does not mean that he proved his case "beyond a reasonable doubt," meaning a separate criminal trial is required to make that determination.

Practical Legal Tip:

While a criminal case requires the government to meet the high burden of "beyond a reasonable doubt," a civil suit only requires the plaintiff to prove a claim by a "preponderance of the evidence" — or more likely than not. One of the best examples of how these standards differ is found in the O.J. Simpson case. In the criminal case, the jury found that the government did not prove "beyond a reasonable doubt" that Simpson was guilty. In the civil lawsuit that followed, however, the jury found that the plaintiffs proved that it was more likely than not that Simpson was liable. -*Mike*

The one area where a civil case can impact a criminal case is the potential overlapping use of evidence and testimony. Your admission in one case can almost always be used against you in another case. Meaning, your sworn testimony in the civil case ("Yes, I shot the guy") can almost always be used against you in the criminal case, and vice versa.

II. What might you be sued for? Gun related claims in civil courts

A. *Liability for unintentional discharge*

This section deals with accidental or unintentional discharges of your firearm. Common unintentional discharges are associated with hunting and cleaning accidents or the mishandling of a weapon. Intentional shootings are addressed in the following section.

With that said, the following are the types of civil claims that may be asserted in connection with an unintentional discharge:

1. Negligence/gross negligence

Most civil cases for damages resulting from an accidental discharge will include a negligence or gross negligence claim. What does this mean and what does a plaintiff have to prove before they can win? Under Pennsylvania law, negligence is defined as the failure to use ordinary care. *Merlini ex rel. Merlini v. Gallitzin Water Auth.*, 980 A.2d 502, 506 (Pa. 2009). That is failure to do that which a person of ordinary prudence would have done under the same or similar circumstances, or doing that which a person of ordinary prudence would not have done under the same or similar circumstances. *Id.* If a person fails to use ordinary care, then they have acted negligently and will be liable for damages resulting from their conduct. "Ordinary care" means that degree of care that would be used by a person of ordinary prudence under the same or similar circumstances. This is an "objective standard," meaning the test is not whether you believed you acted prudently, but whether the judge or jury believes you acted as a person of ordinary prudence would have acted. Of course, this is the definition of negligence in the civil context. There is actually a different definition of criminal negligence, which is beyond the scope of this book's discussion.

What is gross negligence and how is it different than "regular" negligence? Gun cases could potentially include a claim alleging "gross negligence." The primary reason for this is that if a plaintiff establishes gross negligence by a defendant, the plaintiff may be entitled to additional types or amounts of money beyond what is legally available if mere negligence is established. In Pennsylvania, "gross negligence constitutes conduct more egregious than ordinary negligence but does not rise to the level of intentional indifference to the consequences of one's acts." *In re Scheidmantel*, 2005 868 A.2d 464, 485 (Pa. Super. 2005) (quoting *Ratti v. Wheeling Pittsburgh Steel Corporation*, 758 A.2d 695 (Pa.Super. 2000), appeal denied, 785 A.2d 90 (Pa. 2001) (internal quotations omitted).

Pennsylvania law is widely unsettled when it comes to gross negligence. Gross negligence is not a separate cause of action in and of itself in Pennsylvania, however, pertinent allegations of gross negligence may be used to support a claim for punitive damages. *See Fiorentino v. Cabot Oil & Gas Corp.*, 750 F.Supp.2d 506, 513 (M.D.Pa. 2010). In the context of the Mental Health Procedures Act, the Superior Court of Pennsylvania has held that gross negligence is "more than ordinary carelessness, inadvertence, laxity, or indifference." Furthermore, the defendant's actions "must be flagrant, grossly deviating from the ordinary standard of care."

Keeping in mind that Pennsylvania law is widely unsettled when it comes to gross negligence, what are some potential examples of what may constitute gross negligence as opposed to negligence?

Example:

> *Donnie has a Glock 22 that he keeps in his bedroom. It sits in his dresser in a holster. One day, his friend Ned comes over and asks to see the handgun. Donnie retrieves the Glock from his dresser and takes it out of the holster. Pointing it in a safe direction, he racks the slide to clear the chamber. The round in the chamber flies out onto the floor. Unfortunately, Donnie did not release the magazine, so another round was fed into the chamber. Donnie, thinking the gun is now unloaded, turns toward Ned, pointing the barrel towards the floor to let Ned see, but not touch the*

handgun. When they are finished, Donnie picks up the holster to put the gun away. As he attempts to slide the gun into the holster, his finger gets caught on the trigger and the gun fires. The bullet grazes Ned's foot.

Donnie likely breached the standard of care, and in turn, his conduct was likely negligent. Even though Donnie thought the handgun was unloaded, he failed to take certain precautions that a person of ordinary prudence would likely take. He failed to release the magazine and failed to visually inspect the chamber to ensure that it was clear. While he made an effort to point the barrel in a safe direction, he obviously failed to do so as the bullet ultimately struck Ned. Finally, he failed to keep his finger off of the trigger while putting the gun back into the holster.

Consider this situation instead.

Example:

Artie is at a crowded gathering with some friends, and begins to brag about his brand new Smith & Wesson M&P Shield. Artie's friend, Eric, asks about how the Shield feels in the hand. Artie happens to be carrying his Shield inside his waistband with a round in the chamber. Eager to let Eric see for himself, Artie hastily takes the Shield out from his holster with his finger on the trigger and attempts to hand it to Eric. Artie fumbles the gun and accidentally squeezes the trigger, shooting Eric.

Artie's conduct may constitute gross negligence. First, a person of ordinary prudence would not point the barrel of a firearm towards someone or something he or she does not intend to destroy. Artie did just that. Additionally, a person of ordinary prudence would not handle a loaded gun with his finger on the trigger and would not hand a loaded gun to another person. Artie knew the gun was loaded, but handed it to Eric with his finger on the trigger anyway. Because Artie did so many things wrong, a jury could find that Artie's conduct grossly deviated from the standard of care. While

Artie did not intentionally shoot Eric, his breach of the standard of care caused Eric harm.

Ultimately, whether conduct is negligent or grossly negligent will be determined by the jury. As a result, it is impossible to state with absolute certainty whether conduct rises to the level of negligence or gross negligence. However, it is important to understand that if conduct strays too far from the standard of care, it can trigger the additional damages associated with gross negligence.

Pennsylvania law applies differing standards of care depending on the conduct. Accordingly, activities that carry a high degree of risk demand a high degree of care. In other words, "the reasonable man must exercise care in proportion to the danger involved in his act." *Stewart v. Motts*, 654 A.2d 535, 539 (Pa. 1995). Handling firearms, because of their inherent danger, ostensibly requires a high degree of care. As a result, it may not take much to constitute a gross deviation from the high standard of care.

2. Negligent entrustment of a firearm

Pennsylvania recognizes a claim for negligently entrusting (*e.g.,* giving, lending, transferring) a firearm to another person. Under Pennsylvania law, "[i]t is negligence to permit a third person to use a thing . . . which is under the control of the actor, if the actor knows or should know that such person intends or is likely to use the thing or to conduct himself in the activity in such a manner as to create an unreasonable risk of harm to others." *Wittrien v. Burkholder*, 965 A.2d 1229, 1232 (Pa. Super. 2009) (*quoting* Restatement (Second) of Torts, §308).

Example:

> *Shaun lets his adult son Gordon borrow a shotgun to take on a fishing trip because he knows there are water moccasins in the spot where they plan to fish. Gordon has never been in trouble with the law, has repeatedly been trained in firearms safety, and has never had an incident with a gun. However,*

> *while on the trip, Gordon accidentally shoots a fellow fishing buddy with Shaun's shotgun. The fishing buddy, now turned plaintiff, sues Gordon for negligence and Shaun for negligent entrustment of a firearm.*

Can the plaintiff win his claim for negligence? Probably not. Shaun might get sued for giving the shotgun to his son, but the facts described do not meet the elements necessary to establish negligence under Pennsylvania law; and Shaun should prevail in any lawsuit. There are no facts that suggest Gordon would likely act in a way that creates an unreasonable risk of harm to others, or that he intended to do so. Thus, the negligent entrustment claim would likely fail.

Some plaintiffs have urged Pennsylvania appellate courts to adopt a "strict liability" standard when looking at gun cases. In other words, some have argued that guns are inherently dangerous and people who own and/or handle them should be automatically liable for any harm that results, regardless of how careful they may have been. Pennsylvania appellate courts have, to-date, uniformly rejected a strict liability standard. In fact, the Supreme Court of Pennsylvania has recognized that "accidents involving firearms are to be governed not by strict liability principles, but by negligence principles." *Stewart,* 654 A.2d at 539 N. 1.

Although Pennsylvania does not impose strict liability upon gun owners, it does impose an elevated degree of care as discussed above. *See Stewart,* 654 A.2d at 539. Because of the inherent danger associated with firearms, gun owners must be extremely careful in entrusting others with firearms.

3. <u>Is negligent storage of a firearm recognized in Pennsylvania?</u>

A question commonly asked by gun owners is "if someone steals my gun, am I liable if they shoot someone?" In other words, if I store my gun and a criminal or another less-than-responsible person gets the gun, am I liable if they shoot someone? The answer in Pennsylvania is "it depends." Pennsylvania negligence principles are applied to this type of situation, and as discussed earlier, gun owners must exercise an elevated degree of care. Although a gun owner is not necessarily responsible to insure against any and all harm that may result from another's unpermitted misuse of his firearm, it does "impose upon him a very serious and grave responsibility." *Kuhns v. Brugger*, 135 A.2d 395, 403 (Pa. 1957).

In *Kuhns*, a man left a loaded pistol in his bedroom to which his grandchildren had frequent and unrestricted access. One grandchild took the loaded pistol without permission and ultimately shot another grandchild. The injuries rendered the victim severely and permanently disabled.

At trial, the jury found the grandfather liable for damages based upon principles of negligence. The Supreme Court of Pennsylvania upheld the jury's findings. The Court noted the grandfather's duty to exercise an elevated standard of care, that he knew or should have known that his grandchildren could misuse the loaded firearm, and the foreseeable injuries stemming from such misuse. *Kuhns*, 135 A.2d at 403. Furthermore, the Court analyzed the grandfather's liability using the standard of negligent entrustment principles discussed earlier, even though he did not *intentionally* provide the children with access to his firearm. *Id.*

It is less clear whether the same liability could be imposed upon a gun owner for the burglary or theft of a firearm. Due to the elevated degree of care demanded of gun owners, it seems that precautions to prevent theft and ultimate misuse are required to avoid civil liability. Whether this standard of care is met by locking one's doors, using trigger locks, storing firearms in a safe, or all of the above remains unsettled.

As a result, it remains extraordinarily important to exercise the utmost care in the storage of your firearms.

D. *Intentional discharge: a person intended to shoot*
1. Negligence/gross negligence

Just because you intend to shoot someone or otherwise "use" your gun does not necessarily mean that the plaintiff will not assert negligence or gross negligence claims. In other words, you may have fully intended to pull the trigger, but the plaintiff may claim that you were negligent for any number of reasons. For example, you mistook the mailman for a burglar, or the criminal was retreating and you were negligent in using deadly force. The negligence claims, as defined above, can be brought even if you intended to pull the trigger.

2. Assault and battery

If a person has shot at or shot someone, if they are sued, it may include claims for assault and battery. This is an intentional act, not an accident or a claim based on a deviation from a standard of care. An assault is "an act intended to put another person in reasonable apprehension of an immediate battery, and which succeeds in causing an apprehension of such battery." *Cucinotti v. Ortmann*, 159 A.2d 216, 217 (Pa. 1960). This invites the question "what is a battery?" In Pennsylvania, battery is defined as "harmful or offensive contact." *Dalrymple v. Brown*, 701 A.2d 164, 170 (Pa. 1997).

Example:

> *Bill is startled while driving. Martha is standing next to his passenger window at a light screaming that he cut her off in traffic but taking no action to indicate she intends to harm Bill or do anything besides verbally lodge her complaints. In response, Bill points his gun at Martha and says "You're dead!" He fires his gun but misses.*

Bill has committed a civil assault. He took action putting Martha in imminent apprehension of harmful or offensive contact —in this case, death or serious bodily injury— with no legal justification.

Example:

> *Bill is startled while driving. Martha is standing next to his passenger window at a light screaming that he cut her off in traffic but taking no action to indicate she intends to harm Bill or do anything besides verbally lodge her complaints. In response, Bill fires a shot at Martha to make her go away, and hits her in the leg.*

Bill has committed a civil assault *and* battery. In this case, he put Martha in imminent apprehension of harmful or offensive contact and *successfully caused* that harmful contact. Therefore, a civil jury would likely find Bill liable and award damages to Martha.

3. <u>False imprisonment: being sued for detaining people</u>

What if a gun owner detains someone at gun point? If the person who was detained later decides to sue, it will likely include a claim for "false imprisonment." Pennsylvania recognizes a civil claim for false imprisonment. This claim can arise when someone detains persons waiting for police, *e.g.* homeowners detaining burglars, *etc.* However, it can also come up commonly in shoplifting cases (*see* Chapter Seven). The elements of false imprisonment are: (1) the detention of another person, and (2) the unlawfulness of such detention. *Renk v. City of Pittsburgh*, 641 A.2d 289, 293 (Pa. 1994).

Example:

> *Emily fears she is about to be attacked in a grocery store parking lot by Randall. Randall follows her step-by-step through the parking lot and stops right next to Emily's car. Emily draws her .380 and tells Randall to "stay right there while I call the police." Randall complies, and Emily holds him at gunpoint until the police arrive. When the police arrive, they determine that Randall was an out-of-uniform store employee tasked with rounding up the grocery*

> *carts in the parking lot and was no threat to*
> *Emily.*

If a jury determines that Emily acted without justification (*i.e.*, she was not reasonably in fear of death or serious bodily injury or sexual assault or kidnapping), Emily could be civilly liable for falsely imprisoning Randall and owe him damages, if any.

4.   Wrongful death and survival actions

If a person is in the unfortunate position that they have shot and killed another individual and a civil suit occurs because of the shooting, it likely will include claims under Pennsylvania's wrongful death and survival statutes. A wrongful death claim allows the deceased's spouse, children and/or parents to recover damages "for the death of an individual caused by the wrongful act or neglect or unlawful violence or negligence of another." 42 Pa.C.S. §8301. Pennsylvania's survival statute additionally ensures that causes of action survive a person's death. 42 Pa.C.S. §8302. In other words, any independent causes of action (*e.g.* assault, battery, negligence) may be brought even after a person has died.

A wrongful death claim can be proven by establishing that one of the other claims described in this chapter caused the death of another person. In other words, the "wrongful act or neglect or unlawful violence or negligence" needed to establish a wrongful death claim can be established by proving that the defendant was liable for a tort such as battery or negligence and that the tort caused the death of a person. The survival statute permits one to bring claims for those torts following the death of the injured party. If successful, the damages are distributed to the deceased's heirs. In Pennsylvania, these claims must be presented simultaneously to prevent duplicitous recovery.

III. What can the plaintiff recover?

If a person is sued in civil court and the plaintiff convinces a jury that the defendant was liable for damages, what and how much can a plaintiff get? There are scores of cases discussing the details of each category of damages that a plaintiff can recover in a civil lawsuit. The following is a brief description of two very important concepts: (1) "proximate cause," which is essential to recover damages in most circumstances, and (2) the basic types of damages that a plaintiff may typically seek in a gun case.

A. *Proximate cause*

One basic concept that is important to most civil claims and is usually required to recover damages is "proximate cause." Virtually every tort claim will require the plaintiff to prove that his damages were proximately caused by the defendant. "Proximate cause" looks to "whether the defendant's conduct was a 'substantial factor' in producing the injury." *Vattimo v. Lower Bucks Hosp., Inc.*, 465 A.2d 1231, 1233 (Pa. 1983) (citing Restatement of Torts, Second §431 (1965)). This concept has few bright line tests.

For a gun owner, the most obvious cases of proximate cause are pulling the trigger on a firearm and hitting the person or thing at which you aimed. The law will hold that your action proximately caused whatever physical damage the bullet did to persons or property. But what about those circumstances where the use of the gun is so far removed from the damages claimed? This is where the doctrine of proximate cause will cut off liability. If the damage is too far removed from the act, then the act cannot be a proximate cause of that damage. *See Vattimo* 465 A.2d 1231 N. 4.

Example:

> *Anthony is cleaning his AR-15 one night in his apartment and is negligent in his handling of the rifle. He has an unintentional (negligent or accidental) discharge and the bullet goes through the wall of his apartment and strikes his neighbor, Ray, in the leg. Ray, although in massive pain, received prompt medical care from his wife, Gail, and made a speedy recovery.*

If Anthony is later sued by Ray and his wife Gail, Anthony's negligence undoubtedly "proximately caused" damages for things like Ray's medical bills, hospital stay, and perhaps even lost wages. But what if Gail claims that because of her having to treat Ray's wounds that she missed a big job interview and lost out on a big raise in pay and that she wants Anthony to pay that as a component of damages? The law would likely hold that Gail could not recover damages for her lost raise in pay because the loss would not be "proximately caused" by the act being sued for. To put it another way, it is reasonably foreseeable that the negligent discharge of a firearm will cause medical bills and the like for someone struck by a bullet. Therefore, this is recoverable. However, the law would likely say that the loss of a possible job opportunity for the wife who treated the person who was actually shot is not a reasonably foreseeable consequence of negligently discharging a firearm, therefore, was not proximately caused by the act of negligence. In that case, there will be no recovery for the plaintiff, Gail. Proximate cause must be established in every case and may appear to be arbitrary legal line drawing because it is.

As discussed later, Pennsylvania law also recognizes the doctrine that unforeseeable criminal conduct breaks the causal link between an action and a third-party's injuries.

B.   *What types of damages can a plaintiff recover?*
The following is merely a brief snapshot of the types of damages recoverable in a firearms case. To recover any of the damages below, the plaintiff must first prove one of the claims above by a preponderance of the evidence. For example, if the jury determines a defendant was not negligent, a plaintiff cannot recover his or her medical costs, no matter how severe the plaintiff's injuries. Some of the damages a plaintiff can try to recover include:

- Lost Wages
- Medical Costs
- Disability
- Pain & Suffering (Physical, Mental & Emotional)
- Funeral and Burial Costs

- Disfigurement
- Loss of Companionship
- Loss of Household Services
- Lost Future Wages
- Future Medical Costs
- Punitive or exemplary damages (punitive damages are to "punish outrageous and egregious conduct done in a reckless disregard of another's rights . . . a court may award punitive damages only if an actor's conduct was malicious, wanton, willful, oppressive, or exhibited a reckless indifference to the rights of others." *Johnson v. Hyundai Motor America,* 698 A.2d 631, 639 (Pa. Super. 1997).

A court can find the defendant 100% at fault but award no damages because the plaintiff failed to prove damages by a preponderance of the evidence. For example, a plaintiff who seeks reimbursement for medical expenses but has no evidence that they ever went to a doctor or hospital will unlikely be able to recover those medical expenses.

IV. How good are Pennsylvania civil immunity laws for gun owners?

A. *No immunity from lawsuits*

There is a common misunderstanding that there exists a law that if you are legally justified in using your gun then you can't be sued. This is just not the case. First, if a person has the filing fee, anyone can sue anyone else in the Commonwealth of Pennsylvania. There is no one stopping anyone else from filing a lawsuit. Winning a lawsuit is a different issue entirely. If someone files the lawsuit, no matter how frivolous, it still must be dealt with, and it still must be shown to the court that there is a defense that bars this lawsuit. This process can take significant time, money, and legal energy even for the most loser of cases. In short, lawyers get paid and even if you beat the "rap," you still have to take the civil "ride." So, if there is no immunity to lawsuits for gun owners, what protection is there?

Practical Legal Tip:

In Pennsylvania, it only takes the proper paperwork and a filing fee to file a civil lawsuit. The lawsuit need not be based upon a legitimate claim. For instance, a person can file a lawsuit because they don't like somebody's hat. The Defendant (with the annoying hat) must still respond to this lawsuit and raise his defenses in court to have the lawsuit dismissed. No matter how ridiculous you might think a claim is, you must respond! -*Justin*

B. *Beware of the default judgment*

If you're served with a lawsuit, it's important to see an attorney immediately. Just because a lawsuit is ridiculous, or even frivolous, doesn't mean you can just throw it in the garbage. Much like medical issues, the sooner you "catch" a legal problem, the better chance you'll have of dealing with it effectively. When served, you only have a limited time —20 days— to file your responsive pleading. Pa.R.C.P. No. 1026. Failure to do so gives the plaintiff the opportunity to obtain a default judgment. Once the 20-day period has elapsed, the prothonotary can upon request enter default judgment on behalf of the plaintiff so long as the plaintiff provided the defendant with at least 10 days' notice of their intent to file default judgment. Even though the prothonotary will not review the merits of the case, a default judgment is valid and binding just like any other judgment.

A judgment isn't just a piece of paper either. If the defendant doesn't pay in accordance with the order, several bad things can happen. First, the defendant can be held in contempt of court for failing to comply with a court order. The plaintiff will also have other alternatives to collect on the judgment, such as garnishment and levy. Perhaps the least of all, yet still unfavorable, an unsatisfied judgment also has a serious negative impact on a defendant's credit score.

In some situations, it is not too late for the defendant, even if default judgment is entered. A defendant can petition to have the default judgment set aside. For a judge to grant this application, there must be a reasonable explanation or legitimate excuse for the inactivity or delay. Defective service can be a reasonable explanation or legitimate excuse worthy of setting aside a default judgment. For example, if the plaintiff served the wrong guy and the real defendant had no idea that the lawsuit existed, a judge would not be inclined to let the default judgment stand. On the contrary, "the lawsuit was nonsense, so I crumbled it up and threw it in the garbage" is neither a reasonable explanation nor a legitimate excuse.

C.   *Immunity for certain claims*
Most important for gun owners if they find themselves included in a civil suit after a justified use of force will be 42 Pa.C.S. §8340.2.

This section provides that a person who uses force or deadly force that is justified under Chapter 5 of the Pennsylvania Crimes Code is immune from *civil liability* for personal injury or death that results from the defendant's use of force or deadly force, as applicable. This statute does not prevent lawsuits; it just makes the ones filed harder to win. Immunity from liability is an affirmative defense, and, as such, this defense will be considered only after a plaintiff is well into the pain a civil suit may cause an innocent defendant. Immunity from a claim does not mean that a person cannot sue based upon their claim. It means immunity from damages if the defense is proven during the case.

§8340.2. Civil immunity for use of force
   (a) **General rule.**—An actor who uses force:
      (1) in self-protection as provided in 18 Pa.C.S.
      §505 (relating to use of force in self-protection);

> (2) in the protection of other persons as provided in 18 Pa.C.S. §506 (relating to use of force for the protection of other persons);
> (3) for the protection of property as provided in 18 Pa.C.S. §507 (relating to use of force for the protection of property);
> (4) in law enforcement as provided in 18 Pa.C.S. §508 (relating to use of force in law enforcement); or
> (5) consistent with the actor's special responsibility for care, discipline or safety of others as provided in 18 Pa.C.S. §509 (relating to use of force by persons with special responsibility for care, discipline or safety of others);
> is justified in using such force and shall be immune from civil liability for personal injuries sustained by a perpetrator which were caused by the acts or omissions of the actor as a result of the use of force.

Also, note the language in section 8340.2 is "liability for personal injury sustained." While it has not yet been interpreted by the appellate courts, this language could mean that property damage is not covered.

Example:

> John is the victim of a home invasion. He fires several shots at the intruder. The intruder is hit and stopped. One shot, however, misses the intruder and hits a propane tank at the house across the street. The propane tank explodes and burns down the neighbor's home.

The resulting damage to the neighbor's home is not a personal injury sustained. It is unlikely that the immunity statute will provide John with any protection from a civil suit by the neighbor for the damages to the house.

D. _Justification_

All of the justifications under Chapter 5 of the Pennsylvania Crimes Code can also be asserted as affirmative defenses in a civil action. _See generally, Kitay v. Halpern,_ 158 A. 309 (Pa. Super. 1932). This means, for example, if you shoot someone in defense of yourself, others, or your property and are sued as a result, you may assert the applicable sections of the Penal Code as a defense to the civil claims. If the judge or jury agrees that you acted in self-defense, or properly used force to defend others or property, the plaintiff will be barred from recovery. _See_ Chapters Four through Seven of this book.

E. _Statute of limitations for civil claims_

The statute of limitations is a doctrine in Pennsylvania (and almost every other jurisdiction) that requires civil claims to be brought within a certain period of time after the incident. If the claim is not brought within the statute of limitations period, it is barred. There are a number of issues relating to _when_ the statute of limitations starts to run in many cases, but for the most part, limitations will start to run immediately after a shooting incident. The statute of limitations can vary from claim to claim. Most, however, are between one and four years. In Pennsylvania, the limitations period most likely to apply to gun cases is going to be two years. Assault and battery, negligence, wrongful death, and false imprisonment claims all provide two-year limitations periods. 42 Pa.C.S. §5524.

What does this mean for gun owners? If you "use" your gun, the plaintiff must bring a civil suit against you within two years of the incident in almost all cases or else the claim will be barred.

F. _Superseding or intervening criminal conduct_

Pennsylvania law recognizes a doctrine that may absolve someone from responsibility for conduct that might otherwise be a tort (_e.g._, negligence) if a superseding criminal act breaks the causal connection between the tort and the injury. However, while a third party's criminal conduct can be a superseding cause which relieves the negligent actor from liability, this is *not* always the case. The actor's negligence will not be excused where the criminal conduct is a foreseeable result of the actor's negligence. *See Smith v. Cohen, 176 A. 869, 870 (Pa. Super. 1935) ("If an intervening act which ought to have been foreseen contributes to the original negligence, the original wrongdoer will not be excused; his negligence remains the direct cause of the loss.").*

Example:

> *Jeff allows his nephew Randall to use his handgun for protection. Jeff knows Randall has been in trouble with the law repeatedly and has been accused of armed robbery. While Randall has the handgun, his apartment is burglarized and the gun is stolen and used in a crime spree. During the crime spree, Melanie is shot and injured.*

Melanie would not be able to recover from Jeff. Even though Jeff may have been negligent in giving his gun to Randall, the criminal act of burglarizing Randall's apartment and subsequent crime spree were likely superseding causes that broke the link between Jeff's actions and the resulting injuries. Had Randall used the firearm in an armed robbery, this may have been a foreseeable result of Jeff's negligence. However, in this instance, the gun was misused following a random burglary.

G. *Comparative negligence/proportionate responsibility*

Pennsylvania has adopted a modified comparative negligence system by statute. If comparative negligence is applicable and properly raised, either the judge or the jury will be asked to determine the percentage of fault or responsibility of the parties involved in the incident. The damages are then apportioned based upon the percentages assigned by the judge or jury.

Example:

> *Richard is a young adult trick-or-treater. He uses a very realistic fake gun as a part of his costume*

and knocks loudly on Nancy's door at 11:30 p.m. on October 31. Nancy, having forgotten about Halloween as it is 11:30 p.m. and most child trick or treaters are well past visiting, is frightened by the knock, the fake gun, and the late hour of Richard's arrival. She fires through the door, injuring Richard.

In the civil suit filed by Richard against Nancy, the jury will be permitted to consider whether Richard's negligence, if any, contributed to cause the resulting injuries. The jury could determine that Richard was 0% at fault, 100%, or anything in between. By way of example only, if the jury awarded Richard $100,000 in damages, but found he was 30% at fault and Nancy 70%, Richard would only be able to recover $70,000 of his damages.

In Pennsylvania, this rule only applies where the damaged party is 50% or less at fault. If the plaintiff bringing the lawsuit is determined to be more than 50% responsible for the injuries, he or she cannot recover any damages. This can be important for the average gun owner in that a carjacker/home invader/general troublemaker who is the overwhelming cause of an incident cannot recover just because the judge or jury finds you made a slight misstep in defending yourself or your home. This concept is known as modified comparative negligence.

V.   What about third parties?

Pennsylvania law provides a different standard when it comes to injuries to third parties. In this section, a "third party" generally means someone who is not a party to the encounter with the firearm; *e.g.*, bystanders, witnesses, folks nearby who were not the intended target, *etc.*

The Superior Court of Pennsylvania has held that "a person who unintentionally injures a third party bystander while using justifiable force in self-defense [cannot] be *criminally* liable for his injury to the bystander." *Commonwealth v. Fowlin*, 710 A.2d 1130, 1131 (Pa. Super. 1998) (emphasis added).

There is no case law in Pennsylvania directly addressing whether justified use of deadly force that injures a third party carries civil liability. As a result, nothing would prevent an injured third party from bringing a civil claim against a justified shooter.

Claims in this context would realistically be grounded in negligence. Remember that one must exercise an elevated degree of care when handling a firearm. This means that even if you defend yourself, others or property, but you create an unreasonable risk to others in doing so, you can be liable if a third-party is injured.

Example:

> *Mel shoots Anthony as he unlawfully breaks into Mel's occupied home at night. She fires a single shot with her .223 that narrowly misses Anthony but hits a man washing his car down the street.*

Mel is probably not liable to the man down the street, because it does not appear that her conduct unreasonably placed third-parties at risk. But, there is a strong possibility she will have to answer to a civil suit.

Example:

> *Ben is in a crowded movie theater one evening. He has a LTCF and is carrying his Glock 19 in his waistband. Ben has not trained with his handgun on a single occasion since he bought it. Ben has very poor eyesight and left his glasses at home. In fact, that is why Ben is sitting in the front row. To top it off, it is obviously dark in the theater. Suddenly, Anthony storms into the theater with intentions of killing random patrons. He begins to fire shots, when Ben pulls out his Glock 19. Though he cannot see Anthony, Ben fires his*

> *Glock repeatedly in what he believes to be Anthony's general direction until the magazine is empty. Although Ben hits and stops Anthony with the thirteenth shot, he also hit a fleeing elderly woman with shots 3, 4 and 5.*

Ben could possibly be liable to the elderly lady based on negligence principles. Though deadly force against Anthony was justified under the circumstances, he unreasonably placed third-parties at risk by repeatedly firing his weapon in a crowded movie theater without even picking a target. To add to that, he knew that his vision was poor and that he lacked meaningful training.

VI. Traps and spring guns

Pennsylvania governs the use of "devices" to protect land or tangible movable property in 18 Pa.C.S. §507. Use of a device as force to protect property is justified *ONLY IF:*

- the device is not designed to cause —or known to create— a substantial risk of death or serious bodily injury;
- using that kind of device to protect property is reasonable under the circumstances as the actor reasonably believes them to be; *AND*
- the device is customarily used to protect property *OR* the actor takes reasonable care to let the probable intruders know that the device is used.

Therefore, non-lethal devices can be completely permissible in Pennsylvania. However, a "trap" or "spring gun" that discharges a firearm is designed to cause, and is known to cause death or serious bodily injury and is illegal. Basically, any "device" with a loaded firearm capable of discharging will be prohibited by section 507.

What types of "devices" are permitted? Anything not designed to or known to cause death or serious bodily injury, that is reasonable under the circumstances, and that is customarily used to protect property. If it is not customarily used to protect property, the actor must take reasonable care to let the probable intruders know that the device is used.

Examples:

1. *Barbed wire around a business in the warehouse district of town*

Likely permitted. Barbed wire is typically a reasonable security measure, is not designed to or known to cause death or serious bodily injury, and is customarily used to protect property.

2. *Razor wire around a playground across from an elementary school*

Likely unlawful. While probably not designed to cause death, it is arguably unreasonable under these circumstances. In this case, we have a dangerous "device" near an elementary school, particularly around a playground, and it is likely to attract children.

Also, note that the statute addresses providing adequate notice or warning to probable intruders. It *does not* suggest that a warning or notice shields one from liability. Notice, warning, or knowledge of the maintenance of a spring gun or similar device, by the very wording of the statute, does not constitute a defense to a criminal prosecution and is unlikely to shield a person from civil liability for such a device.

VII. Will insurance cover it if I shoot someone?

A. *Homeowner's insurance*

With few exceptions, almost every homeowner's insurance policy excludes coverage for intentional acts. The act of using your firearm in self-defense is almost always an intentional act. You intended to stop the threat. Plaintiffs' attorneys will very likely assert a negligence claim against a homeowner in an attempt to fall within the coverage, but at the end of the day, if the only evidence is that you intentionally shot the plaintiff because you intended to stop a threat, it is likely that any policy with an intentional act exclusion will not provide coverage for any damages awarded.

B. _Auto insurance_

Scores of cases around the country exist where the parties allege that a gun incident is covered by automobile insurance merely because the use of the firearm occurs in the auto or involves an auto. Almost universally, courts have held that these incidents are not covered merely because the discharge occurs in a car or involves a car.

For an injury to fall into coverage, it must generally arise out of the ownership, maintenance or use of the insured's vehicle. Pennsylvania courts have denied coverage for intentional criminal acts unrelated to operation of a motor vehicle. For instance, in one case, a bus driver abused his passengers. In finding that the act was _not_ covered under the auto insurance policy, the Superior Court of Pennsylvania reasoned that "no causal connection exists between the operation [of the vehicle] and the injuries suffered" by its passengers. _See generally, Erie Ins. Exch. v. Claypoole,_ 673 A.2d 348, 356 (1996).

Example:
> _Jeff is cleaning his 9mm handgun in the car. He unintentionally discharges it causing his passenger Edwin severe injuries._

There seems to exist no "causal connection" between the operation of the vehicle and the injuries suffered (a gunshot wound). As a result, this event will almost certainly not be covered by auto insurance.

Example:
> _Jeff discharges his 9mm handgun in the car at Edwin during an attempted carjacking, causing Edwin severe injuries and also hitting a bystander._

Similarly, the gunshot wound does not seem to be sufficiently connected to operation of the vehicle. Accordingly, this event will almost certainly not be covered by auto insurance.

VIII. <u>What civil liability does a person face if their children access their firearms?</u>

A. *<u>Parents are partially responsible for minor children's actions merely because they are parents!</u>*

As a general rule, minors are civilly liable for their own torts (that is, their wrongful actions such as negligence, gross negligence, assault, *etc.*). The mere fact of paternity or maternity does not make a parent totally liable to third parties for the torts of his or her minor children.

Pennsylvania law, however, does impose a degree of financial responsibility on a parent, rendering them partially liable. The law provides that any parent whose child is found liable or is adjudged guilty for a tortious act "shall be liable to the person who suffers the injury *to the extent set forth in this chapter*." 23 Pa.C.S. §5502. What is the "extent" of this liability as noted? A parent's statutory "automatic liability" is limited to (1) $1,000 for injuries suffered by any one person as a result of one tortious act or continuous series of tortious acts or (2) $2,500 regardless of the number of persons who suffer injury as a result of one tortious act or continuous series of tortious acts. 23 Pa.C.S. §5505. A parent will *not* be liable if the parent (1) does not have, and is not entitled to custody of the child, (2) the child is institutionalized, or (3) the child is emancipated.

This particular liability imposed on parents by statute *does not* limit a parent's liability for their role in their child's harmful behavior. Instead, it only provides for a limited amount of "automatic" liability, even if the *parent* didn't necessarily do anything wrong.

B. *<u>Parents who fail to "parent" may become responsible for minor children's actions</u>*

While parents are not automatically liable for the torts of their children, a parent's actions, or failures to act may render him or her liable. As stated by the Supreme Court of Pennsylvania, "[a]lthough a parent/child relationship by itself is insufficient to render the parents liable for the tortious acts of their children, liability may attach where the negligence of the parents makes the injury possible." *K.H. v. J.R.,* 826 A.2d 863, 873 (Pa. 2003).

In this context, a parent has a duty to exercise reasonable care to control a child's conduct when the parent (1) knows or should know of the need to exercise parental control, (2) has the ability to control the child, and (3) has the opportunity to control the child. *K.H. v. J.R.,* 826 A.2d at 874 (quoting *J.H. v. Pellak,* 764 A.2d 64, 68-69).

In other words, a parent must "parent" when appropriate, or face liability! In *K.H. v. J.R.,* a child shot his friend with a BB gun. The injured friend sued the shooter's father, alleging negligence for providing the BB gun. The trial court granted summary judgment for the defendant, finding that the record did not support the plaintiff's claim that the parent was negligent. The court noted that the parent instructed his son on the handling of firearms, he directed that the gun be kept at the parent's home, and had taken his son to and completed a gun safety course. *K.H. v. J.R.,* 826 A.2d at 867. Although the Supreme Court of Pennsylvania's evaluation focused on the "ability" and "opportunity" requirements, it ultimately found that summary judgment on the defendant's behalf to be proper.

Example:
> *Jon, your 17-year-old son, has been hunting since he was 11. You have taught him the principles of firearm safety and have taken him to several firearms training courses.*

If you take Jon hunting and for some reason Jon accidentally discharges his shotgun, injuring another person, it is unlikely that you, the parent, will be civilly liable for an accident that occurs while hunting. Like the parent in *K.H. v. J.R.,* you took affirmative steps to prevent unreasonable risks.

Example:

> *Gordon, your 12-year-old son, has never handled a gun or taken a firearms training course. You decide to take him to the range for the first time, but you are both asked to leave the range after Gordon repeatedly fires into the ceiling and the floor. Fed up, you take Gordon to another range with no additional instruction or training.*

If Gordon shoots and injures someone at the second range, it is likely that you will be liable because you allowed him to act in a manner likely to harm another, and you did not restrain him despite his dangerous conduct. You knew of Gordon's lack of training. Furthermore, you knew or at least should have known that a risk existed because of Gordon's previous conduct. Instead of using your ability and opportunity to control Gordon, prohibiting him from shooting without additional training, you brought him to continue to engage in unreasonably dangerous conduct.

CHAPTER THIRTEEN
BEYOND FIREARMS:
KNIVES, CLUBS, AND TASERS

I. Introduction

In addition to Pennsylvania's many firearms laws, there also exist state laws governing the possession and use of "other weapons." This includes any object that is not a firearm, but could be used as a weapon. This chapter will briefly discuss the laws governing these other weapons, including the various restrictions Pennsylvania law places on these weapons.

II. Prohibited offensive weapons

A. *What is a prohibited offensive weapon?*

Section 908 of the Pennsylvania Crimes Code is entitled "Prohibited Offensive Weapons." It states that it is a misdemeanor of the first degree if a person "except as authorized by law … makes repairs, sells, or otherwise deals in, uses, or possesses any offensive weapon." 18 Pa.C.S. §908. It is important to note that a Pennsylvania License to Carry Firearms does *not* cover weapons other than firearms. For more on what is, and is not covered by a Pennsylvania License to Carry Firearms, *see* Chapter Nine.

The following are classified as "prohibited offensive weapons" under section 908:

- a bomb
- a grenade
- a machine gun
- a sawed-off shotgun with a barrel less than 18 inches
- a firearm specially made or specially adapted for concealment or silent discharge
- any blackjack
- any sandbag
- metal knuckles
- a dagger

- a knife, razor or cutting instrument, the blade of which is exposed in an automatic way by switch, push-button, spring mechanism, or otherwise
- any stun gun, stun baton, taser or other electronic or electric weapon
- any other implement for the infliction of serious bodily injury which serves no common lawful purpose

As opposed to many laws which merely prohibit the *carrying* of a weapon in a public place, this section of the Crimes Code prohibits a person from even *possessing* such a weapon—including in their home or on any property under their control or influence if an exception does not apply.

B. *Defenses*

The law provides that certain defenses exist to the prohibitions on prohibited offensive weapons. However, the statute also provides that it is the defendant's burden to prove that these defenses apply "by a preponderance of the evidence." As discussed in Chapter Twelve, this means that the defendant must prove that it is more likely than not that his conduct met the requirements of the defense. Consequently, these defenses do not act as a bar to prosecution.

If a person "possessed or dealt with the weapon solely as a curio or in a dramatic performance" it is a defense to the crime defined in section 908. There are no appellate cases clarifying what is meant by "curio" or what qualifies as a "dramatic performance." Accordingly, it is important to be extra cautious if relying upon one of these defenses.

It also a defense that, "with the exception of a bomb, grenade or incendiary device, the person complied with the National Firearms Act." 18 Pa.C.S. §908. As a practical matter, it may be less difficult to prove compliance with the National Firearms Act (NFA) than proving participation in a theatrical performance or possession as a curio. Because the NFA requires specific documentation to evidence compliance (tax stamps), these documents should suffice as proof. This is just another reason why it is important to keep copies of this documentation available when possessing items subject to the NFA. It is vital to note once again that this defense does *not* apply to a bomb, grenade or incendiary device under Pennsylvania law.

Finally, that same statute provides a defense for a person who shows that he "possessed it briefly in consequence of having found it or taken it from an aggressor, or under circumstances similarly negativing any intent or likelihood that the weapon would be used unlawfully." There is no authoritative Pennsylvania case law addressing brief possession of a prohibited offensive weapon after finding it or having taken it from an aggressor. The Superior Court of Pennsylvania has, however, found possession in and of itself to be sufficient to establish intent that the weapon would be used unlawfully. *See Commonwealth v. Karlson*, 674 A.2d 249, 253 (Pa. Super. 1996); *Commonwealth v. Gatto,* 344 A.2d 566 (Pa. Super. 1975). As a result, this provision *should not* be construed to permit possession of prohibited offensive weapons as long as no criminal intent exists.

C. *Specific prohibited offensive weapons*
   1. Unregistered NFA Items, Bombs, Grenades, Incendiary Devices

Section 908 also prohibits the following weapons and devices which are discussed in greater detail in Chapter Fourteen, "National Firearms Act." While possession of the following items are generally prohibited, Pennsylvania law provides a defense if the person complied with the National Firearms Act (NFA):

- a machine gun
- a sawed-off shotgun with a barrel less than 18 inches
- a firearm specially made or specially adapted for concealment or silent discharge

While compliance with the NFA is a defense for possessing the items above, it specifically does not apply to bombs, grenades, or incendiary devices. Consequently, possession of a bomb, grenade or incendiary device is absolutely prohibited. The Superior Court of Pennsylvania has specifically deemed a "pipe bomb" a prohibited offensive weapon, even if the parts viewed separately serve a common lawful purpose. *Commonwealth v. Devlin*, 448 A.2d 594, 597 (Pa. Super. 1982).

2. Blackjacks

Under section 908, blackjacks are specifically classified as a prohibited offensive weapon. The statute does not define "blackjack" nor have the Pennsylvania appellate courts provided guidance as to what qualifies as a blackjack.

Classic Blackjack

a. *Exemptions for blackjacks*

Section 908 provides specific exemptions to the prohibitions on blackjacks. They apply to certain officials in the scope of their duties. The prohibitions applicable to blackjacks do *not* apply to the following persons in the course of official duties:

(1) Police officers, as defined by and who meet the requirements of the act of June 18, 1974 (P.L. 359, No. 120), referred to as the Municipal Police Education and Training Law. (2) Police officers of first class cities who have successfully completed training which is substantially equivalent to the program under the Municipal Police Education and Training Law.

(3) Pennsylvania State Police officers.

(4) Sheriffs and deputy sheriffs of the various counties who have satisfactorily met the requirements of the Municipal Police Education and Training Law.

(5) Police officers employed by the Commonwealth who have satisfactorily met the requirements of the Municipal Police Education and Training Law.

(6) Deputy Sheriffs with adequate training as determined by the Pennsylvania Commission on Crime and Delinquency.

(7) Liquor Control Board agents who have satisfactorily met the requirements of the Municipal Police Education and Training Law.

3. Sandbags

If Pennsylvania once had issues with criminals misusing sandbags, it appears that this is no longer the case. There is no case law discussing the possession of a sandbag as a prohibited offensive weapon. Furthermore, one would be hard pressed to find any examples of offensive uses of sandbags. Nevertheless, they remain on the list of prohibited offensive weapons in Pennsylvania, and are therefore illegal. Want to know what a sandbag is? So do we!

4. Metal Knuckles

Metal knuckles are a prohibited offensive weapon under 18 Pa.C.S. §908. The law does not specifically define what items constitute "metal knuckles." The common use of "metal knuckles" typically refers to "brass knuckles." However, the statute covers more than just "brass knuckles." So the use of a metal other than brass will not render the item legal.

Traditional "Metal Knuckles"

5. Daggers

Daggers expressly qualify as prohibited offensive weapons under section 908. There is no Pennsylvania appellate case law interpreting what is, or is not a dagger. Moreover, the statute does not define dagger. Other states have defined the term "dagger" differently, and until Pennsylvania courts interpret this term, there is no possible way to give a clear definition. It is important to note that although some states require a blade to be double-edged in order to qualify as a dagger, others define "dagger" more broadly. California, for instance, defines it as an *"instrument with or without a handguard that is capable of ready use as a stabbing weapon ..."* Cal. Penal Code §11164. Accordingly, it is best to use extreme caution with any item that may be potentially construed as a dagger.

Dagger

6. Knives, razors or cutting instruments, the blade of which is exposed in an automatic way by switch, push-button, spring mechanism, or otherwise

People use knives on a daily basis for normal everyday activities such as cooking and opening boxes. They aren't *all* illegal. What is an illegal knife? Under section 908 a knife, razor or cutting instrument is a prohibited offensive weapon if the blade is exposed automatically. The statute specifically notes automatic blades that use switches, push-buttons and spring mechanisms, but includes the catch-all phrase "or otherwise." Therefore, the fact that a mechanism opens it automatically seems to be determinative. The specific *kind* of mechanism that allows it to open automatically is not necessarily relevant.

What is a blade that is *not* exposed "automatically?" The Superior Court of Pennsylvania has recognized that "the key" is that the blade has to be "manually exposed." *Commonwealth v. Ashford*, 397 A.2d 420, 422 (Pa. Sup. 1979). In that case, the Superior Court found that a knife with a blade exposed by a flick of the wrist is *not* a prohibited offensive weapon. *Id.* While it seems that knives requiring physical effort to bring a knife from its natural closed state fall outside of the "automatic" exposure category. In light of the little guidance we have from the Pennsylvania appellate courts, however, it is extremely important to be careful not to run afoul of the prohibition on blades that are automatically exposed. Specifically, spring assisted knives are allowed.

It is important to note that some knives, even if not automatically exposed, may be prohibited if they are technically "daggers" or if they serve no common lawful purpose. For more on these classifications, *see* sections II C(5) & C(8) of this chapter.

Local governments that prohibit the public carry of knives
At the time of publication, ordinances prohibiting knives are not expressly preempted in Pennsylvania. There have been efforts by the General Assembly to relax knife laws, and even remove them altogether from Pennsylvania law. However, to date, no substantial change has proven successful. Furthermore, local governments are not expressly forbidden from enacting and upholding knife laws, and many have done so.

i. Philadelphia

Philadelphia has its own ordinance restricting the use and possession of knives. In fact, the Philadelphia law on knives is about as restrictive as the mind can imagine. The restriction on knives in Philadelphia reads, in pertinent part, as follows:

> Prohibited Conduct. No person shall use or possess any cutting weapon upon the public streets or upon any public property at any time. Philadelphia City Ordinance §10-820.

The prohibitive language in and of itself, however, does not begin to encompass the coverage of this prohibition. Let us look to the definition of "cutting weapon":

> Cutting Weapon. Any knife or other cutting instrument which can be used as a weapon that has a cutting edge similar to that of a knife. No tool or instrument commonly or ordinarily used in a trade, profession or calling shall be considered a cutting weapon while actually being used in the active exercise of that trade, profession or calling. Id.

Including "any knife or other cutting instrument," the definition seemingly includes any and all sharp objects. Furthermore, the exception only includes tools or instruments commonly or ordinarily used in a trade, profession or calling *while actually being used in the active exercise of that trade, profession or calling.* In other words, if the object is not being used for a specific "common" purpose, it is illegal! It is difficult, and perhaps impossible to understand where the line is drawn in this definition. When a person is at a cash register purchasing ordinary cutting objects such as knives or scissors, they are not using the item for the "common purpose" at that time. Similarly, one is not using these objects for a "common purpose" when transporting the items from one place to another. Although these conclusions seem absurd, they are the results necessarily drawn by a plain reading of the ordinance. As a result, a person must be extremely cautious when traveling to or through Philadelphia with any and all sharp objects!

Like some other local governments in Pennsylvania, Philadelphia additionally prohibits the "[sale], offer for sale or carry [of] any knife with a blade which is released by a spring mechanism including knives known as 'switchblades.'" *Id.*

ii. *Township of Abington*
Like Philadelphia, the Ordinances of the Township of Abington §83-6 prohibit the sale, offering for sale, or possession of "any knife

where the blade is released by a spring mechanism, including knives known as 'switchblades.'"

iii. *Township of Haverford*

Similarly, the Ordinances of the Township of Haverford contain the same prohibition in §83-6.

iv. *Township of West Lampeter*

In the Township of West Lampeter, local ordinances §278-1, prohibit the sale, offering for sale, possession with intent to sell, or possession with intent to use a "switchblade knife, the blade of which can be opened or released by mechanical means, or any similar device or devices."

v. *City of Coatesville*

The Ordinances of the City of Coatesville §112-1, prohibit the sale, offering for sale, possession with intent to sell, or possession with intent to use a "switchblade knife, the blade of which can be opened or released by mechanical means, or any similar device or devices."

vi. *Township of Warwick*

The Ordinances of the Township of Warwick §131-3, prohibit the possession of "any type of weapon, including but not limited to firearms, knives, archery bows, *etc.*" in its parks.

vii. *Township of Lower Makefield*

The Township of Lower Makefield prohibits, by ordinance §141-26, the possession of "any type of hatchet, ax, saw or knife while within the park system."

viii. *Township of Bristol*

Under the Bristol Township Code of Ordinances §140-4, the use of any "Oriental ninja or stars, wrist rockets, slingshots, fireworks, flare guns, knives or other contraband is strictly prohibited."

ix. *Bucks County*

Ordinance 95, §31 of Bucks County prohibits possession of "any type of knife, hatchet or ax in any area of the park except for those park users camping in campsites."

7. *Stun guns, stun batons, tasers or other electronic or electric weapons*

Section 908 imposes a general prohibition on stun guns, stun batons, tasers or other electronic or electric weapons. Section 908.1, however, clarifies the laws of electric or electronic incapacitation devices. The law makes it a crime to (1) use an electric or electronic incapacitation device on another person for an unlawful purpose, or (2) possess an electric or electronic incapacitation device with the intent to use it on another person for an unlawful purpose.

The law specifically provides that an electronic incapacitation device can be lawfully possessed for self-defense purposes (as defined in section 5 of the Pennsylvania Crimes Code) if the electric or electronic incapacitation device is labeled with or accompanied by clearly written instructions as to its use and the damages involved in its use. Interestingly, Pennsylvania provides no minimum age requirement when it comes to electronic incapacitation devices.

Remember that as a general proposition, force must be necessary and proportional to be justified. It is possible that the improper use of an incapacitation device could result in excessive use of force under the circumstances, which would strip the user of an otherwise available justification. The requirement for written instructions facilitates the use of "proportional" force in self-defense. However, it remains the user's responsibility to use force that is appropriate under the circumstances.

The term "electric or electronic incapacitation device" is defined as:

> [A] portable device which is designed or intended by the manufacturer to be used, offensively or defensively, to temporarily immobilize or incapacitate persons by means of electric pulse or current, including devices operating by means of carbon dioxide propellant.

18 Pa.C.S. §908.1(f).

This definition specifically excludes "cattle prods, electric fences or other electric devices when used in agricultural, animal husbandry or food production activities." *Id.*

Handheld "StunGun"   Cartridge Taser

Under Pennsylvania law, those who are prohibited from possessing firearms under state law are also prohibited from possessing electronic incapacitation devices. As a result, electronic incapacitation devices are *not* legal alternatives for those prohibited from possessing firearms under 18 Pa.C.S. §6105. For more on those prohibited from possessing firearms, *see* Chapter Three.

Many people ask whether one can legally possess a taser in Pennsylvania. Although tasers look like firearms, they do not meet the restrictive definition of a "firearm" found in the Pennsylvania Uniform Firearms Act. Furthermore, they do not meet the broader definition provided by some specific parts of the Uniform Firearms Act or federal law because they do not expel projectiles "by the action of an explosive."

Keep in mind, because tasers are not firearms, they are not protected by the safe passage provision of 18 U.S.C. §926A. As a result, it is extremely important to know the laws covering tasers when traveling out of state.

Practical Legal Tip:

Keep in mind that tasers are *not* firearms! Some of the protections we get for firearms (*e.g.* "federal safe passage") do not apply to tasers. However, those who are prohibited from possessing firearms under Pennsylvania law are also prohibited from possessing tasers! -*Mike*

The City of Philadelphia has a specific prohibition on electronic incapacitation devices, or as they call them, "stun guns." Under Philadelphia City Ordinance §10-825, "No person shall own, use, possess, sell or otherwise transfer any 'stun gun'." The ordinance defines the term "stun gun" as "[a]ny device which expels or projects a projectile which, upon coming in contact with a person, is capable of inflicting injury or an electric shock to such person," which would include the weapon commonly known as a taser. As discussed above, tasers are not "firearms," so one must be careful even when traveling through Philadelphia while possessing a taser or stun gun.

8. _Any other implement for the infliction of serious bodily injury which serves no common lawful purpose_

Finally, we have the "catch-all" provision provided in section 908. Under this provision, certain items may be "prohibited offensive weapons" even if they are not specifically mentioned by statute. In other words, even if the law doesn't overtly prohibit a specific item by name, it may still be illegal to possess that item under section 908.

The Pennsylvania Courts have wrestled with how to approach this broad and vague prohibition. There is no bright line test as to whether an object serves a "common lawful purpose." There exists no book of items that serve a common lawful purpose, and there is no answer to *how common* the lawful purpose must be. Just how many people must use the item in that manner, and how often must they use it? Due to the malleability of this prohibition, the outcome of a case will likely depend on how an attorney fashions his or her argument to prove that an item serves a common lawful purpose. The Superior Court of Pennsylvania has made clear that there is "no need to consider the particular circumstances of the case" when determining whether an object has a "common lawful purpose." *Commonwealth v. Karlson*, 674 A.2d 249, 251 (Pa. Super. 1996). Instead, the Superior Court held that "common lawful purpose" should be interpreted in a reasonable and commonsense manner.

Practical Legal Tip:

What is a lawful weapon may depend on how the lawyer marshals the facts to prove that it has a common lawful purpose (or really, from preventing the Commonwealth from proving that it does not have a common lawful purpose). Where was it bought? Can you buy it in a retail store in the Commonwealth? In what section? These will prove to be relevant factors in such an argument. *-Justin*

a. *Items found to have no common lawful purpose*

Although as discussed above, there is no bright line test for "common lawful purpose," Pennsylvania courts have found that the following items, in the following cases, have no common lawful purpose.

The Superior Court of Pennsylvania found there was sufficient evidence to conclude that the "Guard Father," a six-inch cylindrical steel shaft, served no common lawful purpose. As a result, this was classified as a prohibited offensive weapon. *Commonwealth v. Hitchon*, 549 A.2d 943, 948 (Pa. Super. 1988).

Similarly, in *Commonwealth v. Walton*, the Superior Court found that a cane sword (a cane incorporating a concealed blade) serves no common lawful purpose. *Commonwealth v. Walton*, 380 A.2d 1278 (Pa. Super. 1977).

Recently, the Superior Court of Pennsylvania found that "a knife in a sheath that could be locked in a 90–degree position as well as in a straight position" had no common lawful purpose. *Commonwealth v. Lawson*, 977 A.2d 583, 583 (Pa. Super. 2009).

Although not binding on all Pennsylvania Courts, the United States District Court of the Western District of Pennsylvania concluded that the following items were properly confiscated as prohibited offensive weapons under section 908: slim jims, clubs, socks filled with glass bottles, and a sawed-off baseball bat. *Erret v. Com. of Pa.*, 713 F. Supp. 837, 843 (W.D. Pa. 1989).

b. *Items that may have a common lawful purpose*

The Superior Court of Pennsylvania has found that nunchaku sticks do serve a common lawful purpose. *Commonwealth v. Adams*, 369 A.2d 479, 480 (Pa. Super. 1976). The Court reasoned that "a student or instructor of the martial arts would have occasion to use the nunchaku in the peaceful practice of karate exercises. The martial arts are practiced by many citizens of this Commonwealth as a sport and an exercise." *Id.* at 482.

In *Commonwealth v. Karlson*, the Superior Court found that *the prosecution failed to prove* that a Cobra Knife serves no common awful purpose, noting the defendant's daily use of the tool in his line of work. 674 A.2d 249, 251 (Pa. Super. 1996).

Similarly, in *Commonwealth v. Artis,* in question was a six-inch knife purchased "at a sporting goods store, to use for hunting and fishing." 418 A.2d 644, 645 (Pa. Super. 1980). The Superior Court refused to evaluate the knife in the context that defendant used it, but rather looked to its common lawful purpose: hunting and fishing.

Along the same lines, according to the Supreme Court of Pennsylvania, a Wyoming Knife (a metal handle, with two finger holes, which incorporates two cutting blades, one facing outward, the other inward) is "a hunting implement which has common lawful purpose." *Commonwealth v. Fisher,* 400 A.2d 1284, 1288 Pa. 1979).

For obvious reasons, and due to clear common lawful purposes, the prohibitions of section 908 "[do] not encompass a simple kitchen knife." *Commonwealth v. Cartagena,* 393 A.2d 350, 362 Pa. 1978).

Finally, truly exemplifying the "common lawful purpose" analysis, in *Commonwealth v. Myers*, the defendant charged down the street with a thirteen-inch butcher knife threatening to kill somebody. 417 A.2d 700, 701 (Pa. Super. 1980). The Superior Court of Pennsylvania found that "[t]he 13 inch butcher knife which appellant possessed in the instant case had a common, lawful purpose. Thus, although another section of the Crimes Code may have been violated, section 908(c) was not violated." *Id.*

Pennsylvania courts evaluate whether the object itself has a common lawful purpose. The analysis does not evaluate whether the object was used for that purpose at the relevant time. Similarly, it does not examine whether an item has some conceivable, yet uncommon, lawful purpose. With the lack of clear and defining guidelines, it is important to exercise caution to avoid possession of prohibited offensive weapons!

CHAPTER FOURTEEN
SUPPRESSORS, SHORT-BARRELED WEAPONS, AND MACHINE GUNS: THE NATIONAL FIREARMS ACT

Can an individual in Pennsylvania legally own a suppressor (sometimes called a silencer), short-barreled shotgun, short-barreled rifle, or machine gun? Yes, if all NFA regulations are satisfied. This chapter deals with the laws regarding the possession and use of firearms that are subject to the provisions of the National Firearms Act (NFA) codified in 26 U.S.C. Chapter 53, specifically, silencers, short-barreled firearms, machine guns, and firearms that are otherwise illegal. These firearms are illegal to purchase or possess without possessing the proper paperwork and a "tax stamp." In this chapter, we will discuss the history and the practical aspects of the NFA, what firearms are regulated by the NFA, as well as the process and procedure for legally possessing weapons that are subject to the NFA's provisions.

I.   What is the National Firearms Act?
The National Firearms Act (NFA) was enacted in 1934 in response to media sensationalizing gangster crimes. Prior to the NFA's passage, at the federal level, any person over 18 could buy a machine gun at a store or even through the mail. Before the NFA, as far as federal authorities were concerned, nothing prevented someone from shortening the barrel on their rifle or shotgun. President Roosevelt pushed for the passage of the NFA in an attempt to diminish a gangster's ability to possess and carry supposedly inherently dangerous and/or easily concealable firearms, such as machine guns and short-barreled rifles and shotguns.

NFA is firearms regulation using a registration and tax requirement
The NFA requires both the registration of and tax on the manufacture and transfer of certain firearms. The law created a tax of $200 on the transfer of the following firearms: short-barreled shotguns, short-barreled rifles, machine guns, suppressors

(silencers), and destructive devices. The tax is only $5 for firearms that are classified as "Any Other Weapons" or AOWs. Back in 1934, a $200 tax was the approximate equivalent to about $3,500 today!

Five years after the NFA's passage, the Supreme Court held in *United States v. Miller* that the right to bear arms can be subject to federal regulation. Miller defended himself against the United States government by stating that the NFA infringed upon his Constitutional right to bear arms under the Second Amendment. While the Court agreed that the Constitution does guarantee *a right* to bear arms, it held that the right does not extend to every firearm. *See United States v. Miller*, 307 U.S. 174 (1939).

II. What firearms does the NFA regulate?
A. *Short-barreled rifles and shotguns*
In order to be legal, short-barreled shotguns and rifles must be registered, and a tax must be paid on the firearm. What is a short-barreled shotgun? Under federal law, short-barreled shotguns have one or more barrels less than 18 inches in length and the overall length of the shotgun is less than 26 inches. What is a short-barreled rifle? It is any rifle with one or more barrels less than 16 inches in length, and the overall length of the rifle is less than 26 inches. *See* 27 CFR §478.11.

Short-barreled shotguns and rifles may be purchased from an FFL that deals in NFA items. The FFL must have what is referred to as a Special Occupational Taxpayers (SOT) license. Also, short-barreled firearms are very popular for individuals to build and/or modify on their own. This is legal if the person has properly registered the firearm to be modified into a short-barreled firearm with the ATF and paid the tax *before* it is modified. Once approved, a person may alter or produce a short-barreled firearm and must engrave legally required information on the receiver of the firearm such as manufacturer, location, *etc. See* discussion later in this chapter for detailed requirements.

B. *Machine guns*

If the requirements of the NFA are satisfied, machine guns may be legally owned by individuals or other legal entities (such as trusts or corporations), under certain circumstances.

First, what is a machine gun? Federal law defines a machine gun as "any weapon which shoots, is designed to shoot, or can be readily restored to shoot, automatically more than one shot, without manual reloading, by a single function of the trigger. The term shall also include the frame or receiver of any such weapon, any part designed and intended solely and exclusively, or combination of parts designed and intended, for use in converting a weapon into a machine gun, and any combination of parts from which a machine gun can be assembled if such parts are in the possession or under the control of a person." 27 CFR §478.11. This includes three burst fire weapons, but not bump fire weapons. As a result of this definition, the individual metal components that make up a whole machine gun, such as a full-auto sear, individually meet the federal definition of machine gun. The parts for the machine gun do not have to be assembled to constitute a machine gun.

No new manufacturing of machine guns for private ownership

With the passage of the Firearm Owners' Protection Act of 1986 (FOPA), which created section 922(o), the only machine guns available for private, non-FFL07 ownership are limited to the legally registered machine guns that existed prior to May 19, 1986. Thus, the private market is very limited and prices, as a result, are very high. If a person is an FFL07/SOT02, there is a provision for making (with filing an ATF form 2 within 24 hours of 80% construction) and transferring post-ban machine guns. When created, the post-ban machine gun can only be sold to a law enforcement agency or to another SOT02/SOT03 with a demonstration letter.

C. *Firearm suppressors*

What is a suppressor? It is just a muffler for a firearm. It reduces the noise (called the report) of the firearm. It does not eliminate it.

Buying and owning a suppressor is legal if all NFA requirements are met. It is an easy process that takes time. In legal terms, a firearm suppressor is defined in 27 CFR §478.11 as "any device for silencing, muffling, or diminishing the report of a portable firearm, including any combination of parts, designed or redesigned, and intended for use in assembling or fabricating a firearm silencer or firearm muffler, and any part intended only for use in such assembly or fabrication."

Firearm suppressors are very practical instruments. They are great for hunting and recreational shooting not only because it suppresses gunshots in a way so as to not alarm other animals being hunted nearby, but also because it lessens the impact on the shooter's ears. However, firearms owners should be carefully aware that the definition of a suppressor is very broad under federal law. Suppressors do not need to be items manufactured specifically for use as a suppressor. There are some ordinary, everyday items that could be easily converted into a suppressor such as a water bottle or an automotive oil filter. Possession of otherwise legal items when used or modified to be used as a suppressor is illegal.

D. *Destructive devices*

The term "destructive device" (DD) is a legal term given to certain firearms, objects, and munitions that are illegal under the NFA. There is a very important distinction under Pennsylvania law when it comes to DDs. Remember, just because it is permissible under Federal law, does not necessarily mean it is allowed under Pennsylvania state law.

First, we will turn to federal law.

> ### Destructive Devices – Part A;
> ### 27 C.F.R. §478.11
>
> Any explosive, incendiary, or poison gas (1) bomb, (2) grenade, (3) rocket having a propellant charge of more than 4 ounces, (4) missile having an explosive or incendiary charge of more than one-quarter ounce, (5) mine, or (6) device similar to any of the devices described in the preceding paragraphs of this definition.

> ### Destructive Devices – Part B;
> ### 27 C.F.R. §478.11
>
> Any type of weapon (other than a shotgun or shotgun shell which the Director finds is generally recognized as particularly suitable for sporting purposes) by whatever name known which will, or which may be readily converted to, expel a projectile by the action of an explosive or other propellant, and which has any barrel with a bore of more than one-half inch in diameter.

> ### Destructive Devices – Part C;
> ### 27 C.F.R. §478.11
>
> Any combination of parts either designed or intended for use in converting any destructive device described in [part] (A) and (B) of this section and from which a destructive device may be readily assembled.

The "destructive devices" as defined and interpreted by the federal authorities are effectively broken down into three categories: explosive devices, large caliber weapons, and parts easily convertible into a destructive device.

The first portion of the definition of a destructive device concerns explosive, incendiary, and poison gas munitions. The definition designates that any explosive, incendiary, or poison gas bomb, grenade, mine or similar device is a destructive device. In addition, the definition includes a rocket having a propellant charge of more than four ounces and a missile (projectile) having an explosive or incendiary charge of more than one-quarter ounce. These topics and the regulations thereof are beyond the scope of this book's discussion. However, the reader should be aware that as of the time of the writing of this chapter there is significant federal activity in re-classifying by certain previously permissible 40mm grenade launcher rounds such as parachute flares and chalk practice rounds.

The second section of the definition addresses large caliber weapons and states that any type of weapon that has a bore diameter of *more than one-half inch* in diameter is a destructive device with the exception of shotguns (and shotgun shells) that are suitable for sporting purposes. Thus, any caliber in a rifle or handgun more than 0.5 inches or above a fifty caliber rifle is classified as a destructive device. Shotguns are exempt from this prohibition on size *unless* the ATF rules it is not for "sporting purposes." How do you know if a shotgun is suitable for sporting purposes? The ATF keeps a list, and has issued rulings classifying specific shotguns as destructive devices because they are not considered to be particularly "suitable for sporting purposes" including the USAS-12, Striker-12, Streetsweeper, and 37/38mm Beanbags. The ATF does not provide any specific definition of what constitutes being "suitable for sporting purposes" nor does it specify the methodology in which it determines what makes a particular shotgun suitable for sporting purposes. Ultimately, one will have to check with the ATF lists to see whether a particular shotgun with a larger bore-diameter is classified as a destructive device or not.

Finally, a destructive device does not need to be a completed and assembled product to fall under the federal definition and regulation under the NFA. Much like machine guns, if a person possesses parts that can be readily assembled into a destructive device, then whether or not the device has actually been constructed is irrelevant—by law it's already a destructive device.

Although these firearms, munitions, and devices are prohibited by the law on its face pursuant to the NFA, on a federal level a person may nevertheless receive permission to possess them so long as they possess the correct legal authorization and the $200 tax stamp.

<u>Pennsylvania law is stricter than federal law</u>
It is with DDs where Pennsylvania law differs from NFA regulations. As mentioned above, there are large bore NFA items and explosive, incendiary, and poison gas munitions covered under the NFA. If all federal requirements are met, then a large bore NFA item may be owned in Pennsylvania. However, explosive, incendiary, and poison gas munitions that are covered under the NFA are not legal to own in Pennsylvania even if allowed under the NFA. *See* 18 Pa.C.S. §908.

E. *"Any Other Weapons" or AOWs*
The AOW category under the NFA pertains to firearms and weapons that may not fit the traditional definition of some of the

firearms discussed elsewhere in this book due to the way in which they are manufactured or modified. Under federal law, an AOW is "any weapon or device capable of being concealed on the person from which a shot can be discharged through the energy of an explosive, a pistol or revolver having a barrel with a smooth bore designed or redesigned to fire a fixed shotgun shell, weapons with combination shotgun and rifle barrels 12 inches or more, less than 18 inches in length, from which only a single discharge can be made from either barrel without manual reloading, and shall include any such weapon which may be readily restored to fire. Such term shall not include a pistol or a revolver having a rifled bore, or rifled bores, or weapons designed, made, or intended to be fired from the shoulder and not capable of firing fixed ammunition." 26 U.S.C. §5845(e).

1. Concealable weapons and devices

Weapons which are capable of being concealed from which one shot can be discharged are AOWs. This includes such weapons as a pen gun, knife gun, or umbrella gun.

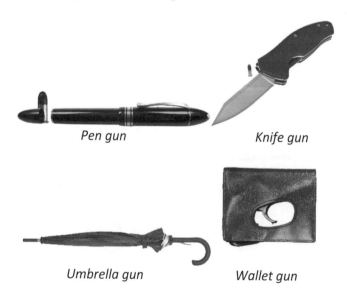

Pen gun   *Knife gun*

Umbrella gun   *Wallet gun*

2. <u>Pistols and revolvers having a smooth-bore barrel for firing shotgun shells</u>

Pistols and revolvers that have a smooth bore (no rifling) that are designed to shoot shotgun ammunition are defined as an AOW. The ATF cites firearms such as the H&R Handy Gun or the Ithaca Auto & Burglar Gun as firearms which fall under the AOW category. *Note:* handguns with partially rifled barrels such as The Judge do not fall under this category due to the rifling of the barrel.

H&R Handy Gun   *Ithaca Auto & Burglar Gun*

3. <u>Weapons with barrels 12 inches or longer and lengths 18 inches or shorter</u>

The definition of AOW also includes any weapon which has a shotgun or rifle barrel of 12 inches or more but is 18 inches or less in overall length from which only a single discharge can be made from either barrel without manual reloading. The ATF identifies the "Marble Game Getter" as the firearm most commonly associated with this definition (excluding the model with an 18" barrel and folding shoulder stock).

4. <u>Pistols and revolvers with vertical handgrips</u>

If a pistol is modified with a vertical grip on the front, it will now be legally classified as an AOW and require registration and a tax stamp. Note, vertical grips are readily available and are legal to own as long as they are not placed on a handgun. The definition of a handgun is a weapon which is intended to be fired by one hand, the addition of the vertical foregrip makes it so the weapon now is intended to be used with two hands to fire. This modification changes the weapon from a handgun to what is known as an "AOW" and is now a prohibited weapon without the proper documentation.

F. _Antique firearms_

Firearms that are defined by the NFA as "antique firearms" are *not* regulated by the NFA. The NFA definition of antique firearm is found in 26 U.S.C. §5845(g) as "any firearm not designed or redesigned for using rim fire or conventional center fire ignition with fixed ammunition and manufactured in or before 1898 (including any matchlock, flintlock, percussion cap, or similar type of ignition system or replica thereof, whether actually manufactured before or after the year 1898) and also any firearm using fixed ammunition manufactured in or before 1898, for which ammunition is no longer manufactured in the United States and is not readily available in the ordinary channels of commercial trade." Under this statute and for NFA purposes, the only firearms that are antiques are firearms which were both actually manufactured in or before 1898 and ones for which fixed ammunition is no longer manufactured in the United States and is not readily available in the ordinary channels of commercial trade.

With this in mind, the ATF states in its NFA guidebook that "it is important to note that a specific type of fixed ammunition that has been out of production for many years may again become available due to increasing interest in older firearms. Therefore, the classification of a specific NFA firearm as an antique can change if ammunition for the weapon becomes readily available in the ordinary channels of commerce."

G. *NFA curio firearms and relics*

Under federal law, curios or relics are defined in 27 CFR §478.11 as "firearms which are of special interest to collectors by reason of some quality other than is associated with firearms intended for sporting use or as offensive or defensive weapons." Persons that collect curios or relics may do so with a special collector's license although one is not required. The impact of an NFA item being classified as a curio or relic, however, is that it allows the item to be transferred interstate to persons possessing a collector's license. The collector's license does not allow the individual to deal in curios or relics, nor does it allow the collector to obtain other firearms interstate as those transactions still require an FFL.

To be classified as a curio or relic, federal law states that the firearm must fall into one of the following three categories:
1. Firearms which were manufactured at least 50 years prior to the current date, but not including replicas thereof;
2. Firearms which are certified by the curator of a municipal, State, or Federal museum which exhibits firearms to be curious or relics of museum interest; or
3. Any other firearms which derive a substantial part of their monetary value from the fact that they are novel, rare, bizarre, or because of their association with some historical figure, period, or event.

See 27 CFR §478.11.

The ATF maintains a list of firearms that are classified as curios or relics.

H. *How can some after-market gun parts make your firearm illegal?*

A number of companies manufacture and sell gun products or parts that alter the appearance or utility of a firearm (*i.e.,* shoulder stocks, forward hand grips, *etc.*). However, some of these after-market products can actually change the firearm you possess from one type of a weapon to another type of weapon for legal purposes whether you realize it or not. As a result, many individuals make the modifications to their firearms thinking that because there was no special process for purchasing the accessory, any modification would be in compliance with the law. Unfortunately, this is not always the case. Consider the example of short-barreled uppers for AR-15s: selling, buying, or possessing AR-15 "uppers" with barrels less than 16 inches is legal. However, it is illegal to put the upper on a receiver of an AR-15 because this would be the act of manufacturing a short-barreled rifle and is legally prohibited unless you receive prior approval via an ATF Form 1. This is equally true of vertical forward grips on a handgun. Vertical foregrips are legal to buy or possess, however, if you actually install one on a handgun, you have manufactured an AOW, and it is illegal, unless registered and a tax stamp is issued. *Note:* there are other types of braces that are permissible in their proper application and illegal in any application or adaptation that would alter the classification of the weapon. For example, the Sig Arm Brace (SB-15 Pistol Stabilizing Brace) is legal to attach to an AR Pistol when used as an arm brace, but illegal when used as a shoulder stock. The ATF has reached similar conclusions when it comes to other stabilizing braces.

Practical Legal Tip:

Even if you don't own a machine gun today, that doesn't mean you won't be the intended owner of one later. A person could always leave you their NFA items in a will. If this happens, you must file the appropriate paperwork with the ATF as soon as possible, or at least before probate is closed. -*Mike*

III. Process and procedure for obtaining NFA firearms

A. *Who can own and possess an NFA firearm?*

Any person may own and possess an NFA firearm as long as they are legally not disqualified to own or possess firearms and live in a state that allows possession of NFA items. *See* Chapters 2 and 3. The ATF also allows for a non-person legal entity to own these items, such as corporations, partnerships, and trusts, *etc.*

B. *What are the usual steps for buying or manufacturing NFA items?*

Whether a person is buying or making (manufacturing) an NFA firearm, there are several steps in the process. The transfer or manufacture of an NFA firearm requires the filing of an appropriate transfer form with the ATF, payment of any federally-mandated transfer tax, approval of the transfer by the ATF, and registration of the firearm to the transferee. Only after these steps have occurred may a buyer legally take possession of the NFA item, or may a person legally assemble or manufacture the NFA item. In this section, we will walk through the process, step-by-step, of (1) purchasing an NFA item that already exists, and (2) manufacturing an NFA firearm.

Steps for buying an existing NFA item (for example, a suppressor):

1. Select and purchase the item (suppressor) from a dealer;
2. Assemble appropriate paperwork (ATF Form 4, *see* Appendix B) and money order for the tax stamp ($200)
   a. If the buyer is an individual, the individual must secure Chief Law Enforcement Officer signature on ATF Form 4, a photograph, and fingerprints. *Note:* though after July 13, 2016, only CLEO notification is required;
   b. If the buyer is a corporation/trust, no Chief Law Enforcement Officer signature, photograph, or fingerprints are required. *Note:* this will change on July 13, 2016, which will require that for each application the "responsible persons" of the trust to submit fingerprints, photographs and a 5320.23, as well as notify the CLEO;
3. Submit paperwork, fingerprints, and money order for the tax stamp to the ATF → ATF review and approval;
4. ATF sends approval (tax stamp affixed to Form 4) to the dealer;
5. Pick up suppressor from the dealer.

Steps for manufacturing an NFA item (such as a short-barreled rifle):

1. Select the item to manufacture or modify, *i.e.,* short-barreled AR-15;
2. Assemble appropriate paperwork (ATF Form 1, *see* Appendix B) and a money order for the tax stamp ($200);
   a. If the maker is an individual, the individual must secure Chief Law Enforcement Officer signature on ATF Form 4, a photograph, and fingerprints. *Note:* though after July 13, 2016, only CLEO notification is required;
   b. If the maker is a corporation/trust, no Chief Law Enforcement Officer signature, photograph, or fingerprints are required. *Note:* this will change on July 13, 2016, which will require that for each application the "responsible persons" of the trust to submit fingerprints, photographs and a 5320.23, as well as notify the CLEO;
3. Submit paperwork and tax to the ATF → ATF review and approval;
4. ATF sends you the approval (tax stamp affixed to Form 1);
5. Maker may then legally assemble the AR-15, *i.e.,* put upper with a barrel length of less than 16 inches on a lower receiver, *etc.* The item must now be engraved and identified, *see* below.

When purchasing an NFA firearm from a dealer, the dealer is required to have the purchaser fill out ATF Form 4473 when the purchaser goes to pick up the item from the dealer. There is a background check for a firearm, but not for a suppressor.

C. *How must an NFA item be engraved and identified if I make it myself?*

Once you receive ATF approval to manufacture your own NFA item (such as the short-barreled AR-15 in the previous section), federal law requires that you engrave, cast, stamp, or otherwise conspicuously place or cause to be engraved, cast, stamped, or placed on the frame, receiver, or barrel of the NFA item the following information:

1. The item's serial number;
2. The item's model (if so designated);
3. Caliber or gauge;
4. The name of the owner whether individual, corporation, or trust; and
5. The city and state where the item was made.

This information must be placed on the item with a minimum depth of .003 inch and in a print size no smaller than 1/16 inch. *See* 27 CFR §479.102.

D. *Which way should I own my NFA item? Paperwork requirements for individuals, trusts, or business entities to own NFA items*

Form 4 and Form 1

The appropriate paperwork that must be assembled and submitted to the ATF under the NFA varies depending on whether an individual, or a legal entity such as a trust, corporation, or partnership is purchasing or manufacturing the NFA item. The paperwork generally starts either with an ATF Form 4 (used for purchasing an existing item), or an ATF Form 1 which is used if a person wishes to manufacture a new NFA item. All relevant portions of the Form must be completed. Both Form 4 and Form 1 have a requirement that a Chief Law Enforcement Officer for the applicant must sign the ATF form. However, this requirement only applies to living, breathing individuals; it does *not* apply to applicants who are legal entities like trusts, corporations, *etc.* Therefore, a Chief Law Enforcement Officer signature is not necessary. The signature of the Chief Law Enforcement Officer may be difficult or impossible to obtain for an individual in Pennsylvania. There is no law that says the Chief Law Enforcement Officer must sign off on the Form 1 or Form 4. *Note:* for trusts, this will change July 13, 2016. For applications submitted after this date, the ATF will require each "responsible person" in the trust to submit fingerprints, photographs, and a completed ATF Form 5320.23, as well as notify their CLEO.

Who may sign a Form 4 or Form 1 as a Chief Law Enforcement Officer?
For the purposes of Form 4, "the chief law enforcement officer is considered to be the Chief of Police for the transferee's city or town of residence, the Sheriff for the transferee's county of residence; the Head of the State Police for the transferee's State of residence; a State or local district attorney or prosecutor having jurisdiction in the transferee's area of residence; or another person whose certification is acceptable to the Director, Bureau of Alcohol, Tobacco and Firearms." ATF Form 1, *Instructions*. Keep in mind, this step will no longer be required for applications submitted after July 13, 2016.

Photograph and fingerprints only required for individual applicants
In addition, if an individual is purchasing or manufacturing an NFA item, the applicant must submit an appropriate photograph and their fingerprints. Neither fingerprints nor photographs are required if the applicant is not an individual. Conversely, an entity such as a trust or corporation must submit the appropriate documents showing its existence, such as the trust or corporate formation documents. *Note:* this will change July 13, 2016. For applications submitted after this date, the ATF will require each "responsible person" in the trust to submit fingerprints, photographs, and a completed ATF Form 5320.23, as well as notify their CLEO.

E. *Why are trusts so popular to own NFA items?*
There are four major reasons trusts are very popular to own NFA items: turnaround time, paperwork, control, and ease of ownership. A trust is a legal entity that can hold property.

The turnaround time for NFA approvals with the ATF varies. For example, in 2014, we were seeing wait times on Form 4 approval for individuals as long as 10 months or longer. In 2014, we were seeing wait times on Form 1 approval for individuals as long as 5 months or longer. In the first quarter of 2015, we saw these times reduced quite a bit. However, one important aspect to note is that the wait time for Form 1 or Form 4 approvals for trusts are reduced by several months when compared to approval times for individuals. In addition, a trust will allow people within the trust to transfer NFA items without the ATF Form 5320.20 approval.

On the paperwork side, trusts are beneficial because they, as of the time of writing, do not require the signature of the Chief Law Enforcement Officer on Form 1 or Form 4. In addition, unlike individuals seeking ownership of an NFA item, no fingerprints or photographs are required. The only paperwork required to own an NFA item under a trust is the trust agreement and the appropriate ATF form or forms. *Note:* this will change July 13, 2016. For applications submitted after this date, the ATF will require each "responsible person" in the trust to submit fingerprints, photographs, and a completed ATF Form 5320.23, as well as notify their CLEO.

A third major reason for having a trust own an NFA item is that it makes owning and using the NFA item easier if more than one person wishes to use the item. If an individual owns the item, then only the individual can ever "possess" it. On the other hand, if the item is owned by a trust, all trustees, including co-trustees, are able to possess and use the items contained in the trust. Therefore, co-trustees may be added or removed. *Note:* non-trustees and non-owners may still use a properly registered NFA firearm, but only when in "the presence" of the owner.

Finally, unlike other entities such as corporations, LLCs, *etc.*, a trust requires no filings with a government to create, which saves expenses and even preserves privacy. Further, these expense savings continue because there are no continuing government fees or compliance requirements. Thus, trusts are one of the best ways currently to own an NFA item.

F.   *The Tax Stamp*

Once the ATF has an applicant's materials in hand, they will be reviewed and checked by NFA researchers and an examiner. The application will then either be approved or denied. A denial will be accompanied by an explanation of why the application was denied and how to remedy it, if possible. If the application is approved, the examiner will affix a tax stamp on one of the submitted Form 1 or Form 4 and send the newly-stamped Form to the applicant.

This tax stamp on the appropriate form is a person's evidence of compliance with the NFA's requirements and is a very important document. A copy should always be kept with the NFA item. *See* below.

G.   *What documents should I have with me when I am in actual possession of my suppressor, short-barreled firearm, or other NFA item?*

If you have an NFA item, always have the proper documentation with you to prove that you legally possess the item. Again, if you are in possession of your suppressor, short-barreled firearm, destructive device, or if you are lucky enough, your machine gun— always have your paperwork showing you are legal, or it may be a long day with law enforcement. To show you are legal, always keep a copy of your ATF Form 4 or Form 1 (whichever is applicable) with the tax stamp affixed for every NFA item in your possession, personal identification, and if the item is held in a trust or corporation, a copy of the trust or articles of incorporation, and the authorization for possession. Care should be given to make sure these documents name the individual so as to show legal ownership, *i.e.*, trust and/or amendments showing the person is a co-trustee or an officer of the corporation.

Practically, individuals should not carry around the original documents as they could be destroyed by wear and tear, rain, or be misplaced, effectively destroying the required evidence of compliance. Photocopies of the stamp and any other pertinent documents are generally enough to satisfy inquisitive law enforcement officials. The more technologically advanced may take pictures on their phone or other mobile device, or even upload them to a cloud database. Keep in mind that if the phone dies or the cloud cannot be reached, and you have no way to access the documents, your proof is gone and you may have a very bad day ahead of you! We recommend keeping photocopies of the ATF form with the tax stamp affixed and appropriate documents to avoid any problems with technology.

H. *Can I take my properly registered NFA item out of state? What if I want to permanently move, but keep my NFA items?*

Yes, provided that you follow all of the published ATF rules and regulations BEFORE you travel or move. In order to do this, the owner or trustee must (1) check to make sure that the NFA item is legal to possess or own in that other state (not all states allow for the ownership or possession of a NFA items), (2) submit in duplicate a ATF Form 5320.20 (sometimes called a "Form 20"). You can seek prior approval to travel with your NFA item or items up to a year in advance. As of the writing of this chapter, we are typically seeing a 2-week turnaround time on approvals, though this can vary.

APPENDICES

APPENDIX A: SELECTED PENNSYLVANIA STATUTES

WARNING:

These appendices contain all of the legislative changes as of the date of this book's publication in 2016. Legislative changes may be made to these statutes after the date of publication. A person seeking to rely on a statute should review complete version of the current statute.

The Pennsylvania Consolidated Statutes Title 18
Chapter 5: General Principals of Justification

§502. Justification a defense.

In any prosecution based on conduct which is justifiable under this chapter, justification is a defense.

§503. Justification generally.

(a) General rule.--Conduct which the actor believes to be necessary to avoid a harm or evil to himself or to another is justifiable if:

(1) the harm or evil sought to be avoided by such conduct is greater than that sought to be prevented by the law defining the offense charged;

(2) neither this title nor other law defining the offense provides exceptions or defenses dealing with the specific situation involved; and

(3) a legislative purpose to exclude the justification claimed does not otherwise plainly appear.

(b) Choice of evils.--When the actor was reckless or negligent in bringing about the situation requiring a choice of harms or evils or in appraising the necessity for his conduct, the justification afforded by this section is unavailable in a prosecution for any offense for which recklessness or negligence, as the case may be, suffices to establish culpability.

§505. Use of force in self-protection.

(a) Use of force justifiable for protection of the person.--The use of force upon or toward another person is justifiable when the actor believes that such force is immediately necessary for the purpose of protecting himself against the use of unlawful force by such other person on the present occasion.

(b) Limitations on justifying necessity for use of force.--

(1) The use of force is not justifiable under this section:

(i) to resist an arrest which the actor knows is being made by a peace officer, although the arrest is unlawful; or

(ii) to resist force used by the occupier or possessor of property or by another person on his behalf, where the actor knows that the person using the force is doing so under a claim of right to protect the property, except that this limitation shall not apply if:

(A) the actor is a public officer acting in the performance of his duties or a person lawfully assisting him therein or a person making or assisting in a lawful arrest;

(B) the actor has been unlawfully dispossessed of the property and is making a reentry or recaption justified by section 507 of this title (relating to use of force for the protection of property); or

(C) the actor believes that such force is necessary to protect himself against death or serious bodily injury.

(2) The use of deadly force is not justifiable under this section unless the actor believes that such force is necessary to protect himself against death, serious bodily injury, kidnapping or sexual intercourse compelled by force or threat; nor is it justifiable if:

(i) the actor, with the intent of causing death or serious bodily injury, provoked the use of force against himself in the same encounter; or

(ii) the actor knows that he can avoid the necessity of using such force with complete safety by retreating, except the actor is not obliged to retreat from his dwelling or place of work, unless he was the initial aggressor or is assailed in his place of work by another person whose place of work the actor knows it to be.

(2.1) Except as otherwise provided in paragraph (2.2), an actor is presumed to have a reasonable belief that deadly force is immediately necessary to protect himself against death, serious bodily injury, kidnapping or sexual intercourse compelled by force or threat if both of the following conditions exist:

    (i) The person against whom the force is used is in the process of unlawfully and forcefully entering, or has unlawfully and forcefully entered and is present within, a dwelling, residence or occupied vehicle; or the person against whom the force is used is or is attempting to unlawfully and forcefully remove another against that other's will from the dwelling, residence or occupied vehicle.

    (ii) The actor knows or has reason to believe that the unlawful and forceful entry or act is occurring or has occurred.

(2.2) The presumption set forth in paragraph (2.1) does not apply if:

    (i) the person against whom the force is used has the right to be in or is a lawful resident of the dwelling, residence or vehicle, such as an owner or lessee;

    (ii) the person sought to be removed is a child or grandchild or is otherwise in the lawful custody or under the lawful guardianship of the person against whom the protective force is used;

    (iii) the actor is engaged in a criminal activity or is using the dwelling, residence or occupied vehicle to further a criminal activity; or

    (iv) the person against whom the force is used is a peace officer acting in the performance of his official duties and the actor using force knew or reasonably should have known that the person was a peace officer.

(2.3) An actor who is not engaged in a criminal activity, who is not in illegal possession of a firearm and who is attacked in any place where the actor would have a duty to retreat under paragraph (2)(ii) has no duty to retreat and has the right to stand his ground and use force, including deadly force, if:

    (i) the actor has a right to be in the place where he was attacked;

    (ii) the actor believes it is immediately necessary to do so to protect himself against death, serious bodily injury, kidnapping or sexual intercourse by force or threat; and

    (iii) the person against whom the force is used displays or otherwise uses:

        (A) a firearm or replica of a firearm as defined in 42 Pa.C.S. §9712 (relating to sentences for offenses committed with firearms); or

        (B) any other weapon readily or apparently capable of lethal use.

(2.4) The exception to the duty to retreat set forth under paragraph (2.3) does not apply if the person against whom the force is used is a peace officer acting in the performance of his official duties and the actor using force knew or reasonably should have known that the person was a peace officer.

(2.5) Unless one of the exceptions under paragraph (2.2) applies, a person who unlawfully and by force enters or attempts to enter an actor's dwelling, residence or occupied vehicle or removes or attempts to remove another against that other's will from the actor's dwelling, residence or occupied vehicle is presumed to be doing so with the intent to commit:

    (i) an act resulting in death or serious bodily injury; or

        (ii) kidnapping or sexual intercourse by force or threat.

(2.6) A public officer justified in using force in the performance of his duties or a person justified in using force in his assistance or a person justified in using force in making an arrest or preventing an escape is not obliged to desist from efforts to perform such duty, effect such arrest or prevent such escape because of resistance or threatened resistance by or on behalf of the person against whom such action is directed.

(3) Except as otherwise required by this subsection, a person employing protective force may estimate the necessity thereof under the circumstances as he believes them to be when the force is used, without retreating, surrendering possession, doing any other act which he has no legal duty to do or abstaining from any lawful action.

(c) Use of confinement as protective force.--The justification afforded by this section extends to the use of confinement as protective force only if the actor takes all reasonable measures to terminate the confinement as soon as he knows that he safely can, unless the person confined has been arrested on a charge of crime.

(d) Definition.--As used in this section, the term "criminal activity" means conduct which is a misdemeanor or felony, is not justifiable under this chapter and is related to the confrontation between an actor and the person against whom force is used.

§506. Use of force for the protection of other persons.

(a) General rule.--The use of force upon or toward the person of another is justifiable to protect a third person when:

    (1) the actor would be justified under section 505 (relating to use of force in self-protection) in using such force to protect himself against the injury he believes to be threatened to the person whom he seeks to protect;

    (2) under the circumstances as the actor believes them to be, the person whom he seeks to protect would be justified in using such protective force; and

    (3) the actor believes that his intervention is necessary for the protection of such other person.

(b) Exception.--Notwithstanding subsection (a), the actor is not obliged to retreat to any greater extent than the person whom he seeks to protect.

§507. Use of force for the protection of property.

(a) Use of force justifiable for protection of property.--The use of force upon or toward the person of another is justifiable when the actor believes that such force is immediately necessary:

    (1) to prevent or terminate an unlawful entry or other trespass upon land or a trespass against or the unlawful carrying away of tangible movable property, if such land or movable property is, or is believed by the actor to be, in his possession or in the possession of another person for whose protection he acts; or

    (2) to effect an entry or reentry upon land or to retake tangible movable property, if:

        (i) the actor believes that he or the person by whose authority he acts or a person from whom he or such other person derives title was unlawfully dispossessed of such land or movable property and is entitled to possession; and

        (ii) (A) the force is used immediately or on fresh pursuit after such dispossession; or

            (B) the actor believes that the person against whom he uses force has no claim of right to the possession of the property and, in the case of land, the circumstances, as the actor believes them to be, are of such urgency that it would be an exceptional hardship to postpone the entry or reentry until a court order is obtained.

(b) Meaning of possession.--For the purpose of subsection (a) of this section:

   (1) A person who has parted with the custody of property to another who refuses to restore it to him is no longer in possession, unless the property is movable and was and still is located on land in his possession.

   (2) A person who has been dispossessed of land does not regain possession thereof merely by setting foot thereon.

   (3) A person who has a license to use or occupy real property is deemed to be in possession thereof except against the licensor acting under claim of right.

(c) Limitations on justifiable use of force.--

   (1) The use of force is justifiable under this section only if the actor first requests the person against whom such force is used to desist from his interference with the property, unless the actor believes that:

      (i) such request would be useless;

      (ii) it would be dangerous to himself or another person to make the request; or

      (iii) substantial harm will be done to the physical condition of the property which is sought to be protected before the request can effectively be made.

   (2) The use of force to prevent or terminate a trespass is not justifiable under this section if the actor knows that the exclusion of the trespasser will expose him to substantial danger of serious bodily injury.

   (3) The use of force to prevent an entry or reentry upon land or the recaption of movable property is not justifiable under this section, although the actor believes that such reentry or caption is unlawful, if:

      (i) the reentry or recaption is made by or on behalf of a person who was actually dispossessed of the property; and

      (ii) it is otherwise justifiable under subsection (a)(2).

(4) (i) The use of deadly force is justifiable under this section if:

    (A) there has been an entry into the actor's dwelling;

    (B) the actor neither believes nor has reason to believe that the entry is lawful; and

    (C) the actor neither believes nor has reason to believe that force less than deadly force would be adequate to terminate the entry.

  (ii) If the conditions of justification provided in subparagraph (i) have not been met, the use of deadly force is not justifiable under this section unless the actor believes that:

    (A) the person against whom the force is used is attempting to dispossess him of his dwelling otherwise than under a claim of right to its possession; or

    (B) such force is necessary to prevent the commission of a felony in the dwelling.

(d) Use of confinement as protective force.--The justification afforded by this section extends to the use of confinement as protective force only if the actor takes all reasonable measures to terminate the confinement as soon as he knows that he can do so with safety to the property, unless the person confined has been arrested on a charge of crime.

(e) Use of device to protect property.--The justification afforded by this section extends to the use of a device for the purpose of protecting property only if:

  (1) the device is not designed to cause or known to create a substantial risk of causing death or serious bodily injury;

  (2) the use of the particular device to protect the property from entry or trespass is reasonable under the circumstances, as the actor believes them to be; and

(3) the device is one customarily used for such a purpose or reasonable care is taken to make known to probable intruders the fact that it is used.

(f) Use of force to pass wrongful obstructor.--The use of force to pass a person whom the actor believes to be intentionally or knowingly and unjustifiably obstructing the actor from going to a place to which he may lawfully go is justifiable, if:

(1) the actor believes that the person against whom he uses force has no claim of right to obstruct the actor;

(2) the actor is not being obstructed from entry or movement on land which he knows to be in the possession or custody of the person obstructing him, or in the possession or custody of another person by whose authority the obstructor acts, unless the circumstances, as the actor believes them to be, are of such urgency that it would not be reasonable to postpone the entry or movement on such land until a court order is obtained; and

(3) the force used is not greater than it would be justifiable if the person obstructing the actor were using force against him to prevent his passage.

§508. Use of force in law enforcement.

(a) Peace officer's use of force in making arrest.--

(1) A peace officer, or any person whom he has summoned or directed to assist him, need not retreat or desist from efforts to make a lawful arrest because of resistance or threatened resistance to the arrest. He is justified in the use of any force which he believes to be necessary to effect the arrest and of any force which he believes to be necessary to defend himself or another from bodily harm while making the arrest. However, he is justified in using deadly force only when he believes that such force is necessary to prevent death or serious bodily injury to himself or such other person, or when he believes both that:

       (i) such force is necessary to prevent the arrest from being defeated by resistance or escape; and

       (ii) the person to be arrested has committed or attempted a forcible felony or is attempting to escape and possesses a deadly weapon, or otherwise indicates that he will endanger human life or inflict serious bodily injury unless arrested without delay.

(2) A peace officer making an arrest pursuant to an invalid warrant is justified in the use of any force which he would be justified in using if the warrant were valid, unless he knows that the warrant is invalid.

(b) Private person's use of force in making arrest.--

(1) A private person who makes, or assists another private person in making a lawful arrest is justified in the use of any force which he would be justified in using if he were summoned or directed by a peace officer to make such arrest, except that he is justified in the use of deadly force only when he believes that such force is necessary to prevent death or serious bodily injury to himself or another.

(2) A private person who is summoned or directed by a peace officer to assist in making an arrest which is unlawful, is justified in the use of any force which he would be justified in using if the arrest were lawful, unless he knows that the arrest is unlawful.

(3) A private person who assists another private person in effecting an unlawful arrest, or who, not being summoned, assists a peace officer in effecting an unlawful arrest, is justified in using any force which he would be justified in using if the arrest were lawful, if:

       (i) he believes the arrest is lawful; and

       (ii) the arrest would be lawful if the facts were as he believes them to be.

(c) Use of force regarding escape.--

   (1) A peace officer, corrections officer or other person who has an arrested or convicted person in his custody is justified in the use of such force to prevent the escape of the person from custody as the officer or other person would be justified in using under subsection (a) if the officer or other person were arresting the person.

   (2) A peace officer or corrections officer is justified in the use of such force, including deadly force, which the officer believes to be necessary to prevent the escape from a correctional institution of a person whom the officer believes to be lawfully detained in such institution under sentence for an offense or awaiting trial or commitment for an offense.

   (3) A corrections officer is justified in the use of such force, which the officer believes to be necessary to defend himself or another from bodily harm during the pursuit of the escaped person. However, the officer is justified in using deadly force only when the officer believes that such force is necessary to prevent death or serious bodily injury to himself or another or when the officer believes that:

      (i) such force is necessary to prevent the apprehension from being defeated by resistance; and

      (ii) the escaped person has been convicted of committing or attempting to commit a forcible felony, possesses a deadly weapon or otherwise indicates that he will endanger human life or inflict serious bodily injury unless apprehended without delay.

(d) Use of force to prevent suicide or the commission of crime.--

   (1) The use of force upon or toward the person of another is justifiable when the actor believes that such force is immediately necessary to prevent such other person from committing suicide, inflicting serious bodily injury upon himself, committing or

consummating the commission of a crime involving or threatening bodily injury, damage to or loss of property or a breach of the peace, except that:

(i) Any limitations imposed by the other provisions of this chapter on the justifiable use of force in self-protection, for the protection of others, the protection of property, the effectuation of an arrest or the prevention of an escape from custody shall apply notwithstanding the criminality of the conduct against which such force is used.

(ii) The use of deadly force is not in any event justifiable under this subsection unless:

(A) the actor believes that there is a substantial risk that the person whom he seeks to prevent from committing a crime will cause death or serious bodily injury to another unless the commission or the consummation of the crime is prevented and that the use of such force presents no substantial risk of injury to innocent persons; or

(B) the actor believes that the use of such force is necessary to suppress a riot or mutiny after the rioters or mutineers have been ordered to disperse and warned, in any particular manner that the law may require, that such force will be used if they do not obey.

(2) The justification afforded by this subsection extends to the use of confinement as preventive force only if the actor takes all reasonable measures to terminate the confinement as soon as he knows that he safely can, unless the person confined has been arrested on a charge of crime.

Title 18, Chapter 9: Inchoate Crimes

§908. Prohibited offensive weapons.
  (a) Offense defined.--A person commits a misdemeanor of the first degree if, except as authorized by law, he makes repairs, sells, or otherwise deals in, uses, or possesses any offensive weapon.
  (b) Exceptions.--
    (1) It is a defense under this section for the defendant to prove by a preponderance of evidence that he possessed or dealt with the weapon solely as a curio or in a dramatic performance, or that, with the exception of a bomb, grenade or incendiary device, he complied with the National Firearms Act (26 U.S.C. § 5801 et seq.), or that he possessed it briefly in consequence of having found it or taken it from an aggressor, or under circumstances similarly negativing any intent or likelihood that the weapon would be used unlawfully.
    (2) This section does not apply to police forensic firearms experts or police forensic firearms laboratories. Also exempt from this section are forensic firearms experts or forensic firearms laboratories operating in the ordinary course of business and engaged in lawful operation who notify in writing, on an annual basis, the chief or head of any police force or police department of a city, and, elsewhere, the sheriff of a county in which they are located, of the possession, type and use of offensive weapons.
    (3) This section shall not apply to any person who makes, repairs, sells or otherwise deals in, uses or possesses any firearm for purposes not prohibited by the laws of this Commonwealth.
  (c) Definitions.--As used in this section, the following words and phrases shall have the meanings given to them in this subsection:
      "Firearm." Any weapon which is designed to or may readily be converted to expel any projectile by the action

of an explosive or the frame or receiver of any such weapon.

"Offensive weapons." Any bomb, grenade, machine gun, sawed-off shotgun with a barrel less than 18 inches, firearm specially made or specially adapted for concealment or silent discharge, any blackjack, sandbag, metal knuckles, dagger, knife, razor or cutting instrument, the blade of which is exposed in an automatic way by switch, push-button, spring mechanism, or otherwise, any stun gun, stun baton, taser or other electronic or electric weapon or other implement for the infliction of serious bodily injury which serves no common lawful purpose.

(d) Exemptions.--The use and possession of blackjacks by the following persons in the course of their duties are exempt from this section:

(1) Police officers, as defined by and who meet the requirements of the act of June 18, 1974 (P.L.359, No.120), referred to as the Municipal Police Education and Training Law.

(2) Police officers of first class cities who have successfully completed training which is substantially equivalent to the program under the Municipal Police Education and Training Law.

(3) Pennsylvania State Police officers.

(4) Sheriffs and deputy sheriffs of the various counties who have satisfactorily met the requirements of the Municipal Police Education and Training Law.

(5) Police officers employed by the Commonwealth who have satisfactorily met the requirements of the Municipal Police Education and Training Law.

(6) Deputy sheriffs with adequate training as determined by the Pennsylvania Commission on Crime and Delinquency.

(7) Liquor Control Board agents who have satisfactorily met the requirements of the Municipal Police Education and Training Law.

§908.1. Use or possession of electric or electronic incapacitation device.

    (a) Offense defined.--Except as set forth in subsection (b), a person commits an offense if the person does any of the following:

      (1) Uses an electric or electronic incapacitation device on another person for an unlawful purpose.

      (2) Possesses, with intent to violate paragraph (1), an electric or electronic incapacitation device.

    (b) Self defense.--A person may possess and use an electric or electronic incapacitation device in the exercise of reasonable force in defense of the person or the person's property pursuant to Chapter 5 (relating to general principles of justification) if the electric or electronic incapacitation device is labeled with or accompanied by clearly written instructions as to its use and the damages involved in its use.

    (c) Prohibited possession.--No person prohibited from possessing a firearm pursuant to section 6105 (relating to persons not to possess, use, manufacture, control, sell or transfer firearms) may possess or use an electric or electronic incapacitation device.

    (d) Grading.--An offense under subsection (a) shall constitute a felony of the second degree if the actor acted with the intent to commit a felony. Otherwise any offense under this section is graded as a misdemeanor of the first degree.

    (e) Exceptions.--Nothing in this section shall prohibit the possession or use by, or the sale or furnishing of any electric or electronic incapacitation device to, a law enforcement agency, peace officer, employee of a correctional institution, county jail or prison or detention center, the National Guard or reserves or a member of the National Guard or reserves for use in their official duties.

    (f) Definition.--As used in this section, the term "electric or electronic incapacitation device" means a portable device which is designed or intended by the manufacturer to be used, offensively or defensively, to temporarily immobilize or incapacitate persons by means of electric pulse or current, including devices operating by means of carbon dioxide propellant. The term does not include cattle prods, electric fences or other electric devices when used in agricultural, animal husbandry or food production activities.

Title 18, Chapter 61: Firearms and Other Dangerous Articles
SUBCHAPTER A
UNIFORM FIREARMS ACT

§6102. Definitions.

Subject to additional definitions contained in subsequent provisions of this subchapter which are applicable to specific provisions of this subchapter, the following words and phrases, when used in this subchapter shall have, unless the context clearly indicates otherwise, the meanings given to them in this section:

"Commissioner." The Commissioner of the Pennsylvania State Police.

"Commonwealth Photo Imaging Network." The computer network administered by the Commonwealth and used to record and store digital photographs of an individual's face and any scars, marks, tattoos or other unique features of the individual.

"Conviction." A conviction, a finding of guilty or the entering of a plea of guilty or nolo contendere, whether or not judgment of sentence has been imposed, as determined by the law of the jurisdiction in which the prosecution was held. The term does not include a conviction which has been expunged or overturned or for which an individual has been pardoned unless the pardon expressly provides that the individual may not possess or transport firearms.

"County treasurer." The county treasurer or, in home rule or optional plan counties, the person whose duties encompass those of a county treasurer.

"Crime punishable by imprisonment exceeding one year." The term does not include any of the following:

(1) Federal or State offenses pertaining to antitrust, unfair trade practices, restraints on trade or regulation of business.

(2) State offenses classified as misdemeanors and punishable by a term of imprisonment not to exceed two years.

"Firearm." Any pistol or revolver with a barrel length less than 15 inches, any shotgun with a barrel length less than 18 inches or any rifle with a barrel length less than 16 inches, or any pistol, revolver, rifle or shotgun with an overall length of less than 26 inches. The barrel length of a firearm shall be determined by measuring from the muzzle of the barrel to the face of the closed action, bolt or cylinder, whichever is applicable.

"Fund." The Firearm Ownership Fund established in section 6111.3 (relating to Firearm Ownership Fund).

"Law enforcement officer." Any person employed by any police department or organization of the Commonwealth or political subdivision thereof who is empowered to effect an arrest with or without warrant and who is authorized to carry a firearm in the performance of that person's duties.

"Loaded." A firearm is loaded if the firing chamber, the nondetachable magazine or, in the case of a revolver, any of the chambers of the cylinder contain ammunition capable of being fired. In the case of a firearm which utilizes a detachable magazine, the term shall mean a magazine suitable for use in said firearm which magazine contains such ammunition and has been inserted in the firearm or is in the same container or, where the container has multiple compartments, the same compartment thereof as the firearm. If the magazine is inserted into a pouch, holder, holster or other protective device that provides for a complete and secure enclosure of the ammunition, then the pouch, holder, holster or other protective device shall be deemed to be a separate compartment.

"Pennsylvania Sheriffs' Association." The State association of sheriffs authorized by the act of June 14, 1923 (P.L.774, No.305), entitled "An act authorizing the sheriffs of the several counties of this Commonwealth to organize themselves into a State Association, for the purpose of holding annual meetings, to secure more uniformity and cooperation in the conduct of their offices, and providing for the payment of certain expenses in connection with such meetings by the various counties."

"Safekeeping permit." As defined in 23 Pa.C.S. §6102 (relating to definitions).

"Sheriff."

    (1) Except as provided in paragraph (2), the sheriff of the county.

    (2) In a city of the first class, the chief or head of the police department.

"State." When used in reference to different parts of the United States, includes the District of Columbia, the Commonwealth of Puerto Rico and territories and possessions of the United States.

§6105. Persons not to possess, use, manufacture, control, sell or transfer firearms.

    (a) Offense defined.--

        (1) A person who has been convicted of an offense enumerated in subsection (b), within or without this Commonwealth, regardless of the length of sentence or whose conduct meets the criteria in subsection (c) shall not possess, use, control, sell, transfer or manufacture or obtain a license to possess, use, control, sell, transfer or manufacture a firearm in this Commonwealth.

        (2) (i) A person who is prohibited from possessing, using, controlling, selling, transferring or manufacturing a firearm under paragraph (1) or subsection (b) or (c) shall have a reasonable period of time, not to exceed 60 days from the date of the imposition of the disability under this subsection, in which to sell or transfer that person's firearms to another eligible person who is not a member of the prohibited person's household.

      (ii) This paragraph shall not apply to any person whose disability is imposed pursuant to subsection (c)(6).

(a.1) Penalty.--

    (1) A person convicted of a felony enumerated under subsection (b) or a felony under the act of April 14, 1972 (P.L.233, No.64), known as The Controlled Substance, Drug, Device and Cosmetic Act, or any equivalent Federal statute or equivalent statute of any other state, who violates subsection (a) commits a felony of the second degree.

    (2) A person who is the subject of an active protection from abuse order issued pursuant to 23 Pa.C.S. §6108 (relating to relief), which order provided for the relinquishment of firearms, other weapons or ammunition during the period of time the order is in effect, commits a misdemeanor of the first degree if he intentionally or knowingly fails to relinquish a firearm, other weapon or ammunition to the sheriff as required by the order unless, in lieu of relinquishment, he provides an affidavit which lists the firearms, other weapons or ammunition to the sheriff in accordance with either 23 Pa.C.S. §6108(a)(7)(i)(B), 6108.2 (relating to relinquishment for consignment sale, lawful transfer or safekeeping) or 6108.3 (relating to relinquishment to third party for safekeeping).

    (3) (i) A person commits a misdemeanor of the third degree if he intentionally or knowingly accepts possession of a firearm, other weapon or ammunition from a person he knows is the subject of an active protection from abuse order issued pursuant to 23 Pa.C.S. §6108, which order provided for the relinquishment of the firearm, other weapon or ammunition during the period of time the order is in effect.

        (ii) This paragraph shall not apply to:

            (A) a third party who accepts possession of a firearm, other weapon or ammunition relinquished pursuant to 23 Pa.C.S. §6108.3; or

(B) a dealer licensed pursuant to section 6113 (relating to licensing of dealers) or subsequent purchaser from a dealer licensed pursuant to section 6113, who accepts possession of a firearm, other weapon or ammunition relinquished pursuant to 23 Pa.C.S. §6108.2.

(4) It shall be an affirmative defense to any prosecution under paragraph (3) that the person accepting possession of a firearm, other weapon or ammunition in violation of paragraph (3):

(i) notified the sheriff as soon as practicable that he has taken possession; and

(ii) relinquished possession of any firearm, other weapon or ammunition possessed in violation of paragraph (3) as directed by the sheriff.

(5) A person who has accepted possession of a firearm, other weapon or ammunition pursuant to 23 Pa.C.S. §6108.3 commits a misdemeanor of the first degree if he intentionally or knowingly returns a firearm, other weapon or ammunition to a defendant or intentionally or knowingly allows a defendant to have access to the firearm, other weapon or ammunition prior to either of the following:

(i) The sheriff accepts return of the safekeeping permit issued to the party pursuant to 23 Pa.C.S. §6108.3(d)(1)(i).

(ii) The issuance of a court order pursuant to subsection (f)(2) or 23 Pa.C.S. §6108.1(b) (relating to return of relinquished firearms, other weapons and ammunition and additional relief) which modifies a valid protection from abuse order issued pursuant to 23 Pa.C.S. §6108, which order provided for the relinquishment of the firearm, other weapon or ammunition by allowing the defendant to take possession of the firearm, other weapon or ammunition that had previously been ordered relinquished.

(b) Enumerated offenses.--The following offenses shall apply to subsection (a):

Section 908 (relating to prohibited offensive weapons).

Section 911 (relating to corrupt organizations).

Section 912 (relating to possession of weapon on school property).

Section 2502 (relating to murder).

Section 2503 (relating to voluntary manslaughter).

Section 2504 (relating to involuntary manslaughter) if the offense is based on the reckless use of a firearm.

Section 2702 (relating to aggravated assault).

Section 2703 (relating to assault by prisoner).

Section 2704 (relating to assault by life prisoner).

Section 2709.1 (relating to stalking).

Section 2716 (relating to weapons of mass destruction).

Section 2901 (relating to kidnapping).

Section 2902 (relating to unlawful restraint).

Section 2910 (relating to luring a child into a motor vehicle or structure).

Section 3121 (relating to rape).

Section 3123 (relating to involuntary deviate sexual intercourse).

Section 3125 (relating to aggravated indecent assault).

Section 3301 (relating to arson and related offenses).

Section 3302 (relating to causing or risking catastrophe).

Section 3502 (relating to burglary).

Section 3503 (relating to criminal trespass) if the offense is graded a felony of the second degree or higher.

Section 3701 (relating to robbery).

Section 3702 (relating to robbery of motor vehicle).

Section 3921 (relating to theft by unlawful taking or disposition) upon conviction of the second felony offense.

Section 3923 (relating to theft by extortion) when the offense is accompanied by threats of violence.

Section 3925 (relating to receiving stolen property) upon conviction of the second felony offense.

Section 4906 (relating to false reports to law enforcement authorities) if the fictitious report involved the theft of a firearm as provided in section 4906(c)(2).

Section 4912 (relating to impersonating a public servant) if the person is impersonating a law enforcement officer.

Section 4952 (relating to intimidation of witnesses or victims).

Section 4953 (relating to retaliation against witness, victim or party).

Section 5121 (relating to escape).

Section 5122 (relating to weapons or implements for escape).

Section 5501(3) (relating to riot).

Section 5515 (relating to prohibiting of paramilitary training).

Section 5516 (relating to facsimile weapons of mass destruction).

Section 6110.1 (relating to possession of firearm by minor).

Section 6301 (relating to corruption of minors).

Section 6302 (relating to sale or lease of weapons and explosives).

Any offense equivalent to any of the above-enumerated offenses under the prior laws of this Commonwealth or any offense equivalent to any of the above-enumerated offenses under the statutes of any other state or of the United States.

(c) Other persons.--In addition to any person who has been convicted of any offense listed under subsection (b), the following persons shall be subject to the prohibition of subsection (a):

(1) A person who is a fugitive from justice. This paragraph does not apply to an individual whose fugitive status is based upon a nonmoving or moving summary offense under Title 75 (relating to vehicles).

(2) A person who has been convicted of an offense under the act of April 14, 1972 (P.L.233, No.64), known as

The Controlled Substance, Drug, Device and Cosmetic Act, or any equivalent Federal statute or equivalent statute of any other state, that may be punishable by a term of imprisonment exceeding two years.

(3) A person who has been convicted of driving under the influence of alcohol or controlled substance as provided in 75 Pa.C.S. §3802 (relating to driving under influence of alcohol or controlled substance) or the former 75 Pa.C.S. §3731, on three or more separate occasions within a five-year period. For the purposes of this paragraph only, the prohibition of subsection (a) shall only apply to transfers or purchases of firearms after the third conviction.

(4) A person who has been adjudicated as an incompetent or who has been involuntarily committed to a mental institution for inpatient care and treatment under section 302, 303 or 304 of the provisions of the act of July 9, 1976 (P.L.817, No.143), known as the Mental Health Procedures Act. This paragraph shall not apply to any proceeding under section 302 of the Mental Health Procedures Act unless the examining physician has issued a certification that inpatient care was necessary or that the person was committable.

(5) A person who, being an alien, is illegally or unlawfully in the United States.

(6) A person who is the subject of an active protection from abuse order issued pursuant to 23 Pa.C.S. §6108, which order provided for the relinquishment of firearms during the period of time the order is in effect. This prohibition shall terminate upon the expiration or vacation of an active protection from abuse order or portion thereof relating to the relinquishment of firearms.

(7) A person who was adjudicated delinquent by a court pursuant to 42 Pa.C.S. §6341 (relating to adjudication) or under any equivalent Federal statute or statute of any other state as a result of

conduct which if committed by an adult would constitute an offense under sections 2502, 2503, 2702, 2703 (relating to assault by prisoner), 2704, 2901, 3121, 3123, 3301, 3502, 3701 and 3923.

(8) A person who was adjudicated delinquent by a court pursuant to 42 Pa.C.S. §6341 or under any equivalent Federal statute or statute of any other state as a result of conduct which if committed by an adult would constitute an offense enumerated in subsection (b) with the exception of those crimes set forth in paragraph (7). This prohibition shall terminate 15 years after the last applicable delinquent adjudication or upon the person reaching the age of 30, whichever is earlier.

(9) A person who is prohibited from possessing or acquiring a firearm under 18 U.S.C. §922(g)(9) (relating to unlawful acts). If the offense which resulted in the prohibition under 18 U.S.C. §922(g)(9) was committed, as provided in 18 U.S.C. §921(a)(33)(A)(ii) (relating to definitions), by a person in any of the following relationships:

    (i) the current or former spouse, parent or guardian of the victim;

    (ii) a person with whom the victim shares a child in common;

    (iii) a person who cohabits with or has cohabited with the victim as a spouse, parent or guardian; or

    (iv) a person similarly situated to a spouse, parent or guardian of the victim; then the relationship need not be an element of the offense to meet the requirements of this paragraph.

(d) Exemption.--A person who has been convicted of a crime specified in subsection (a) or (b) or a person whose conduct meets the criteria in subsection (c)(1), (2), (5), (7) or (9) may make application to the court of common pleas of the county where the principal residence of the applicant is situated for relief from the disability imposed by this section upon the possession, transfer or control of a firearm. The court shall grant such relief if it determines that any of the following apply:

(1) The conviction has been vacated under circumstances where all appeals have been exhausted or where the right to appeal has expired.

(2) The conviction has been the subject of a full pardon by the Governor.

(3) Each of the following conditions is met:

    (i) The Secretary of the Treasury of the United States has relieved the applicant of an applicable disability imposed by Federal law upon the possession, ownership or control of a firearm as a result of the applicant's prior conviction, except that the court may waive this condition if the court determines that the Congress of the United States has not appropriated sufficient funds to enable the Secretary of the Treasury to grant relief to applicants eligible for the relief.

    (ii) A period of ten years, not including any time spent in incarceration, has elapsed since the most recent conviction of the applicant of a crime enumerated in subsection (b), a felony violation of The Controlled Substance, Drug, Device and Cosmetic Act or the offense which resulted in the prohibition under 18 U.S.C. §922(g)(9).

(e) Proceedings.--

(1) If a person convicted of an offense under subsection (a), (b) or (c)(1), (2), (5), (7) or (9) makes application to the court, a hearing shall be held in open court to determine whether the requirements of this section have been met. The commissioner and the district attorney of the county where the application is filed and any victim or survivor of a victim of the offense upon which the disability is based may be parties to the proceeding.

     (2) Upon application to the court of common pleas pursuant to paragraph (1) by an applicant who is subject to the prohibition under subsection (c)(3), the court shall grant such relief if a period of ten years, not including any time spent in incarceration, has passed since the applicant's most recent conviction under subsection (c)(3).

(f) Other exemptions and proceedings.--

     (1) Upon application to the court of common pleas under this subsection by an applicant subject to the prohibitions under subsection (c)(4), the court may grant such relief as it deems appropriate if the court determines that the applicant may possess a firearm without risk to the applicant or any other person.

     (2) If application is made under this subsection for relief from the disability imposed under subsection (c)(6), notice of such application shall be given to the person who had petitioned for the protection from abuse order, and such person shall be a party to the proceedings. Notice of any court order or amendment to a court order restoring firearms possession or control shall be given to the person who had petitioned for the protection from abuse order, to the sheriff and to the Pennsylvania State Police. The application and any proceedings on the application shall comply with 23 Pa.C.S. Ch. 61 (relating to protection from abuse).

     (3) All hearings conducted under this subsection shall be closed unless otherwise requested to be open by the applicant.

     (4) (i) The owner of any seized or confiscated firearms or of any firearms ordered relinquished under 23 Pa.C.S. §6108 shall be provided with a signed and dated written receipt by the appropriate law enforcement agency. This receipt shall include, but not limited to, a detailed identifying description indicating the serial number and condition of the firearm. In addition, the appropriate law enforcement agency shall be liable to the lawful

owner of said confiscated, seized or relinquished firearm for any loss, damage or substantial decrease in value of said firearm that is a direct result of a lack of reasonable care by the appropriate law enforcement agency.

    (ii) Firearms shall not be engraved or permanently marked in any manner, including, but not limited to, engraving of evidence or other identification numbers. Unless reasonable suspicion exists to believe that a particular firearm has been used in the commission of a crime, no firearm shall be test fired. Any reduction in the value of a firearm due to test firing, engraving or permanently marking in violation of this paragraph shall be considered damage, and the law enforcement agency shall be liable to the lawful owner of the firearm for the reduction in value caused by the test firing, engraving or permanently marking.

    (iii) For purposes of this paragraph, the term "firearm" shall include any scope, sight, bipod, sling, light, magazine, clip, ammunition or other firearm accessory attached to or seized, confiscated or relinquished with a firearm.

(g) Other restrictions.--Nothing in this section shall exempt a person from a disability in relation to the possession or control of a firearm which is imposed as a condition of probation or parole or which is imposed pursuant to the provision of any law other than this section.

(h) License prohibition.--Any person who is prohibited from possessing, using, controlling, selling, purchasing, transferring or manufacturing any firearm under this section shall not be eligible for or permitted to obtain a license to carry a firearm under section 6109 (relating to licenses).

(i) Firearm.--As used in this section only, the term "firearm" shall include any weapons which are designed to or may readily be converted to expel any projectile by the action of an explosive or the frame or receiver of any such weapon.

(j) Copy of order to State Police.--If the court grants relief from the disabilities imposed under this section, a copy of the order shall be sent by the prothonotary within ten days of the entry of the order to the Pennsylvania State Police and shall include the name, date of birth and Social Security number of the individual.

§6105.1. Restoration of firearm rights for offenses under prior laws of this Commonwealth.

(a) Restoration.--A person convicted of a disabling offense may make application to the court of common pleas in the county where the principal residence of the applicant is situated for restoration of firearms rights. The court shall grant restoration of firearms rights after a hearing in open court to determine whether the requirements of this section have been met unless:

(1) the applicant has been convicted of any other offense specified in section 6105(a) or (b) (relating to persons not to possess, use, manufacture, control, sell or transfer firearms) or the applicant's conduct meets the criteria in section 6105(c)(1), (2), (3), (4), (5), (6) or (7);

(2) the applicant has been convicted of any other crime punishable by imprisonment exceeding one year as defined in section 6102 (relating to definitions); or

(3) the applicant's character and reputation is such that the applicant would be likely to act in a manner dangerous to public safety.

(b) Notice and standing.--

(1) Notice of an application for restoration of firearms rights shall be provided to the Pennsylvania State Police, the district attorney of the county where the disabling offense occurred and the district attorney of the county where the application is filed. The district attorney of the county where the application is filed, the district attorney of the county where the disabling offense occurred and the Pennsylvania

State Police may, at their option, be parties to the proceeding.

(2) Notwithstanding paragraph (1), the standing of the Pennsylvania State Police as a party to a proceeding under this section shall be limited to determinations of whether the offense meets the definition of the phrase "disabling offense" or whether the provisions of subsection (a)(1) and (2) have been satisfied.

(c) Copy of order to Pennsylvania State Police.--If the court grants restoration of firearms rights to an applicant, a copy of the order shall be sent by the prothonotary within ten days of the entry of the order to the district attorneys and the Pennsylvania State Police, Firearms Division, and shall include the name, date of birth and Social Security number of the applicant.

(d) Expungement and pardon.--A restoration of firearms rights under this section shall not result in the expungement of any criminal history record information nor will it constitute a gubernatorial pardon.

(e) Definitions.--As used in this section, the following words and phrases shall have the meanings given to them in this subsection:

"Disabling offense." A conviction for any offense which:

(1) resulted in a Federal firearms disability and is substantially similar to either an offense currently graded as a crime punishable by a term of imprisonment for not more than two years or conduct which no longer constitutes a violation of law; and

(2) was a violation of either of the following:

(i) the former act of May 1, 1929 (P.L.905, No.403), known as The Vehicle Code, or the former act of April 29, 1959 (P.L.58, No.32), known as The Vehicle Code; or

(ii) the former act of June 24, 1939 (P.L.872, No.375), known as the Penal Code.

The definition shall not include any offense which, if committed under contemporary standards, would constitute a misdemeanor of the second degree or greater under section 2701 (relating to simple assault) and was committed by a current or former spouse, parent or guardian of the victim, by a person with whom the victim shares a child in common, by a person who is cohabitating with or has cohabited with the victim as a spouse, parent or guardian or by a person similarly situated to a spouse, parent or guardian of the victim.

"Restoration of firearms rights." Relieving any and all disabilities with respect to a person's right to own, possess, use, control, sell, purchase, transfer, manufacture, receive, ship or transport firearms, including any disabilities imposed pursuant to this subchapter. The phrase shall also mean the restoration of the right to vote, to hold public office and to serve on a jury.

§6106. Firearms not to be carried without a license.
   (a) Offense defined.--
      (1) Except as provided in paragraph (2), any person who carries a firearm in any vehicle or any person who carries a firearm concealed on or about his person, except in his place of abode or fixed place of business, without a valid and lawfully issued license under this chapter commits a felony of the third degree.
      (2) A person who is otherwise eligible to possess a valid license under this chapter but carries a firearm in any vehicle or any person who carries a firearm concealed on or about his person, except in his place of abode or fixed place of business, without a valid and lawfully issued license and has not committed any other criminal violation commits a misdemeanor of the first degree.
   (b) Exceptions.--The provisions of subsection (a) shall not apply to:
      (1) Constables, sheriffs, prison or jail wardens, or their deputies, policemen of this Commonwealth or its political subdivisions, or other law-enforcement officers.
      (2) Members of the army, navy, marine corps, air force or coast guard of the United States or of the National Guard or organized reserves when on duty.

(3) The regularly enrolled members of any organization duly organized to purchase or receive such firearms from the United States or from this Commonwealth.

(4) Any persons engaged in target shooting with a firearm, if such persons are at or are going to or from their places of assembly or target practice and if, while going to or from their places of assembly or target practice, the firearm is not loaded.

(5) Officers or employees of the United States duly authorized to carry a concealed firearm.

(6) Agents, messengers and other employees of common carriers, banks, or business firms, whose duties require them to protect moneys, valuables and other property in the discharge of such duties.

(7) Any person engaged in the business of manufacturing, repairing, or dealing in firearms, or the agent or representative of any such person, having in his possession, using or carrying a firearm in the usual or ordinary course of such business.

(8) Any person while carrying a firearm which is not loaded and is in a secure wrapper from the place of purchase to his home or place of business, or to a place of repair, sale or appraisal or back to his home or place of business, or in moving from one place of abode or business to another or from his home to a vacation or recreational home or dwelling or back, or to recover stolen property under section 6111.1(b)(4) (relating to Pennsylvania State Police), or to a place of instruction intended to teach the safe handling, use or maintenance of firearms or back or to a location to which the person has been directed to relinquish firearms under 23 Pa.C.S. §6108 (relating to relief) or back upon return of the relinquished firearm or to a licensed dealer's place of business for relinquishment pursuant to 23 Pa.C.S. §6108.2 (relating to relinquishment for consignment sale, lawful transfer or safekeeping) or back upon return of the relinquished firearm or to a location for safekeeping pursuant to 23 Pa.C.S. §6108.3 (relating

to relinquishment to third party for safekeeping) or back upon return of the relinquished firearm.

(9) Persons licensed to hunt, take furbearers or fish in this Commonwealth, if such persons are actually hunting, taking furbearers or fishing as permitted by such license, or are going to the places where they desire to hunt, take furbearers or fish or returning from such places.

(10) Persons training dogs, if such persons are actually training dogs during the regular training season.

(11) Any person while carrying a firearm in any vehicle, which person possesses a valid and lawfully issued license for that firearm which has been issued under the laws of the United States or any other state.

(12) A person who has a lawfully issued license to carry a firearm pursuant to section 6109 (relating to licenses) and that said license expired within six months prior to the date of arrest and that the individual is otherwise eligible for renewal of the license.

(13) Any person who is otherwise eligible to possess a firearm under this chapter and who is operating a motor vehicle which is registered in the person's name or the name of a spouse or parent and which contains a firearm for which a valid license has been issued pursuant to section 6109 to the spouse or parent owning the firearm.

(14) A person lawfully engaged in the interstate transportation of a firearm as defined under 18 U.S.C. §921(a)(3) (relating to definitions) in compliance with 18 U.S.C. §926A (relating to interstate transportation of firearms).

(15) Any person who possesses a valid and lawfully issued license or permit to carry a firearm which has been issued under the laws of another state, regardless of whether a reciprocity agreement exists between the Commonwealth and the state under section 6109(k), provided:

> > > (i) The state provides a reciprocal privilege for individuals licensed to carry firearms under section 6109.
> > > (ii) The Attorney General has determined that the firearm laws of the state are similar to the firearm laws of this Commonwealth.
> > (16) Any person holding a license in accordance with section 6109(f)(3).
> (c) Sportsman's firearm permit.--
> > (1) Before any exception shall be granted under paragraph (b)(9) or (10) of this section to any person 18 years of age or older licensed to hunt, trap or fish or who has been issued a permit relating to hunting dogs, such person shall, at the time of securing his hunting, furtaking or fishing license or any time after such license has been issued, secure a sportsman's firearm permit from the county treasurer. The sportsman's firearm permit shall be issued immediately and be valid throughout this Commonwealth for a period of five years from the date of issue for any legal firearm, when carried in conjunction with a valid hunting, furtaking or fishing license or permit relating to hunting dogs. The sportsman's firearm permit shall be in triplicate on a form to be furnished by the Pennsylvania State Police. The original permit shall be delivered to the person, and the first copy thereof, within seven days, shall be forwarded to the Commissioner of the Pennsylvania State Police by the county treasurer. The second copy shall be retained by the county treasurer for a period of two years from the date of expiration. The county treasurer shall be entitled to collect a fee of not more than $6 for each such permit issued, which shall include the cost of any official form. The Pennsylvania State Police may recover from the county treasurer the cost of any such form, but may not charge more than $1 for each official permit form furnished to the county treasurer.

(2) Any person who sells or attempts to sell a sportsman's firearm permit for a fee in excess of that amount fixed under this subsection commits a summary offense.

(d) Revocation of registration.--Any registration of a firearm under subsection (c) of this section may be revoked by the county treasurer who issued it, upon written notice to the holder thereof.

(e) Definitions.--

(1) For purposes of subsection (b)(3), (4), (5), (7) and (8), the term "firearm" shall include any weapon which is designed to or may readily be converted to expel any projectile by the action of an explosive or the frame or receiver of the weapon.

(2) As used in this section, the phrase "place of instruction" shall include any hunting club, rifle club, rifle range, pistol range, shooting range, the premises of a licensed firearms dealer or a lawful gun show or meet.

§6106.1. Carrying loaded weapons other than firearms.

(a) General rule.--Except as provided in Title 34 (relating to game), no person shall carry a loaded pistol, revolver, shotgun or rifle, other than a firearm as defined in section 6102 (relating to definitions), in any vehicle. The provisions of this section shall not apply to persons excepted from the requirement of a license to carry firearms under section 6106(b)(1), (2), (5) or (6) (relating to firearms not to be carried without a license) nor shall the provisions of this section be construed to permit persons to carry firearms in a vehicle where such conduct is prohibited by section 6106.

(b) Penalty.--A person who violates the provisions of this section commits a summary offense.

§6107. Prohibited conduct during emergency.

(a) General rule.--No person shall carry a firearm upon the public streets or upon any public property during an emergency proclaimed by a State or municipal governmental executive unless that person is:

    (1) Actively engaged in a defense of that person's life or property from peril or threat.

    (2) Licensed to carry firearms under section 6109 (relating to licenses) or is exempt from licensing under section 6106(b) (relating to firearms not to be carried without a license).

(b) Seizure, taking and confiscation.--Except as otherwise provided under subsection (a) and notwithstanding the provisions of 35 Pa.C.S. Ch. 73 (relating to Commonwealth services) or any other provision of law to the contrary, no firearm, accessory or ammunition may be seized, taken or confiscated during an emergency unless the seizure, taking or confiscation would be authorized absent the emergency.

(c) Definitions.--As used in this section, the following words and phrases shall have the meanings given to them in this subsection:

"Accessory." Any scope, sight, bipod, sling, light, magazine, clip or other related item that is attached to or necessary for the operation of a firearm.

"Firearm." The term includes any weapon that is designed to or may readily be converted to expel any projectile by the action of an explosive or the frame or receiver of any weapon.

§6108. Carrying firearms on public streets or public property in Philadelphia.

No person shall carry a firearm, rifle or shotgun at any time upon the public streets or upon any public property in a city of the first class unless:

    (1) such person is licensed to carry a firearm; or

    (2) such person is exempt from licensing under section 6106(b) of this title (relating to firearms not to be carried without a license).

§6109. Licenses.

(a) Purpose of license.--A license to carry a firearm shall be for the purpose of carrying a firearm concealed on or about one's person or in a vehicle throughout this Commonwealth.

(b) Place of application.--An individual who is 21 years of age or older may apply to a sheriff for a license to carry a firearm concealed on or about his person or in a vehicle within this Commonwealth. If the applicant is a resident of this Commonwealth, he shall make application with the sheriff of the county in which he resides or, if a resident of a city of the first class, with the chief of police of that city.

(c) Form of application and content.--The application for a license to carry a firearm shall be uniform throughout this Commonwealth and shall be on a form prescribed by the Pennsylvania State Police. The form may contain provisions, not exceeding one page, to assure compliance with this section. Issuing authorities shall use only the application form prescribed by the Pennsylvania State Police. One of the following reasons for obtaining a firearm license shall be set forth in the application: self-defense, employment, hunting and fishing, target shooting, gun collecting or another proper reason. The application form shall be dated and signed by the applicant and shall contain the following statement:

> I have never been convicted of a crime that prohibits me from possessing or acquiring a firearm under Federal or State law. I am of sound mind and have never been committed to a mental institution. I hereby certify that the statements contained herein are true and correct to the best of my knowledge and belief. I understand that, if I knowingly make any false statements herein, I am subject to penalties prescribed by law. I authorize the sheriff, or his designee, or, in the case of first class cities, the chief or head of the police department, or his designee, to inspect only those records or documents relevant to information required for this application. If I am issued a license and knowingly become ineligible to legally possess or acquire firearms, I will promptly notify the sheriff

of the county in which I reside or, if I reside in a city of the first class, the chief of police of that city.

(d) Sheriff to conduct investigation.--The sheriff to whom the application is made shall:

    (1) investigate the applicant's record of criminal conviction;

    (2) investigate whether or not the applicant is under indictment for or has ever been convicted of a crime punishable by imprisonment exceeding one year;

    (3) investigate whether the applicant's character and reputation are such that the applicant will not be likely to act in a manner dangerous to public safety;

    (4) investigate whether the applicant would be precluded from receiving a license under subsection (e)(1) or section 6105(h) (relating to persons not to possess, use, manufacture, control, sell or transfer firearms); and

    (5) conduct a criminal background, juvenile delinquency and mental health check following the procedures set forth in section 6111 (relating to sale or transfer of firearms), receive a unique approval number for that inquiry and record the date and number on the application.

(e) Issuance of license.--

    (1) A license to carry a firearm shall be for the purpose of carrying a firearm concealed on or about one's person or in a vehicle and shall be issued if, after an investigation not to exceed 45 days, it appears that the applicant is an individual concerning whom no good cause exists to deny the license. A license shall not be issued to any of the following:

        (i) An individual whose character and reputation is such that the individual would be likely to act in a manner dangerous to public safety.

        (ii) An individual who has been convicted of an offense under the act of April 14, 1972 (P.L.233, No.64), known as The Controlled Substance, Drug, Device and Cosmetic Act.

(iii) An individual convicted of a crime enumerated in section 6105.

(iv) An individual who, within the past ten years, has been adjudicated delinquent for a crime enumerated in section 6105 or for an offense under The Controlled Substance, Drug, Device and Cosmetic Act.

(v) An individual who is not of sound mind or who has ever been committed to a mental institution.

(vi) An individual who is addicted to or is an unlawful user of marijuana or a stimulant, depressant or narcotic drug.

(vii) An individual who is a habitual drunkard.

(viii) An individual who is charged with or has been convicted of a crime punishable by imprisonment for a term exceeding one year except as provided for in section 6123 (relating to waiver of disability or pardons).

(ix) A resident of another state who does not possess a current license or permit or similar document to carry a firearm issued by that state if a license is provided for by the laws of that state, as published annually in the Federal Register by the Bureau of Alcohol, Tobacco and Firearms of the Department of the Treasury under 18 U.S.C. §921(a)(19) (relating to definitions).

(x) An alien who is illegally in the United States.

(xi) An individual who has been discharged from the armed forces of the United States under dishonorable conditions.

(xii) An individual who is a fugitive from justice. This subparagraph does not apply to an individual whose fugitive status is based upon nonmoving or moving summary offense under Title 75 (relating to vehicles).

(xiii) An individual who is otherwise prohibited from possessing, using, manufacturing, controlling, purchasing, selling or transferring a firearm as provided by section 6105.

(xiv) An individual who is prohibited from possessing or acquiring a firearm under the statutes of the United States.

(3) The license to carry a firearm shall be designed to be uniform throughout this Commonwealth and shall be in a form prescribed by the Pennsylvania State Police. The license shall bear the following:

(i) The name, address, date of birth, race, sex, citizenship, height, weight, color of hair, color of eyes and signature of the licensee.

(ii) The signature of the sheriff issuing the license.

(iii) A license number of which the first two numbers shall be a county location code followed by numbers issued in numerical sequence.

(iv) The point-of-contact telephone number designated by the Pennsylvania State Police under subsection (l).

(v) The reason for issuance.

(vi) The period of validation.

(4) The sheriff shall require a photograph of the licensee on the license. The photograph shall be in a form compatible with the Commonwealth Photo Imaging Network.

(5) The original license shall be issued to the applicant. The first copy of the license shall be forwarded to the Pennsylvania State Police within seven days of the date of issue. The second copy shall be retained by the issuing authority for a period of seven years. Except pursuant to court order, both copies and the application shall, at the end of the seven-year period, be destroyed unless the license has been renewed within the seven-year period.

(f) Term of license.--

(1) A license to carry a firearm issued under subsection (e) shall be valid throughout this Commonwealth for

a period of five years unless extended under paragraph (3) or sooner revoked.

(2) At least 60 days prior to the expiration of each license, the issuing sheriff shall send to the licensee an application for renewal of license. Failure to receive a renewal application shall not relieve a licensee from the responsibility to renew the license.

(3) Notwithstanding paragraph (1) or any other provision of law to the contrary, a license to carry a firearm that is held by a member of the United States Armed Forces or the Pennsylvania National Guard on Federal active duty and deployed overseas that is scheduled to expire during the period of deployment shall be extended until 90 days after the end of the deployment.

(4) Possession of a license, together with a copy of the person's military orders showing the dates of overseas deployment, including the date that the overseas deployment ends, shall constitute, during the extension period specified in paragraph (3), a defense to any charge filed pursuant to section 6106 (relating to firearms not to be carried without a license) or 6108 (relating to carrying firearms on public streets or public property in Philadelphia).

(g) Grant or denial of license.--Upon the receipt of an application for a license to carry a firearm, the sheriff shall, within 45 days, issue or refuse to issue a license on the basis of the investigation under subsection (d) and the accuracy of the information contained in the application. If the sheriff refuses to issue a license, the sheriff shall notify the applicant in writing of the refusal and the specific reasons. The notice shall be sent by certified mail to the applicant at the address set forth in the application.

(h) Fee.--

(1) In addition to fees described in paragraphs (2)(ii) and (3), the fee for a license to carry a firearm is $19. This includes all of the following:

(i) A renewal notice processing fee of $1.50.

       (ii) An administrative fee of $5 under section 14(2) of the act of July 6, 1984 (P.L.614, No.127), known as the Sheriff Fee Act.

(2) (Expired).

(3) An additional fee of $1 shall be paid by the applicant for a license to carry a firearm and shall be remitted by the sheriff to the Firearms License Validation System Account, which is hereby established as a special restricted receipt account within the General Fund of the State Treasury. The account shall be used for purposes under subsection (l). Moneys credited to the account and any investment income accrued are hereby appropriated on a continuing basis to the Pennsylvania State Police.

(4) No fee other than that provided by this subsection or the Sheriff Fee Act may be assessed by the sheriff for the performance of any background check made pursuant to this act.

(5) The fee is payable to the sheriff to whom the application is submitted and is payable at the time of application for the license.

(6) Except for the administrative fee of $5 under section 14(2) of the Sheriff Fee Act, all other fees shall be refunded if the application is denied but shall not be refunded if a license is issued and subsequently revoked.

(7) A person who sells or attempts to sell a license to carry a firearm for a fee in excess of the amounts fixed under this subsection commits a summary offense.

(i) Revocation.--A license to carry firearms may be revoked by the issuing authority for good cause. A license to carry firearms shall be revoked by the issuing authority for any reason stated in subsection (e)(1) which occurs during the term of the permit. Notice of revocation shall be in writing and shall state the specific reason for revocation. Notice shall be sent by certified mail to the individual whose license is revoked, and, at that time, notice shall also be provided to the Pennsylvania State Police by electronic means, including e-mail or facsimile transmission, that the license is no longer valid. An individual whose license is revoked shall surrender the license to the issuing authority within five days of receipt of the notice. An individual whose license is revoked may appeal to the court of common pleas for the judicial district in which the individual resides. An individual who violates this section commits a summary offense.

(i.1) Notice to sheriff.--Notwithstanding any statute to the contrary:

   (1) Upon conviction of a person for a crime specified in section 6105(a) or (b) or upon conviction of a person for a crime punishable by imprisonment exceeding one year or upon a determination that the conduct of a person meets the criteria specified in section 6105(c)(1), (2), (3), (5), (6) or (9), the court shall determine if the defendant has a license to carry firearms issued pursuant to this section. If the defendant has such a license, the court shall notify the sheriff of the county in which that person resides, on a form developed by the Pennsylvania State Police, of the identity of the person and the nature of the crime or conduct which resulted in the notification. The notification shall be transmitted by the judge within seven days of the conviction or determination.

   (2) Upon adjudication that a person is incompetent or upon the involuntary commitment of a person to a mental institution for inpatient care and treatment under the act of July 9, 1976 (P.L.817, No.143), known as the Mental Health Procedures Act, or upon involuntary treatment of a person as described under section 6105(c)(4), the judge of the court of common pleas, mental health review officer or county mental health and mental retardation administrator shall notify the sheriff of the county in which that person resides, on a form developed by the Pennsylvania State Police, of the identity of the person who has been adjudicated, committed or

treated and the nature of the adjudication, commitment or treatment. The notification shall be transmitted by the judge, mental health review officer or county mental health and mental retardation administrator within seven days of the adjudication, commitment or treatment.

(j) Immunity.--A sheriff who complies in good faith with this section shall be immune from liability resulting or arising from the action or misconduct with a firearm committed by any individual to whom a license to carry a firearm has been issued.

(k) Reciprocity.--

   (1) The Attorney General shall have the power and duty to enter into reciprocity agreements with other states providing for the mutual recognition of a license to carry a firearm issued by the Commonwealth and a license or permit to carry a firearm issued by the other state. To carry out this duty, the Attorney General is authorized to negotiate reciprocity agreements and grant recognition of a license or permit to carry a firearm issued by another state.

   (2) The Attorney General shall report to the General Assembly within 180 days of the effective date of this paragraph and annually thereafter concerning the agreements which have been consummated under this subsection.

(l) Firearms License Validation System.--

   (1) The Pennsylvania State Police shall establish a nationwide toll-free telephone number, known as the Firearms License Validation System, which shall be operational seven days a week, 24 hours per day, for the purpose of responding to law enforcement inquiries regarding the validity of any Pennsylvania license to carry a firearm.

   (2) Notwithstanding any other law regarding the confidentiality of information, inquiries to the Firearms License Validation System regarding the validity of any Pennsylvania license to carry a

firearm may only be made by law enforcement personnel acting within the scope of their official duties.

(3) Law enforcement personnel outside this Commonwealth shall provide their originating agency identifier number and the license number of the license to carry a firearm which is the subject of the inquiry.

(4) Responses to inquiries by law enforcement personnel outside this Commonwealth shall be limited to the name of the licensee, the validity of the license and any information which may be provided to a criminal justice agency pursuant to Chapter 91 (relating to criminal history record information).

(m) Inquiries.--

(1) The Attorney General shall, not later than one year after the effective date of this subsection and not less than once annually, contact in writing the appropriate authorities in any other state which does not have a current reciprocity agreement with the Commonwealth to determine if:

(i) the state will negotiate a reciprocity agreement;

(ii) a licensee may carry a concealed firearm in the state; or

(iii) a licensee may apply for a license or permit to carry a firearm issued by the state.

(2) The Attorney General shall maintain a current list of those states which have a reciprocity agreement with the Commonwealth, those states which allow licensees to carry a concealed firearm and those states which allow licensees to apply for a license or permit to carry a firearm. This list shall be posted on the Internet, provided to the Pennsylvania State Police and made available to the public upon request.

(m.1) Temporary emergency licenses.--

(1) A person seeking a temporary emergency license to carry a concealed firearm shall submit to the sheriff of the county in which the person resides all of the following:

(i) Evidence of imminent danger to the person or the person's minor child. For purposes of this subparagraph, the term "minor" shall have the same meaning as provided in 1 Pa.C.S. §1991 (relating to definitions).

(ii) A sworn affidavit that contains the information required on an application for a license to carry a firearm and attesting that the person is 21 years of age or older, is not prohibited from owning firearms under section 6105 (relating to persons not to possess, use, manufacture, control, sell or transfer firearms) or any other Federal or State law and is not currently subject to a protection from abuse order or a protection order issued by a court of another state.

(iii) In addition to the provisions of subsection (h), a temporary emergency license fee established by the Commissioner of the Pennsylvania State Police for an amount that does not exceed the actual cost of conducting the criminal background check or $10, whichever is less.

(iv) An application for a license to carry a firearm on the form prescribed pursuant to subsection (c).

(2) Upon receipt of the items required under paragraph (1), the sheriff immediately shall conduct a criminal history, juvenile delinquency and mental health record check of the applicant pursuant to section 6105. Immediately upon receipt of the results of the records check, the sheriff shall review the information and shall determine whether the applicant meets the criteria set forth in this subsection. If the sheriff determines that the applicant has met all of the criteria, the sheriff shall immediately issue the applicant a temporary emergency license to carry a concealed firearm.

(3) If the sheriff refuses to issue a temporary emergency license, the sheriff shall specify the grounds for the

denial in a written notice to the applicant. The applicant may appeal the denial or challenge criminal records check results that were the basis of the denial, if applicable, in the same manner as a denial of a license to carry a firearm under this section.

(4) A temporary emergency license issued under this subsection shall be valid for 45 days and may not be renewed. A person who has been issued a temporary emergency license under this subsection shall not be issued another temporary emergency license unless at least five years have expired since the issuance of the prior temporary emergency license. During the 45 days the temporary emergency license is valid, the sheriff shall conduct an additional investigation of the person for the purposes of determining whether the person may be issued a license pursuant to this section. If, during the course of this investigation, the sheriff discovers any information that would have prohibited the issuance of a license pursuant to this section, the sheriff shall be authorized to revoke the temporary emergency license as provided in subsection (i).

(5) The temporary emergency license issued pursuant to this section shall be consistent with the form prescribed in subsection (e)(3), (4) and (5). In addition to the information provided in those paragraphs, the temporary emergency license shall be clearly marked "Temporary."

(6) A person who holds a temporary emergency license to carry a firearm shall have the same rights to carry a firearm as a person issued a license to carry a firearm under this section. A licensee under this subsection shall be subject to all other duties, restrictions and penalties under this section, including revocation pursuant to subsection (i).

(7) A sheriff who issues a temporary emergency license to carry a firearm shall retain, for the entire period during which the temporary emergency license is in effect, the evidence of imminent danger that the

applicant submitted to the sheriff that was the basis for the license, or a copy of the evidence, as appropriate.

(8) A person applying for a temporary emergency license shall complete the application required pursuant to subsection (c) and shall provide at the time of application the information required in paragraph (1).

(9) Prior to the expiration of a temporary emergency license, if the sheriff has determined pursuant to investigation that the person issued a temporary emergency license is not disqualified and if the temporary emergency license has not been revoked pursuant to subsection (i), the sheriff shall issue a license pursuant to this section that is effective for the balance of the five-year period from the date of the issuance of the temporary emergency license. Records and all other information, duties and obligations regarding such licenses shall be applicable as otherwise provided in this section.

(10) As used in this subsection, the term "evidence of imminent danger" means:

(i) a written document prepared by the Attorney General, a district attorney, a chief law enforcement officer, judicial officer or their designees describing the facts that give a person reasonable cause to fear a criminal attack upon the person or the person's minor child. For the purposes of this subparagraph, the term "chief law enforcement officer" shall have the same meaning as provided in 42 Pa.C.S. §8951 (relating to definitions) and "judicial officer" shall have the same meaning as provided in 42 Pa.C.S. §102 (relating to definitions).

(ii) a police report.

(m.2) Inconsistent provisions.--Notwithstanding the provisions of section 7506 (relating to violation of rules regarding conduct on Commonwealth property), 75 Pa.C.S. §7727 (relating to additional limitations on operation) or the act of June 28, 1995 (P.L.89, No.18), known as the Conservation and Natural Resources Act, and regulations promulgated under that act, a firearm may be carried as provided in subsection (a) by:

(1) a law enforcement officer whose current identification as a law enforcement officer shall be construed as a valid license to carry a firearm; or

(2) any licensee.

(m.3) Construction.--Nothing in this section shall be construed to:

(1) Permit the hunting or harvesting of any wildlife with a firearm or ammunition not otherwise permitted by 34 Pa.C.S. (relating to game).

(2) Authorize any Commonwealth agency to regulate the possession of firearms in any manner inconsistent with the provisions of this title.

(n) Definition.--As used in this section, the term "licensee" means an individual who is licensed to carry a firearm under this section.

§6110.1. Possession of firearm by minor.

(a) Firearm.--Except as provided in subsection (b), a person under 18 years of age shall not possess or transport a firearm anywhere in this Commonwealth.

(b) Exception.--Subsection (a) shall not apply to a person under 18 years of age:

(1) who is under the supervision of a parent, grandparent, legal guardian or an adult acting with the expressed consent of the minor's custodial parent or legal guardian and the minor is engaged in lawful activity, including safety training, lawful target shooting, engaging in an organized competition involving the use of a firearm or the firearm is unloaded and the minor is transporting it for a lawful purpose; or

(2) who is lawfully hunting or trapping in accordance with 34 Pa.C.S. (relating to game).

(c) Responsibility of adult.--Any person who knowingly and intentionally delivers or provides to the minor a firearm in violation of subsection (a) commits a felony of the third degree.

(d) Forfeiture.--Any firearm in the possession of a person under 18 years of age in violation of this section shall be promptly seized by the arresting law enforcement officer and upon conviction or adjudication of delinquency shall be forfeited or, if stolen, returned to the lawful owner.

§6110.2. Possession of firearm with altered manufacturer's number.

(a) General rule.--No person shall possess a firearm which has had the manufacturer's number integral to the frame or receiver altered, changed, removed or obliterated.

(b) Penalty.--A person who violates this section commits a felony of the second degree.

(c) Definition.--As used in this section, the term "firearm" shall have the same meaning as that term is defined in section 6105(i) (relating to persons not to possess, use, manufacture, control, sell or transfer firearms), except that the term shall not include antique firearms as defined in section 6118 (relating to antique firearms).

§6111. Sale or transfer of firearms.

(a) Time and manner of delivery.--

(1) Except as provided in paragraph (2), no seller shall deliver a firearm to the purchaser or transferee thereof until 48 hours shall have elapsed from the time of the application for the purchase thereof, and, when delivered, the firearm shall be securely wrapped and shall be unloaded.

(2) Thirty days after publication in the Pennsylvania Bulletin that the Instantaneous Criminal History Records Check System has been established in accordance with the Brady Handgun Violence Prevention Act (Public Law 103-159, 18 U.S.C. §921 et seq.), no seller shall deliver a firearm to the purchaser thereof until the provisions of this section

have been satisfied, and, when delivered, the firearm shall be securely wrapped and shall be unloaded.

(b) Duty of seller.--No licensed importer, licensed manufacturer or licensed dealer shall sell or deliver any firearm to another person, other than a licensed importer, licensed manufacturer, licensed dealer or licensed collector, until the conditions of subsection (a) have been satisfied and until he has:

(1) For purposes of a firearm as defined in section 6102 (relating to definitions), obtained a completed application/record of sale from the potential buyer or transferee to be filled out in triplicate, the original copy to be sent to the Pennsylvania State Police, postmarked via first class mail, within 14 days of the sale, one copy to be retained by the licensed importer, licensed manufacturer or licensed dealer for a period of 20 years and one copy to be provided to the purchaser or transferee. The form of this application/record of sale shall be no more than one page in length and shall be promulgated by the Pennsylvania State Police and provided by the licensed importer, licensed manufacturer or licensed dealer. The application/record of sale shall include the name, address, birthdate, gender, race, physical description and Social Security number of the purchaser or transferee, the date of the application and the caliber, length of barrel, make, model and manufacturer's number of the firearm to be purchased or transferred. The application/record of sale shall also contain the following question:

Are you the actual buyer of the firearm(s), as defined under 18 Pa.C.S. §6102 (relating to definitions), listed on this application/record of sale? Warning: You are not the actual buyer if you are acquiring the firearm(s) on behalf of another person, unless you are legitimately acquiring the firearm as a gift for any of the following individuals who are legally eligible to own a firearm:

(1) spouse;

(2) parent;

(3) child;

(4) grandparent; or

(5) grandchild.

(1.1) On the date of publication in the Pennsylvania Bulletin of a notice by the Pennsylvania State Police that the instantaneous records check has been implemented, all of the following shall apply:

(i) In the event of an electronic failure under section 6111.1(b)(2) (relating to Pennsylvania State Police) for purposes of a firearm which exceeds the barrel and related lengths set forth in section 6102, obtained a completed application/record of sale from the potential buyer or transferee to be filled out in triplicate, the original copy to be sent to the Pennsylvania State Police, postmarked via first class mail, within 14 days of sale, one copy to be retained by the licensed importer, licensed manufacturer or licensed dealer for a period of 20 years and one copy to be provided to the purchaser or transferee.

(ii) The form of the application/record of sale shall be no more than one page in length and shall be promulgated by the Pennsylvania State Police and provided by the licensed importer, licensed manufacturer or licensed dealer.

(iii) For purposes of conducting the criminal history, juvenile delinquency and mental health records background check which shall be completed within ten days of receipt of the information from the dealer, the application/record of sale shall include the name, address, birthdate, gender, race, physical description and Social Security number of the purchaser or transferee and the date of application.

(iv) No information regarding the type of firearm need be included other than an indication that the firearm exceeds the barrel lengths set forth in section 6102.

(v) Unless it has been discovered pursuant to a criminal history, juvenile delinquency and mental health records background check that the potential purchaser or transferee is prohibited from possessing a firearm pursuant to section 6105 (relating to persons not to possess, use, manufacture, control, sell or transfer firearms), no information on the application/record of sale provided pursuant to this subsection shall be retained as precluded by section 6111.4 (relating to registration of firearms) by the Pennsylvania State Police either through retention of the application/record of sale or by entering the information onto a computer, and, further, an application/record of sale received by the Pennsylvania State Police pursuant to this subsection shall be destroyed within 72 hours of the completion of the criminal history, juvenile delinquency and mental health records background check.

(1.2) Fees collected under paragraph (3) and section 6111.2 (relating to firearm sales surcharge) shall be transmitted to the Pennsylvania State Police within 14 days of collection.

(1.3) In addition to the criminal penalty under section 6119 (relating to violation penalty), any person who knowingly and intentionally maintains or fails to destroy any information submitted to the Pennsylvania State Police for purposes of a background check pursuant to paragraphs (1.1) and (1.4) or violates section 6111.4 shall be subject to a civil penalty of $250 per violation, entry or failure to destroy.

(1.4) Following implementation of the instantaneous records check by the Pennsylvania State Police on or before December 1, 1998, no application/record of sale shall be completed for the purchase or transfer of a firearm which exceeds the barrel lengths set forth in section 6102. A statement shall be submitted by the dealer to the Pennsylvania State Police, postmarked via first class mail, within 14 days of the sale, containing the number of firearms sold which exceed the barrel and related lengths set forth in section 6102, the amount of surcharge and other fees remitted and a list of the unique approval numbers given pursuant to paragraph (4), together with a statement that the background checks have been performed on the firearms contained in the statement. The form of the statement relating to performance of background checks shall be promulgated by the Pennsylvania State Police.

(2) Inspected photoidentification of the potential purchaser or transferee, including, but not limited to, a driver's license, official Pennsylvania photoidentification card or official government photoidentification card. In the case of a potential buyer or transferee who is a member of a recognized religious sect or community whose tenets forbid or discourage the taking of photographs of members of that sect or community, a seller shall accept a valid-without-photo driver's license or a combination of documents, as prescribed by the Pennsylvania State Police, containing the applicant's name, address, date of birth and the signature of the applicant.

(3) Requested by means of a telephone call that the Pennsylvania State Police conduct a criminal history, juvenile delinquency history and a mental health record check. The purchaser and the licensed dealer

shall provide such information as is necessary to accurately identify the purchaser. The requester shall be charged a fee equivalent to the cost of providing the service but not to exceed $2 per buyer or transferee.

(4) Received a unique approval number for that inquiry from the Pennsylvania State Police and recorded the date and the number on the application/record of sale form.

(5) Issued a receipt containing the information from paragraph (4), including the unique approval number of the purchaser. This receipt shall be prima facie evidence of the purchaser's or transferee's compliance with the provisions of this section.

(6) Unless it has been discovered pursuant to a criminal history, juvenile delinquency and mental health records background check that the potential purchaser or transferee is prohibited from possessing a firearm pursuant to section 6105, no information received via telephone following the implementation of the instantaneous background check system from a purchaser or transferee who has received a unique approval number shall be retained by the Pennsylvania State Police.

(7) For purposes of the enforcement of 18 U.S.C. §922(d)(9), (g)(1) and (s)(1) (relating to unlawful acts), in the event the criminal history or juvenile delinquency background check indicates a conviction for a misdemeanor that the Pennsylvania State Police cannot determine is or is not related to an act of domestic violence, the Pennsylvania State Police shall issue a temporary delay of the approval of the purchase or transfer. During the temporary delay, the Pennsylvania State Police shall conduct a review or investigation of the conviction with courts, local police departments, district attorneys and other law enforcement or related institutions as necessary to determine whether or not the misdemeanor conviction involved an act of domestic

violence. The Pennsylvania State Police shall conduct the review or investigation as expeditiously as possible. No firearm may be transferred by the dealer to the purchaser who is the subject of the investigation during the temporary delay. The Pennsylvania State Police shall notify the dealer of the termination of the temporary delay and either deny the sale or provide the unique approval number under paragraph (4).

(c) Duty of other persons.--Any person who is not a licensed importer, manufacturer or dealer and who desires to sell or transfer a firearm to another unlicensed person shall do so only upon the place of business of a licensed importer, manufacturer, dealer or county sheriff's office, the latter of whom shall follow the procedure set forth in this section as if he were the seller of the firearm. The provisions of this section shall not apply to transfers between spouses or to transfers between a parent and child or to transfers between grandparent and grandchild.

(d) Defense.--Compliance with the provisions of this section shall be a defense to any criminal complaint under the laws of this Commonwealth or other claim or cause of action under this chapter arising from the sale or transfer of any firearm.

(e) Nonapplicability of section.--This section shall not apply to the following:

(1) Any firearm manufactured on or before 1898.

(2) Any firearm with a matchlock, flintlock or percussion cap type of ignition system.

(3) Any replica of any firearm described in paragraph (1) if the replica:

(i) is not designed or redesigned to use rimfire or conventional center fire fixed ammunition; or

(ii) uses rimfire or conventional center fire fixed ammunition which is no longer manufactured in the United States and which is not readily available in the ordinary channels of commercial trade.

(f) Application of section.--

    (1) For the purposes of this section only, except as provided by paragraph (2), "firearm" shall mean any weapon which is designed to or may readily be converted to expel any projectile by the action of an explosive or the frame or receiver of any such weapon.

    (2) The provisions contained in subsections (a) and (c) shall only apply to pistols or revolvers with a barrel length of less than 15 inches, any shotgun with a barrel length of less than 18 inches, any rifle with a barrel length of less than 16 inches or any firearm with an overall length of less than 26 inches.

    (3) The provisions contained in subsection (a) shall not apply to any law enforcement officer whose current identification as a law enforcement officer shall be construed as a valid license to carry a firearm or any person who possesses a valid license to carry a firearm under section 6109 (relating to licenses).

    (4) (i) The provisions of subsection (a) shall not apply to any person who presents to the seller or transferor a written statement issued by the official described in subparagraph (iii) during the ten-day period ending on the date of the most recent proposal of such transfer or sale by the transferee or purchaser stating that the transferee or purchaser requires access to a firearm because of a threat to the life of the transferee or purchaser or any member of the household of that transferee or purchaser.

        (ii) The issuing official shall notify the applicant's local police authority that such a statement has been issued. In counties of the first class the chief of police shall notify the police station or substation closest to the applicant's residence.

        (iii) The statement issued under subparagraph (ii) shall be issued by the district attorney, or his designee, of the county of residence if the transferee or purchaser resides in a municipality where there is no chief of police.

Otherwise, the statement shall be issued by the chief of police in the municipality in which the purchaser or transferee resides.

(g) Penalties.--

(1) Any person, licensed dealer, licensed manufacturer or licensed importer who knowingly or intentionally sells, delivers or transfers a firearm in violation of this section commits a misdemeanor of the second degree.

(2) Any person, licensed dealer, licensed manufacturer or licensed importer who knowingly or intentionally sells, delivers or transfers a firearm under circumstances intended to provide a firearm to any person, purchaser or transferee who is unqualified or ineligible to control, possess or use a firearm under this chapter commits a felony of the third degree and shall in addition be subject to revocation of the license to sell firearms for a period of three years.

(3) Any person, licensed dealer, licensed manufacturer or licensed importer who knowingly and intentionally requests a criminal history, juvenile delinquency or mental health record check or other confidential information from the Pennsylvania State Police under this chapter for any purpose other than compliance with this chapter or knowingly and intentionally disseminates any criminal history, juvenile delinquency or mental health record or other confidential information to any person other than the subject of the information commits a felony of the third degree.

(3.1) Any person, licensed dealer, licensed manufacturer or licensed importer who knowingly and intentionally obtains or furnishes information collected or maintained pursuant to section 6109 for any purpose other than compliance with this chapter or who knowingly or intentionally disseminates, publishes or otherwise makes available such information to any person other than the subject of the information commits a felony of the third degree.

(4) Any person, purchaser or transferee commits a felony of the third degree if, in connection with the purchase, delivery or transfer of a firearm under this chapter, he knowingly and intentionally:

(i) makes any materially false oral statement;

(ii) makes any materially false written statement, including a statement on any form promulgated by Federal or State agencies; or

(iii) willfully furnishes or exhibits any false identification intended or likely to deceive the seller, licensed dealer or licensed manufacturer.

(5) Notwithstanding section 306 (relating to liability for conduct of another; complicity) or any other statute to the contrary, any person, licensed importer, licensed dealer or licensed manufacturer who knowingly and intentionally sells, delivers or transfers a firearm in violation of this chapter who has reason to believe that the firearm is intended to be used in the commission of a crime or attempt to commit a crime shall be criminally liable for such crime or attempted crime.

(6) Notwithstanding any act or statute to the contrary, any person, licensed importer, licensed manufacturer or licensed dealer who knowingly and intentionally sells or delivers a firearm in violation of this chapter who has reason to believe that the firearm is intended to be used in the commission of a crime or attempt to commit a crime shall be liable in the amount of the civil judgment for injuries suffered by any person so injured by such crime or attempted crime.

(h) Subsequent violation penalty.--

(1) A second or subsequent violation of this section shall be a felony of the second degree. A person who at the time of sentencing has been convicted of another offense under this section shall be

sentenced to a mandatory minimum sentence of imprisonment of five years. A second or subsequent offense shall also result in permanent revocation of any license to sell, import or manufacture a firearm.

(2) Notice of the applicability of this subsection to the defendant and reasonable notice of the Commonwealth's intention to proceed under this section shall be provided prior to trial. The applicability of this section shall be determined at sentencing. The court shall consider evidence presented at trial, shall afford the Commonwealth and the defendant an opportunity to present necessary additional evidence and shall determine by a preponderance of the evidence if this section is applicable.

(3) There shall be no authority for a court to impose on a defendant to which this subsection is applicable a lesser sentence than provided for in paragraph (1), to place the defendant on probation or to suspend sentence. Nothing in this section shall prevent the sentencing court from imposing a sentence greater than that provided in this section. Sentencing guidelines promulgated by the Pennsylvania Commission on Sentencing shall not supersede the mandatory sentences provided in this section.

(4) If a sentencing court refuses to apply this subsection where applicable, the Commonwealth shall have the right to appellate review of the action of the sentencing court. The appellate court shall vacate the sentence and remand the case to the sentencing court for imposition of a sentence in accordance with this section if it finds that the sentence was imposed in violation of this subsection.

(5) For the purposes of this subsection, a person shall be deemed to have been convicted of another offense under this section whether or not judgment of sentence has been imposed for that violation.

(i) Confidentiality.--All information provided by the potential purchaser, transferee or applicant, including, but not limited to, the potential purchaser, transferee or applicant's name or identity, furnished by a potential purchaser or transferee under this section or any applicant for a license to carry a firearm as provided by section 6109 shall be confidential and not subject to public disclosure. In addition to any other sanction or penalty imposed by this chapter, any person, licensed dealer, State or local governmental agency or department that violates this subsection shall be liable in civil damages in the amount of $1,000 per occurrence or three times the actual damages incurred as a result of the violation, whichever is greater, as well as reasonable attorney fees.

(j) Exemption.--

   (1) The provisions of subsections (a) and (b) shall not apply to:

      (i) sales between Federal firearms licensees; or

      (ii) the purchase of firearms by a chief law enforcement officer or his designee, for the official use of law enforcement officers.

   (2) For the purposes of this subsection, the term "chief law enforcement officer" shall include the Commissioner of the Pennsylvania State Police, the chief or head of a police department, a county sheriff or any equivalent law enforcement official.

§6111.4. Registration of firearms.

Notwithstanding any section of this chapter to the contrary, nothing in this chapter shall be construed to allow any government or law enforcement agency or any agent thereof to create, maintain or operate any registry of firearm ownership within this Commonwealth. For the purposes of this section only, the term "firearm" shall include any weapon that is designed to or may readily be converted to expel any projectile by the action of an explosive or the frame or receiver of any such weapon.

§6111.5. Rules and regulations.

The Pennsylvania State Police shall in the manner provided by law promulgate the rules and regulations necessary to carry out this chapter, including regulations to ensure the identity, confidentiality and security of all records and data provided pursuant hereto.

§6112. Retail dealer required to be licensed.

No retail dealer shall sell, or otherwise transfer or expose for sale or transfer, or have in his possession with intent to sell or transfer, any firearm as defined in section 6113(d) (relating to licensing of dealers) without being licensed as provided in this chapter.

§6113. Licensing of dealers.

  (a) General rule.--The chief or head of any police force or police department of a city, and, elsewhere, the sheriff of the county, shall grant to reputable applicants licenses, in form prescribed by the Pennsylvania State Police, effective for three years from date of issue, permitting the licensee to sell firearms direct to the consumer, subject to the following conditions in addition to those specified in section 6111 (relating to sale or transfer of firearms), for breach of any of which the license shall be forfeited and the licensee subject to punishment as provided in this subchapter:

    (1) The business shall be carried on only upon the premises designated in the license or at a lawful gun show or meet.

    (2) The license, or a copy thereof, certified by the issuing authority, shall be displayed on the premises where it can easily be read.

    (3) No firearm shall be sold in violation of any provision of this subchapter.

    (4) No firearm shall be sold under any circumstances unless the purchaser is personally known to the seller or shall present clear evidence of the purchaser's identity.

    (5) A true record in triplicate shall be made of every firearm sold, in a book kept for the purpose, the form of which may be prescribed by the Pennsylvania State Police, and shall be personally signed by the purchaser and by the person effecting

the sale, each in the presence of the other, and shall contain the information required by section 6111. The record shall be maintained by the licensee for a period of 20 years.

(6) No firearm as defined in section 6102 (relating to definitions) shall be displayed in any part of any premises where it can readily be seen from the outside. In the event that the Commissioner of the Pennsylvania State Police shall find a clear and present danger to public safety within this Commonwealth or any area thereof, firearms shall be stored and safeguarded pursuant to regulations to be established by the Pennsylvania State Police by the licensee during the hours when the licensee is closed for business.

(7) The dealer shall possess all applicable current revenue licenses.

(b) Fee.--The fee for issuing said license shall be $30, which fee shall be paid into the county treasury.

(c) Revocation.--Any license granted under subsection (a) of this section may be revoked for cause by the person issuing the same, upon written notice to the holder thereof.

(d) Definitions.--For the purposes of this section and section 6112 (relating to retail dealer required to be licensed) only unless otherwise specifically provided, the term "firearm" shall include any weapon that is designed to or may readily be converted to expel any projectile by the action of an explosive or the frame or receiver of any such weapon.

§6114. Judicial review.

The action of the chief of police, sheriff, county treasurer or other officer under this subchapter shall be subject to judicial review in the manner and within the time provided by 2 Pa.C.S. Ch. 7 Subch. B (relating to judicial review of local agency action). A judgment sustaining a refusal to grant a license shall not bar, after one year, a new application; nor shall a judgment in favor of the petitioner prevent the defendant from thereafter revoking or refusing to renew such license for any proper cause which may thereafter occur. The court shall have full power to dispose of all costs.

§6115. Loans on, or lending or giving firearms prohibited.
- (a) Offense defined.--No person shall make any loan secured by mortgage, deposit or pledge of a firearm, nor, except as provided in subsection (b), shall any person lend or give a firearm to another or otherwise deliver a firearm contrary to the provisions of this subchapter.
- (b) Exception.--
  - (1) Subsection (a) shall not apply if any of the following apply:
    - (i) The person who receives the firearm is licensed to carry a firearm under section 6109 (relating to licenses).
    - (ii) The person who receives the firearm is exempt from licensing.
    - (iii) The person who receives the firearm is engaged in a hunter safety program certified by the Pennsylvania Game Commission or a firearm training program or competition sanctioned or approved by the National Rifle Association.
    - (iv) The person who receives the firearm meets all of the following:
      - (A) Is under 18 years of age.
      - (B) Pursuant to section 6110.1 (relating to possession of firearm by minor) is under the supervision, guidance and instruction of a responsible individual who:
        - (I) is 21 years of age or older; and
        - (II) is not prohibited from owning or possessing a firearm under section 6105 (relating to persons not to possess, use, manufacture, control, sell or transfer firearms).
    - (v) The person who receives the firearm is lawfully hunting or trapping and is in compliance with the provisions of Title 34 (relating to game).

(vi) A bank or other chartered lending institution is able to adequately secure firearms in its possession.

(2) Nothing in this section shall be construed to prohibit the transfer of a firearm under 20 Pa.C.S. Ch. 21 (relating to intestate succession) or by bequest if the individual receiving the firearm is not precluded from owning or possessing a firearm under section 6105.

(3) Nothing in this section shall be construed to prohibit the loaning or giving of a firearm to another in one's dwelling or place of business if the firearm is retained within the dwelling or place of business.

(4) Nothing in this section shall prohibit the relinquishment of firearms to a third party in accordance with 23 Pa.C.S. §6108.3 (relating to relinquishment to third party for safekeeping).

§6116. False evidence of identity.

In addition to any other penalty provided in this chapter, the furnishing of false information or offering false evidence of identity is a violation of section 4904 (relating to unsworn falsification to authorities).

§6117. Altering or obliterating marks of identification.

(a) Offense defined.--No person shall change, alter, remove, or obliterate the manufacturer's number integral to the frame or receiver of any firearm which shall have the same meaning as provided in section 6105 (relating to persons not to possess, use, manufacture, control, sell or transfer firearms).

(b) Presumption.--(Deleted by amendment).

(c) Penalty.--A violation of this section constitutes a felony of the second degree.

(d) Appellate review.--(Deleted by amendment).

§6118. Antique firearms.

(a) General rule.--This subchapter shall not apply to antique firearms.

(b) Exception.--Subsection (a) shall not apply to the extent that such antique firearms, reproductions or replicas of firearms are concealed weapons as provided in section 6106 (relating to firearms not be carried without a license), nor shall it apply to the provisions of section 6105 (relating to persons not to possess, use, manufacture, control, sell or transfer firearms) if such antique firearms, reproductions or replicas of firearms are suitable for use.

(c) Definition.--As used in this section, the term "antique firearm" means:

    (1) Any firearm with a matchlock, flintlock or percussion cap type of ignition system.

    (2) Any firearm manufactured on or before 1898.

    (3) Any replica of any firearm described in paragraph (2) if such replica:

        (i) is not designed or redesigned for using rimfire or conventional center fire fixed ammunition; or

        (ii) uses rimfire or conventional center fire fixed ammunition which is no longer manufactured in the United States and which is not readily available in the ordinary channels of commercial trade.

§6119. Violation penalty.

Except as otherwise specifically provided, an offense under this subchapter constitutes a misdemeanor of the first degree.

§6120. Limitation on the regulation of firearms and ammunition.

(a) General rule.--No county, municipality or township may in any manner regulate the lawful ownership, possession, transfer or transportation of firearms, ammunition or ammunition components when carried or transported for purposes not prohibited by the laws of this Commonwealth.

(a.1) No right of action.--

    (1) No political subdivision may bring or maintain an action at law or in equity against any firearms or ammunition manufacturer, trade association or

dealer for damages, abatement, injunctive relief or any other relief or remedy resulting from or relating to either the lawful design or manufacture of firearms or ammunition or the lawful marketing or sale of firearms or ammunition to the public.

(2) Nothing in this subsection shall be construed to prohibit a political subdivision from bringing or maintaining an action against a firearms or ammunition manufacturer or dealer for breach of contract or warranty as to firearms or ammunition purchased by the political subdivision.

(a.2) Relief.--A person adversely affected by an ordinance, a resolution, regulation, rule, practice or any other action promulgated or enforced by a county, municipality or township prohibited under subsection (a) or 53 Pa.C.S. §2962(g) (relating to limitation on municipal powers) may seek declaratory or injunctive relief and actual damages in an appropriate court.

(a.3) Reasonable expenses.--A court shall award reasonable expenses to a person adversely affected in an action under subsection (a.2) for any of the following:

(1) A final determination by the court is granted in favor of the person adversely affected.

(2) The regulation in question is rescinded, repealed or otherwise abrogated after suit has been filed under subsection (a.2) but before the final determination by the court.

(b) Definitions.--As used in this section, the following words and phrases shall have the meanings given to them in this subsection:

"Dealer." The term shall include any person engaged in the business of selling at wholesale or retail a firearm or ammunition.

"Firearms." This term shall have the meaning given to it in section 5515 (relating to prohibiting of paramilitary training) but shall not include air rifles as that term is defined in section 6304 (relating to sale and use of air rifles).

"Person adversely affected." Any of the following:

(1) A resident of this Commonwealth who may legally possess a firearm under Federal and State law.

(2) A person who otherwise has standing under the laws of this Commonwealth to bring an action under subsection (a.2).

(3) A membership organization, in which a member is a person described under paragraph (1) or (2).

"Political subdivision." The term shall include any home rule charter municipality, county, city, borough, incorporated town, township or school district.

"Reasonable expenses." The term includes, but is not limited to, attorney fees, expert witness fees, court costs and compensation for loss of income.

§6121. Certain bullets prohibited.

(a) Offense defined.--It is unlawful for any person to possess, use or attempt to use a KTW teflon-coated bullet or other armor-piercing ammunition while committing or attempting to commit a crime of violence as defined in section 6102 (relating to definitions).

(b) Grading.--An offense under this section constitutes a felony of the third degree.

(c) Sentencing.--Any person who is convicted in any court of this Commonwealth of a crime of violence and who uses or carries, in the commission of that crime, a firearm loaded with KTW ammunition or any person who violates this section shall, in addition to the punishment provided for the commission of the crime, be sentenced to a term of imprisonment for not less than five years. Notwithstanding any other provision of law, the court shall not suspend the sentence of any person convicted of a crime subject to this subsection nor place him on probation nor shall the term of imprisonment run concurrently with any other term of imprisonment including that imposed for the crime in which the KTW ammunition was being used or carried. No person sentenced under this subsection shall be eligible for parole.

(d) Definition.--As used in this section the term "armor-piercing ammunition" means ammunition which, when or if fired from any firearm as defined in section 6102 that is used or attempted to be used in violation of subsection (a) under the test procedure of the National Institute of Law Enforcement and Criminal Justice Standard for the Ballistics Resistance of Police Body Armor promulgated December 1978, is determined to be capable of penetrating bullet-resistant apparel or body armor meeting the requirements of Type IIA of Standard NILECJ-STD-0101.01 as formulated by the United States Department of Justice and published in December of 1978.

§6122. Proof of license and exception.

    (a) General rule.--When carrying a firearm concealed on or about one's person or in a vehicle, an individual licensed to carry a firearm shall, upon lawful demand of a law enforcement officer, produce the license for inspection. Failure to produce such license either at the time of arrest or at the preliminary hearing shall create a rebuttable presumption of nonlicensure.

    (b) Exception.--An individual carrying a firearm on or about his person or in a vehicle and claiming an exception under section 6106(b) (relating to firearms not to be carried without a license) shall, upon lawful demand of a law enforcement officer, produce satisfactory evidence of qualification for exception.

§6123. Waiver of disability or pardons.

A waiver of disability from Federal authorities as provided for in 18 U.S.C. § 925 (relating to exceptions; relief from disabilities), a full pardon from the Governor or an overturning of a conviction shall remove any corresponding disability under this subchapter except the disability under section 6105 (relating to persons not to possess, use, manufacture, control, sell or transfer firearms).

§6124. Administrative regulations.

The commissioner may establish form specifications and regulations, consistent with section 6109(c) (relating to licenses), with respect to uniform forms control, including the following:

    (1) License to carry firearms.

    (2) Firearm registration.

(3) Dealer's license.
(4) Application for purchase of a firearm.
(5) Record of sale of firearms.

§6125. Distribution of uniform firearm laws and firearm safety brochures.

It shall be the duty of the Pennsylvania State Police beginning January 1, 1996, to distribute to every licensed firearm dealer in this Commonwealth firearms safety brochures at no cost to the dealer. The brochures shall be written by the Pennsylvania State Police, with the cooperation of the Pennsylvania Game Commission, and shall include a summary of the major provisions of this subchapter, including, but not limited to, the duties of the sellers and purchasers and the transferees of firearms. The brochure or a copy thereof shall be provided without charge to each purchaser.

§6127. Firearm tracing.

(a) Illegal possession.--Upon confiscating or recovering a firearm from the possession of anyone who is not permitted by Federal or State law to possess a firearm, a local law enforcement agency shall use the best available information, including a firearms trace where necessary, to determine how and from where the person gained possession of the firearm.

(b) Tracing.--Local law enforcement shall use the National Tracing Center of the Federal Bureau of Alcohol, Tobacco, Firearms and Explosives in complying with subsection (a).

(c) Notification.--Local law enforcement agencies shall advise the Pennsylvania State Police of all firearms that are recovered in accordance with this section.

SUBCHAPTER B
FIREARMS GENERALLY

§6141.1. Purchase of rifles and shotguns outside this Commonwealth.

Nothing in this chapter shall be construed to prohibit a person in this Commonwealth who may lawfully purchase, possess, use, control, sell, transfer or manufacture a firearm which exceeds the barrel and related lengths set forth in section 6102 (relating to definitions) from lawfully purchasing or otherwise obtaining such a firearm in a jurisdiction outside this Commonwealth.

§6142. Locking device for firearms.

(a) Offense defined.--It shall be unlawful for any licensee to sell, deliver or transfer any firearm as defined in section 6102 (relating to definitions), other than an antique firearm as defined in section 6118 (relating to antique firearms), to any other person, other than another licensee, unless the transferee is provided with or purchases a locking device for that firearm or the design of the firearm incorporates a locking device.

(b) Exceptions.--Firearms for transfer to or possession by any law enforcement officer employed by any Federal, State or local government entity or rail police employed and certified by a rail carrier as a police officer are not subject to the provisions of this section.

(c) Penalties.--A violation of the provisions of this section shall be a summary offense.

(d) Good faith compliance.--A licensee who in good faith complies with this section shall not be civilly liable as a result of such compliance with this section, except for any acts or omissions intentionally designed to harm or for grossly negligent acts or omissions which result in harm.

(e) Admissibility of evidence.--A transferee's purchase or receipt of a locking device in conjunction with the purchase of a firearm pursuant to this section shall not be admissible as evidence in any civil action brought against the transferee.

(f) Definitions.--As used in this section, the following words and phrases shall have the meanings given to them in this subsection:

"Licensee." Any licensed manufacturer, importer or dealer of firearms.

"Locking device." Either of the following:

(1) a device that, when installed on a firearm, is designed to prevent the firearm from being operated without first deactivating the device; or

(2) a device that is incorporated into the design of a firearm and that is designed to prevent the operation of the firearm by anyone not having access to the device.

APPENDIX B: SELECTED FEDERAL FORMS

ATF Form 4473   *Page 1*

OMB No. 1140-0020

U.S. Department of Justice
Bureau of Alcohol, Tobacco, Firearms and Explosives

Firearms Transaction Record Part I - Over-the-Counter

WARNING: You may not receive a firearm if prohibited by Federal or State law. The information you provide will be used to determine whether you are prohibited under law from receiving a firearm. Certain violations of the Gun Control Act, 18 U.S.C. §§ 921 et. seq., are punishable by up to 10 years imprisonment and/or up to a $250,000 fine.

Prepare in original only. All entries must be handwritten in ink. Read the Notices, Instructions, and Definitions on this form. "PLEASE PRINT."

Transferor's Transaction Serial Number (If any)

Section A - Must Be Completed Personally By Transferee (Buyer)

1. Transferee's Full Name
Last Name | First Name | Middle Name (If no middle name, state "NMN")

2. Current Residence Address (U.S. Postal abbreviations are acceptable. Cannot be a post office box.)
Number and Street Address | City | County | State | ZIP Code

3. Place of Birth
U.S. City and State -OR- Foreign Country

4. Height
Ft. ___
In. ___

5. Weight (Lbs.)

6. Gender
☐ Male
☐ Female

7. Birth Date
Month | Day | Year

8. Social Security Number (Optional, but will help prevent misidentification)

9. Unique Personal Identification Number (UPIN) if applicable (See Instructions for Question 9.)

10.a. Ethnicity
☐ Hispanic or Latino
☐ Not Hispanic or Latino

10.b. Race (Check one or more boxes.)
☐ American Indian or Alaska Native
☐ Asian
☐ Black or African American
☐ Native Hawaiian or Other Pacific Islander
☐ White

11. Answer questions 11.a. (see exceptions) through 11.l. and 12 (if applicable) by checking or marking "yes" or "no" in the boxes to the right of the questions.

		Yes	No
a.	Are you the actual transferee/buyer of the firearm(s) listed on this form Warning: You are not the actual buyer if you are acquiring the firearm(s) on behalf of another person. If you are not the actual buyer, the dealer cannot transfer the firearm(s) to you. (See Instructions for Question 11.a.) Exception: If you are picking up a repaired firearm(s) for another person, you are not required to answer 11.a. and may proceed to question 11.b.	☐	☐
b.	Are you under indictment or information in any court for a felony, or any other crime, for which the judge could imprison you for more than one year (See Instructions for Question 11.b.)	☐	☐
c.	Have you ever been convicted in any court of a felony, or any other crime, for which the judge could have imprisoned you for more than one year, even if you received a shorter sentence including probation (See Instructions for Question 11.c.)	☐	☐
d.	Are you a fugitive from justice	☐	☐
e.	Are you an unlawful user of, or addicted to, marijuana or any depressant, stimulant, narcotic drug, or any other controlled substance	☐	☐
f.	Have you ever been adjudicated mentally defective (which includes a determination by a court, board, commission, or other lawful authority that you are a danger to yourself or to others or are incompetent to manage your own affairs) OR have you ever been committed to a mental institution (See Instructions for Question 11.f.)	☐	☐
g.	Have you been discharged from the Armed Forces under dishonorable conditions	☐	☐
h.	Are you subject to a court order restraining you from harassing, stalking, or threatening your child or an intimate partner or child of such partner (See Instructions for Question 11.h.)	☐	☐
i.	Have you ever been convicted in any court of a misdemeanor crime of domestic violence (See Instructions for Question 11.i.)	☐	☐
j.	Have you ever renounced your United States citizenship	☐	☐
k.	Are you an alien illegally in the United States	☐	☐
l.	Are you an alien admitted to the United States under a nonimmigrant visa (See Instructions for Question 11.l.) If you answered "no" to this question, do NOT respond to question 12 and proceed to question 13.	☐	☐
12.	If you are an alien admitted to the United States under a nonimmigrant visa, do you fall within any of the exceptions set forth in the instructions (If "yes," the licensee must complete question 20c.) (See Instructions for Question 12.) If question 11.l. is answered with a "no" response, then do NOT respond to question 12 and proceed to question 13.	☐	☐

13. What is your State of residence (if any) (See Instructions for Question 13.)

14. What is your country of citizenship (List/check more than one, if applicable. If you are a citizen of the United States, proceed to question 16.) ☐ United States of America
☐ Other (Specify) _____

15. If you are not a citizen of the United States, what is your U.S.-issued alien number or admission number

Note: Previous Editions Are Obsolete
Page 1 of 6

Transferee (Buyer) Continue to Next Page
STAPLE IF PAGES BECOME SEPARATED

ATF Form 4473 (5300.9) Part I
Revised April 2012

ATF Form 4473

I certify that my answers to Section A are true, correct, and complete. I have read and understand the Notices, Instructions, and Definitions on ATF Form 4473. I understand that answering "yes" to question 11.a. if I am not the actual buyer is a crime punishable as a felony under Federal law, and may also violate State and/or local law. I understand that a person who answers "yes" to any of the questions 11.b. through 11.k. is prohibited from purchasing or receiving a firearm. I understand that a person who answers "yes" to question 11.l. is prohibited from purchasing or receiving a firearm, unless the person also answers "Yes" to question 12. I also understand that making any false oral or written statement, or exhibiting any false or misrepresented identification with respect to this transaction, is a crime punishable as a felony under Federal law, and may also violate State and/or local law. I further understand that the repetitive purchase of firearms for the purpose of resale for livelihood and profit without a Federal firearms license is a violation of law (See Instructions for Question 16).

16. Transferee's/Buyer's Signature	17. Certification Date

Section B - Must Be Completed By Transferor (Seller)

18. Type of firearm(s) to be transferred (check or mark all that apply):	19. If sale at a gun show or other qualifying event.
☐ Handgun ☐ Long Gun ☐ Other Firearm (Frame, Receiver, etc. (rifles or shotguns) See Instructions for Question 18.)	Name of Event _____ City, State _____

20a. Identification (e.g., Virginia Driver's license (VADL) or other valid government-issued photo identification.) (See Instructions for Question 20.a.)

Issuing Authority and Type of Identification	Number on Identification	Expiration Date of Identification (if any)		
		Month	Day	Year

20b. Alternate Documentation (if driver's license or other identification document does not show current residence address) (See Instructions for Question 20.b.)

20c. Aliens Admitted to the United States Under a Nonimmigrant Visa Must Provide: Type of documentation showing an exception to the nonimmigrant visa prohibition. (See Instructions for Question 20.c.)

Questions 21, 22, or 23 Must Be Completed Prior To The Transfer Of The Firearm(s) (See Instructions for Questions 21, 22 and 23.)

21a. Date the transferee's identifying information in Section A was transmitted to NICS or the appropriate State agency: (Month/Day/Year)	21b. The NICS or State transaction number (if provided) was:
Month Day Year	

21c. The response initially provided by NICS or the appropriate State agency was:	21d. If initial NICS or State response was "Delayed," the following response was received from NICS or the appropriate State agency:
☐ Proceed ☐ Delayed ☐ Denied The firearm(s) may be transferred on ☐ Cancelled _____ (Missing Disposition Information date provided by NICS) if State law permits (optional)	☐ Proceed _____ (date) ☐ Denied _____ (date) ☐ Cancelled _____ (date) ☐ No resolution was provided within 3 business days.

21e. (Complete if applicable.) After the firearm was transferred, the following response was received from NICS or the appropriate State agency on: _____ (date).   ☐ Proceed   ☐ Denied   ☐ Cancelled

21f. The name and Brady identification number of the NICS examiner (Optional)

_____ (name)   _____ (number)

22.	☐ No NICS check was required because the transfer involved only National Firearms Act firearm(s). (See Instructions for Question 22.)

23. ☐ No NICS check was required because the buyer has a valid permit from the State where the transfer is to take place, which qualifies as an exemption to NICS (See Instructions for Question 23.)

Issuing State and Permit Type	Date of Issuance (if any)	Expiration Date (if any)	Permit Number (if any)

Section C - Must Be Completed Personally By Transferee (Buyer)

If the transfer of the firearm(s) takes place on a different day from the date that the transferee (buyer) signed Section A, the transferee must complete Section C immediately prior to the transfer of the firearm(s). (See Instructions for Question 24 and 25.)

I certify that my answers to the questions in Section A of this form are still true, correct and complete.

24. Transferee's/Buyer's Signature	25. Recertification Date

Transferor (Seller) Continue to Next Page
STAPLE IF PAGES BECOME SEPARATED

ATF Form 4473 (5300.9) Part I
Revised April 2012

ATF Form 4473   *Page 3*

26. Manufacturer and/or Importer (If the manufacturer and importer are different, the FFL should include both.)	27. Model	28. Serial Number	29. Type (pistol, revolver, rifle, shotgun, receiver, frame, etc.) (See instructions for question 29)	30. Caliber or Gauge
Section D - Must Be Completed By Transferor (Seller)				

30a. Total Number of Firearms (Please handwrite by printing e.g., one, two, three, etc. Do not use numerals.)	30b. Is any part of this transaction a Pawn Redemption ☐ Yes ☐ No

30c. For Use by FFL (See Instructions for Question 30c.)

Complete ATF Form 3310.4 For Multiple Purchases of Handguns Within 5 Consecutive Business Days

31. Trade/corporate name and address of transferor (seller) (Hand stamp may be used.)	32. Federal Firearms License Number (Must contain at least first three and last five digits of FFL Number X-XX-XXXXX.) (Hand stamp may be used.)

The Person Transferring The Firearm(s) Must Complete Questions 33-36. For Denied/Cancelled Transactions, The Person Who Completed Section B Must Complete Questions 33-35.

I certify that my answers in Sections B and D are true, correct, and complete. I have read and understand the Notices, Instructions, and Definitions on ATF Form 4473. On the basis of: (1) the statements in Section A (and Section C if the transfer does not occur on the day Section A was completed); (2) my verification of the identification noted in question 20a (and my reverification at the time of transfer if the transfer does not occur on the day Section A was completed); and (3) the information in the current State Laws and Published Ordinances, it is my belief that it is not unlawful for me to sell, deliver, transport, or otherwise dispose of the firearm(s) listed on this form to the person identified in Section A.

33. Transferor's/Seller's Name (Please print)	34. Transferor's/Seller's Signature	35. Transferor's/Seller's Title	36. Date Transferred

NOTICES, INSTRUCTIONS AND DEFINITIONS

Purpose of the Form: The information and certification on this form are designed so that a person licensed under 18 U.S.C. § 923 may determine if he or she may lawfully sell or deliver a firearm to the person identified in Section A, and to alert the buyer of certain restrictions on the receipt and possession of firearms. This form should only be used for sales or transfers where the seller is licensed under 18 U.S.C. § 923. The seller of a firearm must determine the lawfulness of the transaction and maintain proper records of the transaction. Consequently, the seller must be familiar with the provisions of 18 U.S.C. §§ 921-931 and the regulations in 27 CFR Part 478. In determining the lawfulness of the sale or delivery of a long gun (rifle or shotgun) to a resident of another State, the seller is presumed to know the applicable State laws and published ordinances in both the seller's State and the buyer's State.

After the seller has completed the firearms transaction, he or she must make the completed, original ATF Form 4473 (which includes the Notices, General Instructions, and Definitions), and any supporting documents, part of his or her permanent records. Such Forms 4473 must be retained for at least 20 years. Filing may be chronological (by date), alphabetical (by name), or numerical (by transaction serial number), as long as all of the seller's completed Forms 4473 are filed in the same manner. FORMS 4473 FOR DENIED/CANCELLED TRANSFERS MUST BE RETAINED: If the transfer of a firearm is denied/cancelled by NICS, or if for any other reason the transfer is not complete after a NICS check is initiated, the licensee must retain the ATF Form 4473 in his or her records for at least 5 years. Forms 4473 with respect to which a sale, delivery, or transfer did not take place shall be separately retained in alphabetical (by name) or chronological (by date of transferee's certification) order.

If you or the buyer discover that an ATF Form 4473 is incomplete or improperly completed after the firearm has been transferred, and you or the buyer wish to make a record of your discovery, then photocopy the inaccurate form and make any necessary additions or revisions to the photocopy. You only should make changes to Sections B and D. The buyer should only make changes to Sections A and C. Whoever made the changes should initial and date the changes. The corrected photocopy should be attached to the original Form 4473 and retained as part of your permanent records.

Over-the-Counter Transaction: The sale or other disposition of a firearm by a seller to a buyer, at the seller's licensed premises. This includes the sale or other disposition of a rifle or shotgun to a nonresident buyer on such premises.

State Laws and Published Ordinances: The publication (ATF P 5300.5) of State firearms laws and local ordinances ATF distributes to licensees.

Exportation of Firearms: The State or Commerce Departments may require you to obtain a license prior to export.

Section A

Question 1. Transferee's Full Name: The buyer must personally complete Section A of this form and certify (sign) that the answers are true, correct, and complete. However, if the buyer is unable to read and/or write, the answers (other than the signature) may be completed by another person, excluding the seller. Two persons (other than the seller) must then sign as witnesses to the buyer's answers and signature.

When the buyer of a firearm is a corporation, company, association, partnership, or other such business entity, an officer authorized to act on behalf of the

ATF Form 4   *Page 1*

U.S. Department of Justice
Bureau of Alcohol, Tobacco, Firearms and Explosives

OMB No. 1140-0014 (01/31/2014)

Application for Tax Paid Transfer and Registration of Firearm

ATF Control Number		Submit in Duplicate to: National Firearms Act Branch Bureau of Alcohol, Tobacco, Firearms and Explosives, P.O. Box 530298 Atlanta, GA 30353-0298
2a. Transferee's Name and Address *(Including tradename, if any) (See instruction 2)*		1. Type of Transfer *(Check one)* ☐ $5 ☐ $200 Submit with your application a check or money order for the appropriate amount made payable to the Bureau of Alcohol, Tobacco, Firearms and Explosives. Upon approval of this application, this office will acquire, affix and cancel the required "National Firearms Act" stamp for you. *(See instructions 2h, 2i and 3.)*
	2b. County	
3a. Transferor's Name and Address *(Including trade name, if any) (Executors: see instruction 2k)*		3d. Number, Street, City, State and Zip Code of Residence *(or Firearms Business Premises)* if Different from Item 3a.
	3b. Transferor's Telephone Number and Area Code	
3c. If Applicable: Decedent's Name, Address, and Date of Death		

The above-named and undersigned transferor hereby makes application as required by Section 5812 of the National Firearms Act to transfer and register the firearm described below to the transferee.

4. Description of Firearm *(Complete items a through h)*

a. Name and Address of Manufacturer and/or Importer of Firearm	b. Type of Firearm *(See instruction 1c)*	c. Caliber, Gauge or Size *(Specify)*	d. Model		
			Length (Inches)	e. Of Barrel:	f Overall:
		g. Serial Number			

h. Additional Description or Data Appearing on Firearm *(Attach additional sheet if necessary)*

5. Transferee's Federal Firearms License *(If any)* (Give complete 15-digit number) *(See instruction 2b)*				6. Transferee's Special (Occupational) Tax Status *(If any)*	
First 6 digits	2 digits	2 digits	5 digits	a. Employer Identification Number	b. Class

7. Transferor's Federal Firearms License *(If any)* (Give complete 15-digit number) *(See instruction 2b)*				8. Transferor's Special (Occupational) Tax Status *(If any)*	
First 6 digits	2 digits	2 digits	5 digits	a. Employer Identification Number	b. Class

Under Penalties of Perjury, I Declare that I have examined this application, and to the best of my knowledge and belief it is true, correct and complete, and that the transfer of the described firearm to the transferee and receipt and possession of it by the transferee are not prohibited by the provisions of Chapter 44, Title 18, United States Code; Chapter 53, Title 26, United States Code; or Title VII of the Omnibus Crime Control and Safe Streets Act, as amended; or any provisions of State or local law.

9. Consent to Disclosure of Information to Transferee *(See instruction 8)* . I Do or Do Not *(Circle one)* Authorize ATF to Provide Information Relating to this Application to the Above-Named Transferee .

10. Signature of Transferor *(or authorized official)*	11. Name and Title of Authorized Official *(Print or type)*	12. Date

The Space Below is for the use of the Bureau of Alcohol, Tobacco, Firearms and Explosives

By authority of the Director, This Application has been Examined, and the Transfer and Registration of the Firearm Described herein and the Interstate Movement of that Firearm, when Applicable, to the Transferee are:	Stamp Denomination
☐ Approved *(with the following conditions, if any)*	☐ Disapproved *(For the following reasons)*
Signature of Authorized ATF Official	Date

ATF Form 4 (5320.4)
Revised March 2006

ATF Form 4   *Page 2*

Transferee Information

The following questions must be answered by any transferee who is **not** a Federal firearms licensee or government agency. The transferee shall give full details on a separate sheet for all "YES" answers. *(See instruction 2d)*

13. Are You:	Yes	No	14. Have You:	Yes	No
a. Charged by information or under indictment in any court for a crime punishable by imprisonment for a term exceeding one year?	☐	☐	a. Been convicted in any court of a crime for which the judge could have imprisoned you for more than one year, even if the judge actually gave you a shorter sentence?	☐	☐
b. A fugitive from justice?	☐	☐	b. Been discharged from the armed forces under dishonorable conditions?	☐	☐
c. An alien who is illegally or unlawfully in the United States?	☐	☐	c. Been adjudicated mentally defective or been committed to a mental institution?	☐	☐
d. Under 21 years of age?	☐	☐	d. Renounced your United States citizenship?	☐	☐
e. An unlawful user of or addicted to, marijuana, or any depressant, stimulant, or narcotic drug, or any other controlled substance?	☐	☐	e. Been convicted in any court of a misdemeanor crime of domestic violence? This includes any misdemeanor conviction involving the use or attempted use of physical force committed by a current or former spouse, parent, or guardian of the victim, or by a person with a similar relationship with the victim.	☐	☐
f. Subject to a court order restraining you from harassing, stalking or threatening an intimate partner or child of such partner?	☐	☐			

15. Transferee's Certification *(See instruction 2e)*

I, _____ , have a reasonable necessity to
(Name of Transferee)
possess the machinegun, short-barreled rifle, short-barreled shotgun, or destructive device described on this application
for the following reason(s) _____

and my possession of the device or weapon would be consistent with public safety (18 U.S.C. 922(b) (4) and 27 CFR 478.98).

UNDER PENALTIES OF PERJURY, I declare that I have examined this application and the documents submitted in support thereof, and to the best of my knowledge and belief it is true, correct and complete.

_____   _____
(Signature of Transferee)   (Date)

16. Photograph

Affix
Recent Photograph Here
(Approximately 2" x 2")
(See instruction 2f.)

17. Law Enforcement Certification *(See instruction 2e)*

I certify that I am the chief law enforcement officer of the organization named below having jurisdiction in the area of residence of
_____ . I have no information indicating that the transferee will use the firearm or device
(Name of Transferee)
described on this application for other than lawful purposes. I have no information that the receipt or possession of the firearm or device described in item 4 would be place the transferee in violation of State or local law.

_____   _____
(Signature and Title of Chief Law Enforcement Officer)   (Date)

_____
(Organization and Street Address)

_____   _____
(County)   (Telephone Number)

Important Information for Currently Registered Firearms

If this registration document evidences the current registration of the firearm described on it, please note the following information.

Estate Procedures: For procedures regarding the transfer of firearms in an estate resulting from the death of the registrant identified in item 2a, the executor should contact the NFA Branch, Bureau of Alcohol, Tobacco, Firearms and Explosives, 244 Needy Road, Martinsburg, WV 25405.

Change of Address: Unless currently licensed under the Gun Control Act, the registrant shall notify the NFA Branch, Bureau of Alcohol, Tobacco, Firearms and Explosives, 244 Needy Road, Martinsburg, WV 25405, in writing, of any change to the address in Item 2a.

Change of Description: The registrant shall notify the NFA Branch, Bureau of Alcohol, Tobacco, Firearms and Explosives, 244 Needy Road, Martinsburg, WV 25405, in writing, of any change to the description of the firearm in Item 4.

Interstate Movement: If the firearm identified in item 4 is a machinegun, short-barreled rifle, short-barreled shotgun, or destructive device, the registrant may be required by 18 U.S.C. § 922(a)(4) to obtain permission from ATF prior to any transportation in interstate or foreign commerce.

Restrictions on Possession: Any restriction *(see approval block on face of form)* on the possession of the firearm identified in item 4 continues with the further transfer of the firearm.

Persons Prohibited from Possessing Firearms: If the registrant becomes prohibited by 18 U.S.C. § 922 from possessing a firearm, the registrant shall notify the NFA Branch, Bureau of Alcohol, Tobacco, Firearms and Explosives, 244 Needy Road, Martinsburg, WV 25405, in writing, immediately upon becoming prohibited for guidance on the disposal of the firearm.

Proof of Registration: This approved application is the registrant's proof of registration and it shall be made available to any ATF officer upon request.

ATF Form 4 (5320.4)
Revised March 2006

ATF Form 1   *Page 1*

OMB No. 1140-0011 (06/30/2016)

U.S. Department of Justice
Bureau of Alcohol, Tobacco, Firearms and Explosives

Application to Make and Register a Firearm

ATF Control Number

To: National Firearms Act Branch, Bureau of Alcohol, Tobacco, Firearms and Explosives, P.O. Box 530298, Atlanta, GA 30353-0298

(Submit in duplicate. See Instructions attached.)

As required by Sections 5821(b), 5822, and 5841 of the National Firearms Act, Title 26 U.S.C., Chapter 53, the undersigned hereby submits application to make and register the firearm described below.	1. Type of Application (check one)
2. Application is made by: ☐ Individual ☐ Corporation or Other Legal Entity ☐ Government Entity 3a. Trade Name (If any)	☐ a. Tax Paid. Submit your tax payment of $200 with the application. The tax may be paid by credit or debit card, check, or money order. Please complete item 17. Upon approval of the application, we will affix and cancel the required National Firearms Act Stamp. (See instructions 2c and 3)
3b. Applicant's Name and Mailing Address (Type or print below and between the dots) (See instruction 2d) ◆ ●	☐ b. Tax Exempt because firearm is being made on behalf of the United States, or any department, independent establishment, or agency thereof.
3c. If P.O. Box is Shown Above, Street Address Must Be Given Here	☐ c. Tax Exempt because firearm is being made by or on behalf of any State or possession of the United States, or any political subdivison thereof, or any official police organization of such a government entity engaged in criminal investigations.
3d. County 3e. Telephone Area Code and Number	

4. Description of Firearm (complete items a through i) (See instruction 2j)

a. Name and Location of Original Manufacturer of Firearm (Receiver) (If prototype, furnish plans and specifications)	b. Type of Firearm to be made (See instruction 1c)	c. Caliber or Gauge (Specify one)	d. Model		
			Length (Inches)	e. Of Barrel:	f. Overall:
			g. Serial Number		

h. Additional Description (Include all numbers and other identifying data to include maker's name, city and state which will appear on the firearm) (use additional sheet if necessary)	i. State Why You Intend To Make Firearm (Use additional sheet if necessary)

j. Is this firearm being reactivated? ☐ Yes ☐ No (See Definition 1k)

5. Applicant's Federal Firearms License (If any)	6. Special (Occupational) Tax Status (If applicable) (See definition 1f)	
(Give complete 15-digit Number)	a. Employer Identification Number	b. Class

Important: All individual applicants (including Federally Licensed Collectors) must complete the reverse side of this form and submit, in duplicate, FBI Form FD-258, Fingerprint Card.

Under Penalties of Perjury, I Declare that I have examined this application, including accompanying documents, and to the best of my knowledge and belief it is true, accurate and complete and the making and possession of the firearm described above would not constitute a violation of Chapter 44, Title 18, U.S.C., Chapter 53, Title 26, U.S.C., or any provisions of State or local law.

7. Signature of Applicant	8. Name and Title of Authorized Official	9. Date

The space below is for the use of the Bureau of Alcohol, Tobacco, Firearms and Explosives

By authority of the Director, Bureau of Alcohol, Tobacco, Firearms and Explosives, this application has been examined and the applicant's making and registration of the firearm described above is:

☐ Approved (With the following conditions, if any)	☐ Disapproved (For the following reasons)

Authorized ATF Official	Date

ATF Form 1 (5320.1)
Revised June 2014

ATF Form 1   *Page 2*

---

10. Law Enforcement Certification (See instruction 2g)

I certify that I am the chief law enforcement officer of the organization named below having jurisdiction in the area of residence of

_____

(Name of maker)

I have no information that the maker will use the firearm or device described on this application for other than lawful purposes. I have no information that Possession of the firearm described in Item 4 on the front of this form would place the maker in Violation of State or Local Law.

_____   _____   _____

(Signature of Chief Law Enforcement Officer)   (Printed name)   (Title and agency name)

_____

(Street address, city, State and zip code)

_____   _____

(Telephone Number)   (Date)

By (if delegated authority to sign for the chief law enforcement official):

_____   _____   _____

(Signature)   (Printed name)   (Title and agency name)

_____

(Street address, city, State and zip code)

_____   _____

(Telephone Number)   (Date)

Maker's Certification

A maker who is an individual must complete this Section.

11. Answer questions 11.a. through 11.j. Answer questions 13 through 16 if applicable. For any YES answer (other than for 11.i.), the applicant shall provide details on a separate sheet. (See instructions 7c and definitions)

	Yes	No	12. Photograph
a. Are you under indictment or information in any court for a felony, or any other crime, for which the judge could imprison you for more than one year?			
b. Have you ever been convicted in any court for a felony, or any other crime, for which the judge could imprison you for than one year, even if you received a shorter sentence including probation?			Affix Recent Photograph Here (Approximately 2" x 2") (See instruction 2e)
c. Are you a fugitive from justice?			
d. Are you an unlawful user of, or addicted to, marijuana or any depressant, stimulant, narcotic drug, or any other controlled substance?			
e. Have you ever been adjudicated mentally defective (which includes a determination by a court, board, commission, or other lawful authority that you are a danger to yourself or others or are incompetent to manage your own affairs) OR have you ever been committed to a mental institution?			
f. Have you been discharged from the Armed Forces under dishonorable conditions?			
g. Are you subject to a court order restraining you from harassing, stalking, or threatening your child or an intimate partner or child of such partner?			
h. Have you ever been convicted in any court of a misdemeanor crime of domestic violence?			
i. Are you a United States citizen?			
j. Have you ever renounced your United States citizenship?			

If you answered "NO" to question 11.i, please answer questions 13, 14, 15 and 16.

13. Answer questions 13.a. through 13.b., and 14 by checking or marking "Yes or "No" or "NA" in the boxes to the right of the questions.

	Yes	No
Are you an alien Illegally in the United States?		
Are you an alien admitted to the United States under a nonimmigrant visa? If the answer is "NO", do not respond to question 14 and proceed to questions 15 and 16.		

14. If you are an alien admitted to the United States under a nonimmigrant visa, do you fall within any of the exceptions set forth in the instructions (see definition 2.u.)? If the answer is "YES", a copy of the Documentation must be attached to the Application. ☐ Yes ☐ No ☐ N/A

15. What is your country of Citizenship if other than the United States? (Specify Country)

16. If you are not a Citizen of the United States, what is your U.S.-issued alien number or admission number?

CERTIFICATION: Under penalties imposed by 26 U.S.C. 5861, I certify that the statements contained in this Certification, and any attached documents in support thereof, are true and correct to the best of my knowledge and belief.

_____   _____

Signature of Maker   Date

ATF Form 1 (5320.1)
Revised June 2014

ATF Form 1   *Page 3*

---

17. Method of Payment Check one) See Instruction 2h)

☐ Check Enclosed)   ☐ Cashier's Check or Money Order Enclosed)   ☐ Visa   ☐ Mastercard   ☐ American Express   ☐ Discover   ☐ Diners Club

Credit/Debit Card Number No dashes)	Name as Printed on the Credit/Debit Card	Expiration Date Month year)

Credit/Debit Card Billing Address:	Address:		
	City:	State:	Ip Code:

Please Complete to Ensure Payment Is Credited to the Correct Application:

I am Paying the making Tax for the Applicant:	Total Amount:

I Authori e ATF to Charge my Credit/Debit Card the Above Amount.

_____   _____
Signature of Cardholder   Date

Your credit/debit card will be charged the above stated amount upon receipt of your application. The charge will be reflected on your credit/debit card statement. In the event your application is NOT approved, the above amount will be credited to the credit/debit card noted above.

Important Information for Currently Registered Firearms

If this registration document evidences the current registration of the firearm described on it, please note the following information.

Estate Procedures: For procedures regarding the transfer of firearms in an estate resulting from the death of the registrant identified in item , the executor should contact the NFA Branch, Bureau of ATF, 244 Needy Road, Martinsburg, WV 25405.

Interstate Movement: If the firearm identified in item 4 is a machinegun, short barreled rifle, short barreled shotgun, or destructive device, the registrant may be required by 18 U.S.C. 22 a) 4) to obtain permission from ATF prior to any transportation in interstate or foreign commerce.

Change of Description or Address: The registrant shall notify the NFA Branch, Bureau of Alcohol, Tobacco, Firearms and Explosives, 244 Needy Road, Martinsburg, WV 25405, in writing, of any change to the description of the firearms in item 4, or any change to the address of the registrant.

Restrictions on Possession: Any restriction see approval block on face of form) on the possession of the firearm identified in item 4 continues with the further transfer of the firearm.

Persons Prohibited from Possessing Firearms: If the registrant becomes prohibited from possessing a firearm, please contact the NFA Branch for procedures on how to dispose of the firearm.

Proof of Registration: A person possessing a firearm registered as required by the NFA shall retain proof of registration which shall be made available to an ATF officer upon request.

Paperwork Reduction Act Notice

This form is in accordance with the Paperwork Reduction Act of 1 5. The information you provide is used to establish that a transferee's receipt and possession of the firearm would be in conformance with Federal, State, and local law. The data is used as proof of lawful registration of a firearm to the manufacturer. The furnishing of this information is mandatory 26 U.S.C. 5822).

The estimated average burden associated with this collection of information 1.6 hours per respondent or recordkeeper, depending on individual circumstances. Comments concerning the accuracy of this burden estimate and suggestions for reducing this burden should be addressed to Reports Management Officer, Information Technology Coordination Staff, Bureau of Alcohol, Tobacco, Firearms and Explosives, Washington, DC 20226.

An agency may not conduct or sponsor, and a person is not required to respond to, a collection of information unless it displays a currently valid OMB control number.

Privacy Act Information

1. **Authority.** Solicitation of this information is made pursuant to the National Firearms Act 26 U.S.C. 5821 and 5822). Disclosure of this information by the applicant is mandatory for any person other than a manufacturer qualified under the National Firearms Act) making a firearm as defined in the National Firearms Act.

2. **Purpose.** To verify payment of the tax imposed by 26 U.S.C. 5821 to determine that the making would not be in violation of law and to effect registration of the firearm.

. **Routine Uses.** The information will be used by ATF to make the determinations set forth in paragraph 2. in addition, to effect registration of the firearm, information as to the identification of the firearm, date of registration, and the identification and address of person entitled to possess the firearm will be entered into the National Firearms Registration and Transfer Record. No information obtained from a application, registration, or records required to be submitted by a natural person in order to comply with any provision of the National Firearms Act or regulations issued thereunder, shall, except in connection with prosecution or other action for furnishing false information, be used, directly or indirectly, as evidence against that person in any criminal proceeding with respect to a violation of law occurring prior to or concurrently with the filing of the application. The information from this application may only be disclosed to Federal authorities for purpose of prosecution for violation of the National Firearms Act.

4. **Effects of not Supplying Information Requested.** Failure to supply complete information will delay processing and may cause denial of the application.

ATF Form 1 5 20.1)
Revised June 2014

ABOUT THE ATTORNEY AUTHORS

JUSTIN MCSHANE
LEAD-AUTHOR

Attorney McShane is the lead program attorney for USLS of PA. He is the owner of The McShane Firm, LLC which is an 8 attorney law firm that focuses on firearms law, criminal law defense, forensic science, and DUI law defense. An avid multi-gun competitor, he trains mostly in combative skills and tactical training. He has been to The Site Firearms Training Center as well as other tactical training venues. He practices concealed carry every single day. He has several NFA weapons. He shoots not less than 5 days a week. In terms of his legal experience, he is a trial lawyer. He has been practicing law since 2001. He has personally litigated thousands of criminal cases including several death penalty cases. He has defended scores of people in critical incident situations as well as in self-defense cases. He is a published author. He is a highly sought after featured international speaker on science and the law.

MICHAEL GIARAMITA, JR.
CO-AUTHOR

Attorney Giaramita is the founder of Giaramita Law Offices, P.C., where he focuses on firearms litigation in both civil and criminal arenas. Currently, he is co-counsel for U.S. Law Shield of Pennsylvania in *U.S. Law Shield of Pennsylvania, LLC, et al. v. City of Harrisburg, et al.*, a lawsuit challenging five of Harrisburg's illegal gun ordinances. He helped U.S. Law Shield secure a preliminary injunction, suspending three of the five contested ordinances. Because of his role in this litigation, he was featured as a panelist for "Preemption of Municipal Firearms Ordinances," a seminar hosted by the Pennsylvania Bar Institute. He has also been a featured guest on NRA News on two separate occasions, and was a guest lecturer for the Fall Conference of Townships, Boroughs and Authorities. As a program attorney for U.S. Law Shield of Pennsylvania, he has lectured to law abiding gun owners at over 70 seminars throughout the Commonwealth of Pennsylvania. He graduated from the University of Tulsa College of Law with highest honors, and was awarded Order of the Curule Chair, the highest award granted. Throughout law school he was an active member of the Tulsa Indoor Firearms Range. He is currently a proud member of Harrisburg Hunters & Anglers Association, and a regular attendee of TROP Institute. He is admitted to practice law in both Pennsylvania and New Jersey.